THE PHILOSOPHY
OF RELIGION
1875–1980

Alan P. F. Sell

WIPF & STOCK · Eugene, Oregon

Wipf and Stock Publishers
199 W 8th Ave, Suite 3
Eugene, OR 97401

The Philosophy of Religion 1875 - 1980
By Sell, Alan P.F.
Copyright©1988 by Sell, Alan P.F.
ISBN 13: 978-1-62032-426-4
Publication date 7/31/2012
Previously published by Routledge, 1988

Contents

Preface
Abbreviations
1. Introduction — 1
2. The Impact of Absolute Idealism, 1875–1900 — 8
3. Approaches Old and New, 1900–20 — 32
4. Systems, Silence and Scholasticism, 1920–35 — 62
5. Advancing and Marking Time, 1935–45 — 102
6. Languages, Standpoints and Attitudes, 1945–55 — 128
7. Widening Horizons, 1955–65 — 160
8. Almost Open House, 1965–80 — 205
9. Epilogue — 242
Bibliography — 246
Index of Persons — 247

TO
JOHN HEYWOOD THOMAS

Preface

There is no shortage of books which introduce their readers to such problems in the philosophy of religion as the existence of God, evil, immortality and the soul. Again, general histories of philosophy are readily available. I here attempt something rather different: an account of the history, objectives and methods of one branch of philosophy in the period 1875–1980, with reference to activities elsewhere in the philosophical domain. I hope that the result will be of interest to students and non-professional readers, and that even hard-pressed professionals will find it helpful to be reminded of the size and shape of the wood within which their several trees are set.

Chapters two to seven represent a radically revised and greatly expanded version of a section of a doctoral thesis submitted in the University of Nottingham in 1967. I am indebted to Professors Ronald W. Hepburn, Jonathan Harrison and James Richmond who supervised my studies; and to Professor John Heywood Thomas for his subsequent comments upon the thesis. The Congregational Church in England and Wales, through the good offices of its then Minister Secretary, Dr John Huxtable, financed a three-month sabbatical to enable me to write up my work, and the churches at Worcester, Hallow and Ombersley granted me leave of absence for that period. I am grateful to all concerned.

I thank Dr W. Donald Hudson for reading the draft of the complete book in its present form, and for his encouragement towards publication.

Diligent source critics would be able to trace a few paragraphs to articles of mine which have appeared in *Churchman* (XCVI, 1982), *The Downside Review* (XCIII, 1975), *The Irish Theological Quarterly* (XLIX, 1982), *Philosophical Studies* (XXIII, 1975) and *Scottish Journal of Theology* (XXVII, 1974). I am grateful to the editors of these journals for the hospitality of their pages, and for their kind permission to plunder them here.

For 15 years I taught the philosophy of religion at the West Midlands College of Higher Education, Walsall. I owe much to the first Principal of the College, Dr John Cornwell, and to my first Head of Department, Dr Lawrence Proctor, for their interest and encouragement as I pioneered the discipline in that institution; and to my students who ever reminded me that if clarity is not enough, it is at least indispensable!

Preface

My first steps in the subject were taken 30 years ago this year under the kindly but demanding tutelage of John Heywood Thomas. I have much pleasure in dedicating this book to him as a token of my deep appreciation of his searching criticism and staunch friendship.

Alan P.F. Sell
Geneva

Abbreviations

AJP:	*Australasian Journal of Philosophy* (1923 — known as the *Australasian Journal of Psychology and Philosophy* until 1947)
Anal.:	*Analysis* (1933)
APQ:	*American Philosophical Quarterly* (1964)
B:	*New Blackfriars* (1920)
CQ:	*Constructive Quarterly* (1913-1922)
CQR:	*Church Quarterly Review* (1875-1968)
DR:	*The Downside Review* (1880)
DS:	*Dominican Studies* (1948-1954)
Dub R.:	*The Dublin Review* (1836-1969)
ET:	*The Expository Times* (1889)
FF:	*Faith and Freedom* (1947)
HeyJ:	*The Heythrop Journal* (1960)
HJ:	*The Hibbert Journal* (1902-1968)
HTR:	*Harvard Theological Review* (1908)
IJPR:	*The International Journal for Philosophy of Religion* (1970)
ITQ:	*Irish Theological Quarterly* (1951)
JP:	*Journal of Philosophy* (1904)
JTSA:	*Journal of Theology for Southern Africa* (1972)
JURCHS:	*Journal of the United Reformed Church History Society* (1973)
LQ:	*The London Quarterly and Holborn Review* (1853-1968)
M:	*Mind* (1876)
MC:	*The Modern Churchman* (1911)
P:	*Philosophy* (1925 — known as the *Journal of Philosophical Studies* until 1931)
PAS:	*Proceedings of the Aristotelian Society* (1888)
PASSV:	*Proceedings of the Aristotelian Society, Supplementary Volume* (1918)
PBA:	*Proceedings of the British Academy* (1903)
PPNL:	*The Price-Priestley Newsletter* (1977)
PQ:	*The Philosophical Quarterly* (1950)
PR:	*The Philosophical Review* (1892)
PS:	*Philosophical Studies* (Dublin, 1951)
R:	*Ratio* (1957)
RR:	*Reformed Review* (1947)
RS:	*Religious Studies* (1965)
SJT:	*Scottish Journal of Theology* (1948)
Soc.:	*The Socratic* (1952)

T: *Theology* (1920)
Tab.:   *The Tablet* (1840)
TT: *Theology Today* (1944)

Note

In the interest of keeping footnotes to a minimum the following conventions are observed in the text:
(1) Figures in brackets are page references to the last-named article or book.
(2) References to journals are given in brackets thus: title; volume number; part number, where pagination is not consecutive through the volume; date; page reference. For example (*ET*, IV, 1892–3, 164) = *The Expository Times*, volume 4, 1892–3, page 164.

1
Introduction

The philosophy of religion is a many-sided pursuit. Some of its practitioners have set out to propound a Christian philosophy of life. They have done this in relation to a prevailing philosophical 'ism' — notably idealism in the period here under review; or they have built upon some such concept as encounter, or process. They have attempted to give an account of 'what it all comes to'. Wholeness, coherence of system and consistency of vision have been their watchwords. Others have worked on a smaller canvas. Eschewing the grand systematic task they have devoted themselves to the detailed discussion of such specific problems within the philosophy of religion as the existence of God, the problem of evil, immortality and the soul. Still others have stood back from the statements made by religious believers and have examined their logic. Questions concerning the verifiability and falsifiability — even the possibility — of religious propositions have occupied their attention.

In addition to being multi-faceted, the philosophy of religion is an hospitable discipline. It is as open to interested professional philosophers — whose ranks include atheists, agnostics, secular humanists, Marxists and followers of world religions including Christianity — as it is to philosophically-inclined Christian theologians. Moreover, the questions with which the subject deals are by no means the exclusive preserve of the professional. In their different ways the small child who asks 'Who made God?' and the dying elderly person who wonders whether there is anything 'on the other side' are concerned with matters which fall within the purview of the philosopher of religion.

It would thus have been entirely inappropriate to have decided at the outset that one type of activity only — metaphysical synthesising, philosophical theologising, linguistic analysing — counts as philosophy of religion, or that philosophers of religion must conform to one preconceived pattern. 'Philosophy is the attempt to co-ordinate the totality of our experience'; 'Philosophy is the clearing up of logical muddles' — such are the extremes of definition which have been heard during this century. If we were dogmatically, perhaps even intolerantly, to disregard the variety and the fluidity of the subject we should open ourselves to the danger of saying, for example, that because F.H. Bradley was not an empiricist linguistic analyst he was not a philosopher at all, for philosophy *is* empiricist linguistic analysis. We should on the same basis be tempted to declare that existentialists are mere (denunciatory word!) poets, and neo-Thomists and Reformed Christian presuppositionalists crypto-theologians.

The truth is that analysis, contrary to the impression sometimes conveyed during the 1950s, is not the invention of the 20th century, as any who are familiar with Socrates will readily acknowledge. Neither have the best metaphysicians shunned the analytical task — Aquinas springs at once to mind. Conversely, the more perceptive (or the more honest) empiricist analysts have readily granted that their practice presupposes metaphysical considerations of the most profound kind, and that E.D. Fawcett's dictum of 1909 concerning metaphysicians applies no less certainly to themselves: 'In practice, of course, there is no heaven-born sage, and assuredly no metaphysician, religious or other, without his bias.'[1]

So many have contributed in their differing ways to the philosophy of religion since 1875 that it will be impossible to mention all of them in this book. The relatively brief treatment of existentialism is justifiable on the ground that whatever its merits its impact upon Anglo-Saxon philosophical thought was relatively slight. Again, one older type of philosophy of religion is omitted altogether — not for partisan reasons, but because of what has been happening, and is ever happening, to philosophy. Over the centuries there has been a narrowing-down of the scope of philosophy. In classical times mathematics, music, astronomy and other 'subjects' were all within the purview of the philosopher, the lover of wisdom. With the passage of time these fields and others have developed as disciplines in their own right. Among relatively recent departures from philosophy's nest are the study of world religions and the phenomenology of religion. Thus a work like Atkinson Lee's *Groundwork of the Philosophy of Religion* (1946), with its interest in the nature and roots of religion, naturalism, humanism, spiritualism, mysticism, atheism, dualism, polytheism, pantheism and monotheism, is best regarded as heralding the more specialised studies in the phenomenology of religion that have subsequently been published.

Introduction

Despite the limitations of scope just mentioned, there remains a formidable amount of literature to review. Clearly, we shall not be able to examine the thought of any one thinker in great detail. This is not a disadvantage, however, given that our objective is to follow the course of one branch of philosophical study in relation to others over a period of years. We should fail to attain our objective were we to become so immersed in one thinker or group of thinkers, or in one problem or cluster of related problems, that we never saw the wood for the trees. The attempt from time to time to view the whole and not isolated parts is salutary; and if a certain type of philosopher wished to say, 'But this is history, not philosophy that you are doing', we should avail ourselves of C.D. Broad's ready-made retort: 'It is consoling to a philosopher's vanity not to pry too closely into the history of his subject, for otherwise he is liable to find that his discoveries have been anticipated and his fallacies refuted in advance by predecessors whom he has ignored or despised.'[2] Less pugilistically, it cannot be denied that just as to read a map in the comfort of one's armchair is no substitute for going on a country walk, so to read an account of what has been happening in an intellectual territory is no substitute for venturing in detail into the territory oneself. On the other hand, a map is of great assistance when we are deciding where to walk; it can place our chosen path in context, and it can help us to find our way — not least when we are lost.

It will soon become clear that some major philosophical figures are mentioned but briefly, whilst some lesser writers receive more space. For example, relatively little reference will be made to Gilbert Ryle and P.F. Strawson, and rather more to the all-but-forgotten James Iverach. This is because our focus is upon philosophico-theological *relationships* and (a) not all important philosophers have dwelt upon questions pertaining to the philosophy of religion; and (b) those, like Iverach, who have sought to respond to the prevailing philosophical climate from the theological side are important as enabling us to assess the state of relations, even if their own contribution is not as distinguished as that of those upon whom they comment.

The guiding questions in this study are: What was the relationship between secular philosophy and philosophical theology in the period 1875–1980? To what extent did philosophers and theologians heed and cross-fertilise one another when they met on common territory or, at least, conversed over the same fence? And why, on occasion, were representatives of either side tempted to replace the fence by an impenetrable and unscalable barrier?

It is not at all difficult to test the water in these matters. The following list of quotations, presented in chronological order, will enable us

Introduction

to see how some philosophers and theologians judged the situation:

> Today theology is more closely connected with philosophy than ever.
>
> R.M. Wenley, 1897
>
> Philosophy and theology 'are friendly fellow-students, studying the greatest field of human thoughts from similar points of view'.
>
> W.N. Clarke, 1898
>
> When we discover a believer among men of science we take him by the hand heartily. How much more when we discover a believer among men of philosophy. For is he not much rarer? And is not philosophy the real antagonist of our faith?
>
> *ET*, 1908-9
>
> Is the reunion of philosophy and religion to come to pass even before the reunion of the Churches? The signs are all around us.
>
> *ET*, 1918-19
>
> No philosopher who deals with fundamentals . . . can avoid dealing with religion.
>
> R.F.A. Hoernlé, 1920
>
> It is not likely that the present generation will enjoy the spectacle of a commonly recognised alliance between religion and science, or religion and philosophy.
>
> Charles Gore, 1930
>
> This mention of God brings us to the question of the possibility of religious knowledge. We shall see that this possibility has already been ruled out by our treatment of metaphysics.
>
> A.J. Ayer, 1936
>
> In our half century, philosophy and theology have not been on speaking terms.
>
> Gilbert Ryle
>
> Theology cannot conflict with philosophy because, in a sense, it is based upon philosophy.
>
> Dom I. Trethowan, 1954
>
> The contemporary philosopher . . . is, therefore, neither ally nor rival of the theologian. He is, if anything, his critic.
>
> B. Mitchell, 1957
>
> No serious philosopher can hope to dodge the questions involved in the claim of religious credenda to *truth*.
>
> D.M. MacKinnon, 1961

The very diversity of the judgements just presented further

Introduction

cautions us to beware of making sweeping generalisations concerning our subject; and the intervals of time which separate some verbally similar utterances remind us that we are to be concerned with cycles and fashions rather than with pure linear development. For example, time alone separates the basic attitudes of Hoernlé and MacKinnon as illustrated in the above quotations. Though their methods and results might differ markedly, they share a common conviction that religious questions properly fall within the scope of philosophy. The quotations further suggest, and our study will demonstrate, that this conviction has not been held at all times by all philosophers, and that in broad terms it was still just fashionable to adopt this stance when Hoernlé wrote, and that MacKinnon's reiteration of the conviction comes at a period of heightened interest in the philosophy of religion.

Our pursuit of relationships has necessitated a chronological rather than a thematic approach to the material. Had the primary concern been to discuss particular theories in detail it would have been tidier, for example, to have placed all the idealists within one chapter. But we wish to explore a frontier, to note actions and reactions (or the lack of them), time-lags, and fashions. We wish to discover whether at any given time philosophers and philosophically-inclined theologians were engaged in mutual conversation, whether mutual hostility prevailed, or whether mutual indifference was the order of the day. Moreover, the chronological rather than the thematic approach will dissuade us from the too-easy labelling of philosophers — a practice which results in hurt to tender souls. For example, the outraged laments of some analytical empiricists who were labelled 'positivists' by the unwary had scarcely less emotive force than those of a Greek chorus.

The chronological approach does, however, give rise to a problem in connection with the last 15 years of the period. We are as yet too close to these years to see them in historical perspective; and it is not without significance that the most recent of the 'relationships' quotations given above was dated 1961. The problem is somewhat mitigated by the fact that owing to the adoption of analytical techniques by secular and Christian philosophers alike, the period 1965-80 is marked by more conversation and less exclusivist dogmatism (on both sides) than was customary during the preceding 40 years.

If there is a problem concerning the ending of a book of this kind, there is also a problem concerning the beginning. On the one hand the impression must not be conveyed that philosophy began in 1875!

Introduction

On the other hand we cannot embark upon an extended regress. A brief scene-setting compromise may, however, be in order.

The 19th century was a period of shifting landmarks in theology and philosophy alike. The deism of the 18th century had run into the sand; the older natural theology had suffered under the assaults of Hume and Kant; and those under the influence of the Romantic movement — of whom Coleridge was supreme in England — drove the inward trail and popularised the view that no complete account of man could be given within the constricting frameworks of naturalism and materialism.

The development of evolutionary thought following the publication of Charles Darwin's *The Origin of Species* (1859); the advance of modern biblical criticism which, in keeping with the then novel approaches to historical method, viewed the biblical writings not so much as a collection of chronicles, but as texts of varying kinds which nevertheless evinced a 'progressive revelation'; and concern in Catholic circles with the 'development of doctrine' — all of these elements prompted a degree of theological stock-taking the like of which had seldom been seen before. While some conservative theologians felt that the very foundations of the faith were being shaken, some on the liberal wing were so optimistic as to baptise almost any aspect of 'the newer thought' on the grounds of its importance for 'the higher life'.[3]

As for philosophy, F.D. Maurice's *Moral and Metaphysical Philosophy* (1871-2) with its reflections on the philosophy of the ages, encouraged some to feel that metaphysical speculation was not the moribund pursuit that the empiricism of Hume and Mill made it out to be. But it was the implications for thought of the phenomenal advances in the natural sciences which lay behind the founding of the Metaphysical Society in 1869. The members of the Society included the philosopher Henry Sidgwick, the scientist T.H. Huxley, the churchmen Cardinal Manning and Archbishop Magee, the men of letters Tennyson and Ruskin, and Gladstone the statesman. Their objective was not simply to find a firm foundation for thought, but to synthesise all known knowledge — an objective which invited the sceptical mind to construe the lines of their contemporary, Browning, ironically:

Ah, but a man's reach should exceed his grasp,
   Or what's heaven for?

The Society was disbanded before its objective was attained.

Introduction

In 1896 the Synthetic Society was formed, and once again Sidgwick was a member. The objective of the Synthetic was less grandiose than that of the Metaphysical: the quest was now for the foundations of religious belief. That the deliberations of the group were marked by certain communication difficulties is clear from the remark of its leader, R.B. Haldane the Hegelian, to the effect that one half of the members did not understand what the other half were talking about. At the root of this inability lay the lack of presuppositional contact between those who continued in the line of British empiricism; those who opted for one of the several possible interpretations of Kant; and those who were post-Hegelian idealists of one kind or another. By 1875 this last type of philosophy was coming to the fore in certain British philosophical circles — hence the point of departure of this book. It seemed to match the evolutionary mood of the times admirably, and a number of philosophical theologians came to regard it as a suitable medium for the articulation of their Christian view of the world. That not all were equally enthusiastic will become clear as we turn to two very distinguished and very different philosophers, neither of whom was hostile towards religion.

Notes

1. E.D. Fawcett, *The Individual and Reality* (Longmans, London, 1909,) p. 9.
2. C.D. Broad, 'Two lectures on the nature of philosophy' in H.D. Lewis (ed.), *Clarity is Not Enough* (Allen & Unwin, London, 1963), p. 50.
3. For the general theological developments see A.P.F. Sell, *Theology in Turmoil: The roots, course and significance of the conservative-liberal debate in modern theology* (Baker Book House, Grand Rapids, 1986). For detailed studies of the responses of individual theologians to the changing intellectual environment see A.P.F. Sell, *Robert Mackintosh: Theologian of Integrity* (Peter Lang, Bern, 1977), and *Defending and Declaring the Faith: Some Scottish Examples 1860-1920* (The Paternoster Press, Exeter, 1987).

2
The Impact of Absolute Idealism, 1875-1900

At the beginning of our period two very influential philosophers were at the height of their powers: Robet Flint (1838-1910) and Thomas Hill Green (1836-82). They exemplify radically contrasting approaches in philosophy. Although Flint could declare that 'a richer treasure-house of philosophical thoughts scarcely exists' than Hegel's *Works*, he was no Hegelian. Flint was indeed influenced by post-Hegelian evolutionary thought, with its emphasis upon progress, but methodologically he stood at the end of a line (or at least at a break in the line) of Christian apologetics whose great exponent in the previous century had been Bishop Butler. Flint regarded the dramatic scientific advances of his day as lending support to the traditional theistic argument from, or to, design. His *Theism* (1876) had reached its eleventh edition by 1905, and its thirteenth by 1929; and the general esteem in which he was held is reflected in the fact that after parish ministries at East Church, Aberdeen and Kilconquhar, Flint defeated Green, among others, in his successful application for the Chair of Moral Philosophy at St Andrews. There he served for twelve years (1864-76), and in the latter year he removed to Edinburgh where he held the Chair of Divinity until 1903.

Widely respected though he was, we can with hindsight see that Flint was a somewhat old-fashioned thinker even in his lifetime. As far as truth is concerned he was not necessarily the worse for this, and it is certainly preferable for a thinker to stand aloof from the intellectual fashion of his day for good reasons than to be bowled over by it for no good reasons. The fact remains that from about 1880 the tide was with the neo-Hegelians — though that designation must not tempt us to overlook significant differences between those thus labelled. It is salutary to recall that Green, one of the most influential of the neo-Hegelians, was critical of Hegel's dialectical method, and said of his work, 'It must all be done over again'; and that his pupil, F.H. Bradley, went so far as to say that 'Green was in my opinion no Hegelian and was in some respects anti-Hegelian even'. At the very least we may say that there was no unwholesomely adulatory, unreflective discipleship here.

Robert Flint

Flint, said to be the most learned man of his time in Scotland, poured a wealth of careful scholarship into his major works. He wrote massively on the history of European philosophy, and on the philosophy of history, but our concern is with his philosophy of religion. With his *Anti-Theistic Theories* (1879) and *Agnosticism* (1903) Flint established himself as a doughty defender of the Christian faith against positivism, materialism and agnosticism — doctrines which were being articulated by relatively few Victorian intellectuals, but which were being absorbed into the atmosphere which the less articulate breathed. But his positive foundations were laid in his *Theism*.

Unconvinced that religious belief can be grounded upon feeling, Flint sets out to demonstrate the rationality of belief in God, and to promote theism as thus defined: 'Theism is the doctrine that the universe owes its existence, and continuance in existence, to the reason and will of a self-existent Being, who is infinitely powerful, wise, and good' (18). Flint grants that there can be no logically demonstrable proof of the existence of God, but is convinced that rational philosophy can adduce satisfactory arguments in favour of God's existence. He could not share the enthusiasm of those religious thinkers who rejoiced that Kant, having demolished the traditional arguments for God's existence, had left room for faith. To Flint belief without adequate grounds was a very poor thing indeed. He regards the theistic arguments — the cosmological (from a first mover or a first cause), the teleological (from, or to, design), the moral (from our experience of being under obligation) and the ontological (from the *a priori* idea of the most perfect being) — as stages in a process of rational inference from God's manifestations of himself to the affirmation of God himself.

Flint agrees that the apprehension of God involves intuition, but declares that to rest exclusively upon intuition is 'the merest dogmatism'. Nor is there such a thing as a self-authenticating belief: we can believe only what we know, or think we know, and God is known through his works. The cosmological, teleological and moral arguments are all indications of what God is; they testify to his existence by exhibiting his character. But even when taken together they do not prove God to be infinite, eternal, and absolute in being and perfection. At this point, and on no account before this point, the *a priori* argument may be invoked: 'to get from the ideal to the actual may be impossible, and is certain to be difficult; whereas, if we have allowed facts to teach us all that they legitimately can about the existence, power, wisdom, and righteousness of God, it may be easy to show that our ideas of absolute being and perfection must apply to Him, and to Him only' (*Theism*, 267). No being to whom these ideas did not apply would be a satisfying object of religious worship. (It is not altogether surprising that Flint's contemporary, A. Caldecott, should have wondered why, having conceded so much, Flint did not go right across to the transcendentalist position. It is possible that he was restrained by the appeal of Butler's method, and of the Scottish common sense philosophy which had come down to him from Thomas Reid.)

His quest of rationality notwithstanding, Flint's concluding lecture in *Theism* is headed, 'Mere theism insufficient'. Theism might have sufficed man in his original state of innocence, but man now is a sinner in need of salvation. The revelation of a holy, Saviour God is required, and this revelation is given in Christ. It cannot be said that this insight did much to inform either Flint's method or his epistemology.

For all Flint's learning there is a troublesome ambivalence in his case. He knows that the arguments for the existence of God do not succeed as logically coercive proofs, but he thinks that their cumulative force cannot be gainsaid:

> It is sophistry to attempt to destroy them separately by assailing each as if it had no connection with the other, and as if each isolated fragmentary argument were bound to yield as large a conclusion as all the arguments combined. A man quite unable to break a bundle of rods firmly bound together may be strong enough to break each rod separately. But before proceeding to deal with the bundle in that way, he may be required to establish his right to untie it, and to decline putting forth his strength upon it as it is presented to him. (*Theism*, 74-5)

But what if we do not have a bundle of rods, but just one rod, and that a broken one? Kant had argued that the traditional arguments for the existence of God reduce to the ontological argument, and that that is inadequate. Flint nowhere answers this objection, thereby leaving us with a certain tension between his religion, which may not need an answer, and his philosophical method, which does need an answer. It is not without significance in this connection that for all his determination to tread the *a posteriori* path for as long as possible, he nevertheless believes that 'Platonism is substantially true; that the objections which the empiricism and positivism at present prevalent urge against its fundamental positions are superficial and insufficient; that what is essential in its theory of ideas, and in the theism inseparable from that theory, must abide with our race for ever as a priceless possession' (271). He cannot remove from his mind the forms, the ideas, the eternal verities.

But Flint's streak of idealism is not to be confused with the increasingly fashionable absolute idealism of his day. This immanentist idealism provoked an outburst from Flint in which he put his finger on many points which were to disturb the more orthodox theologians:

> The philosophy of the Absolute was, on the whole, a great advance towards a philosophical theism. And yet it was largely pantheistic, and tended strongly towards pantheism. This was not surprising. Any philosophy which is in thorough earnest to show that God is the ground of all existence and the condition of all knowledge must find it difficult to retain a firm grasp of the personality and transcendence of the Divine and to set them forth with due prominence . . . [Absolutism] regarded too exclusively the necessary and formal in thought, trusted almost entirely to its insight into the significance of the categories and its powers of rational deduction. Hence the idea of the Divine which it attained, if vast and comprehensive, was also vague and abstract, shadowy and unimpressive.[1]

The creator-creature distinction, the historic roots of the faith, and the Scottish common sense philosophy were not thus to be compromised.

Green and those who followed in his wake had fewer reservations. They were quite undeterred by the fact that the idealism by which they were influenced was largely a spent force in Germany its home by the time it kindled their enthusiasm. For the next generation in

Britain Flint's style of natural theology was to be under a cloud; indeed, we shall not hear much more of the *a posteriori* way until the neo-Thomists begin to emerge from their seminaries and take their place on the platform of general philosophical debate.

Towards Hegel-inspired idealism

I use this clumsy sub-heading in preference to the more customary 'neo-Hegelian idealism' in order to caution myself and others that no British philosopher of note adopted Hegelianism uncritically. They took from the barrel what they required, and then diluted it to suit their varying tastes. They did not endorse all that Hegel wrote, and some did not pay much attention to certain aspects of his thought. There was, for example, an early disregard of the *Phenomenology* in favour of the *Logic*. Again, in epistemology both Green and Edward Caird preferred to refurbish Kantian thought rather than to seek to attain knowledge of the absolute *via* Hegel's dialectical path. Bradley went so far as to aver that apart from authors in the philosophical reviews no-one knew of the existence of a neo-Hegelian school. It would not have been so had J.H. Stirling had his way.

A few British writers had devoted some thought to Hegel before Stirling burst into print — T.C. Sandars's account of Hegel's *Philosophy of Right* in *Oxford Essays* (1855) comes to mind. But Stirling was the supreme propagandist. Although almost beaten into submission by a Hegel whom he could call 'a Swabian lout', Stirling nevertheless chirrupped, 'Kant and Hegel have no object but to restore Faith — Faith in God, Faith in the Immortality of the Soul and the Freedom of the Will — nay Faith in Christianity as the revealed religion'. This testimony occurs in Stirling's book *The Secret of Hegel* (1865), concerning which the later idealist J.H. Muirhead said that if Stirling knew what the secret of Hegel was he had successfully kept it secret.

We may charitably allow Stirling the licence of a salesman with a new product. Not indeed that the ground was entirely unprepared for the new variety of thought. Negatively, many had felt for some time that the old-style apologetics was bankrupt, Hume and Kant between them having demolished the traditional arguments for the existence of God. It did not seem likely that the newer enemies of the faith — positivism, naturalism, Darwinism, agnosticism — were to be vanquished by utilising rusty weapons. Positively, from the concern of the Romantic movement with the inward it seemed possible to infer that the whole creation was alive with divinity — an inference consonant with immanentism; and when to this inference there was added the evolutionary theme that a grand purpose was being worked out which could only have been inspired by mind, the relevance of Hegelianism seemed undeniable. As the American philosopher William James opined, Hegelianism supplied British liberal theology with a quasi-metaphysical backbone which it had hitherto lacked. The extent to which this was really to theology's advantage soon came to be questioned — as it was by the largely forgotten philosopher J.D. Morell as early as 1850: 'religion, if not destroyed by the Hegelian philosophy, is absorbed in it'. Again, there was the general bankruptcy of philosophical thought. The Scottish philosophy of common sense had little left to offer, and that empiricism of which J.S. Mill was the chief exponent had been weighed by many and found wanting. There was a void which it seemed sensible to suppose that Hegelianism might fill. Yet again, Hegelian-inspired biblical criticism of the kind offered by D.F. Strauss in his *The Life of Jesus Critically Examined* (Eng. trans. 1846, 1864), with its idealising of Jesus off the stage of history, prompted some theologians to examine the German thought. Finally, although of less direct bearing on theological matters, we should note the need of a transfusion of life into the *laissez-faire* social thought of the day — a transfusion to which Green in particular contributed greatly with his *Lectures on the Principles of Political Obligation* (*Works* II, 1885).

Though not a systematic thinker, and despite the fact that he nowhere names Hegel in print, Coleridge was a harbinger of things to come. He had studied Kant, Fichte and Hegel, and was — at least initially — profoundly moved by the successive stages of Schelling's transition from Fichte's position that the *ego* is all to the congenially (to Coleridge) mystical view that all is the *ego*: that is, that both the natural and spiritual realms are sustained by one and the same intelligible principle. De Quincey, Carlyle and Emerson were among other literary men who imbibed and propagated something of the new intellectual romanticism, though they were not rigorous expositors or critics of philosophical thought. They did, however, have their fingers on the intellectual pulse, and one feels on reading them that the waters of philosophy are to be disturbed, and that new intellectual departures are imminent.

Among philosophers who set their faces against the prevailing empiricism were J.F. Ferrier (1808–64) of St Andrews, and John

Grote (1813–66) of Cambridge. In his *The Institutes of Metaphysics* (1854) Ferrier broke with the Scottish philosophy on the ground that to make common sense the criterion of philosophical truth is to put the cart before the horse. In reality, common sense is governed by rational thought, and intuitionalism will not suffice. Ferrier drew on the long-since-neglected Berkeley's idealism at certain points, but above all he utilised Hegel and Schelling (of whom he had more accurate knowledge than most in his day) in his quest of the absolute conceived as 'unparasitical being'. For his pains he was criticised by J.S. Mill for reasoning in a circle.

Grote defended the view that we can know the truly real, the thing-in-itself, because it is of the same nature as our minds. This is not to deny the existence of, or our knowledge of, phenomena, but it is to say that knowledge of phenomena is but preparatory to philosophic knowledge. This view Grote maintained against phenomenalism and positivism, but it cannot be said that he met all criticisms or presented a fully rounded system. By the time his works were published (and all but one were published posthumously) thought had moved on, and his pioneering work was superseded.

The contribution of Benjamin Jowett of Balliol College, Oxford, in reviving classical studies at Oxford, in acquainting himself with German thought *in situ*, and in inspiring his pupils Green, E. Caird and R.L. Nettleship to investigate Hegel and his circle, was decisive. From Green and Caird above all there flowed ideas which were not simply Hegel regurgitated, but Hegel reprocessed in ways which were sometimes more, sometimes less appealing to theologians. Nor were these thinkers at all inhibited by the fact that in his *On the Philosophy of Discovery* (1860) William Whewell of Cambridge had declared Hegel's triads to be at variance with sound science; or by the fact that Oxford's H.L. Mansel had argued that Hegel's identification of thought with being was nothing but an unproved assumption which could only lead religion down the dangerous road of pantheism.

Thomas Hill Green

In 1874 Green, Fellow of Balliol College, Oxford (and from 1878 to 1882 Professor of Moral Philosophy in that University), published his *Introduction to Hume's 'Treatise of Human Nature'* in which, while making clear his profound opposition to empiricism, he argued in Hegelian fashion that empiricism was not absolutely discardable. It had been a stage in the organic process of thought. Just as there is no such thing as an isolated event, for all events are *related* to other events, so there can be no such thing as an isolated system of thought standing in absolute dissociation from all other varieties of thought. Rather, the earlier grows to become the later. There is a dialectical process at work by means of which we are led through successive stages to an ever more fully rational understanding of reality; and reality itself is rational. No doubt the empiricists from Locke to Hume had erred in their thinking, but they had paved the way for, and to that extent contributed to the thought of, Kant. The anachronism apart, we might almost say that to Green Kant's testimony that Hume awoke him from his dogmatic (rationalist) slumbers is a testimony to the truth of Hegelianism. At all events, Green was convinced that to ignore the history of philosophy 'is not to return to the simplicity of a pre-philosophic age, but to condemn ourselves to grope in the maze of "cultivated opinion" , itself the confused result of those past systems of thought which we will not trouble ourselves to think out' (Introduction, 4-5).

The fact that viewed as a whole Green's conclusions are broadly Hegelian should neither blind us to the large pinch of salt with which he took Hegel's dialectical method of thesis, antithesis and synthesis (by which, for example he thought that John Caird had been 'too much overpowered' in his *Introduction to the Philosophy of Religion*), nor cause us to underestimate his deep indebtedness to Kant, not least in his theory of knowledge and his ethical philosophy. Green, like Kant, insists on the contribution which the mind makes to the acquisition of knowledge. Atomism, whether sensationalist or materialist, is inadequate, since apart from the knowing subject there are no relations and therefore no knowledge. To know a thing is to know it in its relations. But where Kant left us with a dualism between the knowable appearances of the phenomenal realm and the thing-in-itself which, since it belongs to the noumenal realm, is not knowable, Green proceeds to harmonise those two realms. Hegelianism cannot for long tolerate a discontinuity. All is harmonised in spirit — an all-embracing metaphysical principle which Green cashes variously in terms reminiscent of Berkeley's God, Kant's reason and Hegel's spirit. (Not indeed that he espouses Berkeley's empiricist epistemology. Rather, whilst maintaining the unassailable place of thought in perception, he nevertheless holds, echoing Berkeley, that phenomena cannot be conceived except in relation to mind.)

We have limited apprehensions of this underlying spiritual unity only, but any dualism between the individual consciousness and spirit is said to be an illusion created by the inability of the human mind to comprehend the whole, the universal mind. Green's *credo* is that

> The unification of the manifold in the world implies the presence of the manifold to a mind, for which, and through the action of which, it is a related whole. The unification of the manifold of sense *in our consciousness* of a world implies a certain self-realisation of this mind in us through certain processes of the world which, as explained, only exists through it — in particular through the processes of life and feeling.[2]

This same mind underpins morality and renders moral progress inevitable.

How far did Green's philosophy — which was, after all, the work of an earnest evangelical Anglican — comfort theological hearts assailed by materialism, Darwinism, agnosticism and the like? The now unhappily forgotten James Iverach (1839-1922) will supply a typical answer. Iverach, of the Free (later the United Free) Church College, Aberdeen, was among the most perceptive and judicious of commentators on the philosophico-theological frontier, and I refer now to the second part of his article on 'Professor Thomas Hill Green' (*ET* IV, 1892-3, 164).

Green is applauded by Iverach for making personality the essential feature of human nature. This was pioneering work when so much of the psychology to date had contented itself with the discussion of faculties in abstraction from the self. But to Iverach's regret self-consciousness becomes absorbed at crucial points in the universal self, and this raises questions which remain unanswered by Green: How is the universal self-consciousness related to the finite self-consciousness? Is God anything in himself — that is, apart from man? The rueful conclusion is that 'the attempt to unify the divine and human subject seems to destroy the reality of both'.

Nor is this all. Because Green does not recognise the full significance of humanity he cannot recognise the full significance of Christ. In the wake of Baur, Green leaves us with an idealised Christ; as Green says, 'To the modern philosopher the idea itself is the reality. To them Christ is the necessary determination of the eternal subject, the objectification by this subject of himself in the world of nature and humanity.' Iverach has no patience at all with this: 'come what may, men will not give up the Christ, and if philosophy can exist only by attenuating Him to an idea, then so much the worse for philosophy'. Theologians were to find the work of Bradley more disquieting still.

Francis Herbert Bradley

F.H. Bradley (1846-1924), Fellow of Merton College, Oxford, published his *Ethical Studies* in 1876. Like Green and Hegel he argues that the self is to be realised in self-conscious membership of the state; but he goes further in finding moral goals in such fields as art, science and philosophy, which transcend political frontiers whether local or national. We are to realise ourselves as self-conscious members of the infinite whole by realising that whole within ourselves.

Bradley's greatest departure from Hegel lay in his denial of the identity of thought and reality. His absolute is *supra*-rational. In his *The Principles of Logic* (1883, 2nd edn 1922, II, 591) he expressed himself thus: 'The notion that existence could be the same as understanding strikes as cold and ghost-like as the dreariest materialism. That the glory of this world in the end is appearance leaves the world more glorious, if we feel it is a show of some fuller splendour . . .' Religious and other philosophers saw agnosticism in all of this, but Bradley clung to his view, and in his most important work, *Appearance and Reality* (1893), he insists that the (Hegelian) relational way of thought can give appearance only, not truth. Relational thought is a necessary practical compromise, but it is strictly indefensible.

It is a sign of his times that Bradley could say, without fear of much contradiction, that we all reflect and ponder on ultimate truth, and are not likely to cease doing so. Lest not *all* should agree he continues; 'The man who is ready to prove that metaphysical knowledge is wholly impossible . . . has, perhaps unknowingly, entered the arena. He is a brother metaphysician with a rival theory of first principles' (*Appearance*, 1-2). Variations upon this theme were later to be played loudly into the ears of the logical positivists. In his day, however, Bradley could summarily dismiss objectors to metaphysics, for such persons were few. Most philosophers and theologians would have accepted Bradley's definition of metaphysics as being 'the effort to comprehend the universe, not simply piecemeal or by fragments, but somehow as a whole'.

Bradley believed that we have real, though incomplete knowledge of the absolute, of reality, and he spoke of his metaphysical quest with near-homiletical gusto:

> And so, when poetry, art, and religion have ceased wholly to interest, or when they show no longer any tendency to struggle with ultimate problems and come to an understanding with them; when the sense of mystery and enchantment no longer draws the mind to wander aimlessly and to love it knows not what; when, in short, twilight has no charm — then metaphysics will be worthless. (3-4)

The hurt to the pragmatist F.C.S. Schiller, to say nothing of the later positivists, on reading this must have been almost physical. Nevertheless, Bradley thought that the metaphysical pursuit conducted along his lines would serve as a protection against dogmatic superstition, would satisfy a desire experienced by most to understand what is beyond the physical world, and would supply the metaphysic most relevant to the age. His method was to be the unflinching questioning of all views from those of orthodox philosophy to 'commonplace materialism'.

In the result Bradley seemed to undermine all accepted notions of the relation between thought and experience. Some of our most commonly held conceptions, such as space and time are, he urged, subject to inherent and ineradicable contradictions. Therefore they cannot be other than appearances, for reality is and must be entirely free of contradictions. Reality is thus unlike anything about which we can think rationally: it is 'an all-inclusive and super-relational experience'. On the other hand, to the extent to which our customary conceptions are coherent they possess some reality, though they are not ultimate. This latter fact does not represent a defect in our conceptions, for they do not aspire to the finality of the absolute. Each category of human experience enjoys a degree of reality relative to its comprehensiveness and self-consistency, and each is taken into, and is transmuted by, the absolute.

Theologians could only have rested content with Bradley's concessions to our ordinary thought so long as they forgot that God belonged in part to that thought, and was therefore, on Bradley's terms, less than the absolute: 'God is but an aspect, and that must mean an appearance, of the Absolute', said Bradley. He even dispenses with the familiar idealist absolutes: the good, the beautiful and the true. They too are appearances only, and while they may stand closer to the absolute than certain other appearances, for there are degrees in this matter, they are not themselves the absolute. It is hard not to feel that A.E. Taylor had some justification for his remark that having made merry with Spencer's Unknowable, the absolute idealists were now presenting us with an absolute which was none other than the Unknowable in its Sunday best. Theologians could take more comfort from the immanentist philosophy of William Wallace, Green's successor in the Chair of Moral Philosophy at Oxford, who interpreted Hegel as explicating the God who is 'in the actuality and plenitude of the world'. But of all the professional philosophers, none was a greater friend (in intention if not in fact) to theology than Edward Caird.

Edward Caird

Edward Caird (1835-1908) was Professor of Moral Philosophy at Glasgow University from 1866 until 1893, when he succeeded Jowett as Master of Balliol. He was firmly committed to the view that the world is a rational system, intelligible to man and ultimately harmonious. The philosopher's task is to show that what appear as disharmonies may be reconciled in a higher unity. Thus Caird interpreted Kant through Hegelian eyes and held that the epistemological dualism with which Kant left us was resolved by Hegel along ontological lines: it is in the nature of things that there is unity between the knower and the thing known. If Caird saw friction, as for example between science and religion, he maintained that there *must* ultimately be harmony. What is more, he believed that the higher unity of all things was manifesting itself gradually over the years, and that historical study — especially the study of religion — was one of the best ways of detecting this movement.

Utilising decidedly Hegelian triads Caird reminds us of the subjective-objective polarity in human thought. We look out, and the world around us is filled with objects which engage our attention; we may look in and observe the inner life of our own self; and we may look up, and as we do so we are aware that our ability to look out and in presupposes God, the supreme unity, to whom we look up. As he wrote in his Gifford Lectures on *The Evolution of Religion* (1893), 'in a sense . . . we are nearer to God than to ourselves: for the consciousness of self rests upon the idea of God, as at once its first presupposition and its last end and goal' (II, 2): and in his later Gifford Lectures, *The Evolution of Theology in the Greek Philosophers* (1904) he declared that 'to believe in a God is . . . simply to realize that there is a principle of unity in the whole, akin to that which gives unity to our own existence as self-conscious beings (I, 33). Since the spiritual is said to be everywhere present and all-pervasive we are not surprised that when Caird comes to debate the evolution of the idea of God he should seek to show how objective religion (of the Greek kind) and subjective religion (of the Hebraic kind) are synthesised in the universal religion, Christianity. What has happened here is that Caird has transformed Hegel's dialectic from an epistemological method into a dynamic law of life.

Clearly Caird, like Wallace, provides a theistic reading of Hegel, and he makes explicit reference to biblical material and to Christian theology at many points. Indeed he argues that Hegel drew out the essential meaning of Christianity, namely, that the law of the life of spirit — self-realisation through self-abnegation — holds good for God as well as for man. Hegel has learned 'the ultimate lesson of the idealistic movement of thought in Kant, Fichte, and Schelling'.

Despite the fact that Caird regarded Hegelianism as 'but Christianity theorised', he gave some theologians real cause for concern at a number of points. By arguing that nature, humanity and God are all expressions of one spiritual principle he blurred the creator-creature distinction so vital to orthodox theology, and left himself open to the charge of pantheising. True, he was aware — against Bradley, for example — of the pitfall of static monism, and maintained that the realisation of divine-human unity was a dynamic process which entailed 'the overcoming of the deepest of all antagonisms', but this did not silence all theological objectors.

The more conservative objected to the way in which he dispensed with the miraculous understood as the special intervention of God and involving the arrest, or even the breach, of the laws of nature. To Caird the concept of miracle in a world shot through at all times by the immanent divine spirit was redundant. Again, the way in which Caird invoked evolutionary science in support of his dynamic theory upset those who were convinced that Darwinism, with its attack upon the *Genesis* creation narratives, was undermining biblical authority; and his faith in the inevitable organic development of all things towards a higher unity seemed to some almost to require evil as a stage on the way to good, whereas they felt that evil ought not to be at all. This same faith also seemed to make sin all-too-naturally explicable — even excusable; to make the incarnation of Christ simply a witness to God's immanence; and to reduce the cross-resurrection event to a symbol of the dying-and-rising principle, whereas the orthodox regarded it as a radical once-for-all act of rescue on the part of the holy and merciful God.

In a word, Caird sat loose to special revelation. His progressivism could not accommodate a *final* revelation (understanding by 'final' not the last in a series of revelations, but the paradigm revelation which cannot be followed). Thus, in his article 'Edward Caird' (*ET* V, 1893-4, 205) Iverach criticised *The Evolution of Religion*. He found specific fault at a number of places. For example, he could not accept Caird's reading of the religion of Israel as *subjective*. But his general complaint was that Caird typified idealistic philosophers in not doing justice to finite experience, and in distorting history by making it fit their preconceived theory: 'Is this universe as simple as Professor Caird makes it out to be? Have historical matters arranged themselves as he represents them, or has he arranged them so as somehow to reflect his principle?' Above all Iverach objected to the way in which Caird had 'calmly annexed' the domain of revelation and made it part of the natural process. And all of this was done in the name of an underlying unity of subject and object whose nature was left undefined, and on which Caird's entire system rested: 'He calls it God, but the use of that sacred name does not make the meaning more clear.'

Edward Caird's older brother John (1820-98), Professor of Theology at Glasgow and, from 1873, Principal of that University, was the most consistently Hegelian *theologian* of his day. 'Christianity and Idealism,' wrote Edward Caird, 'were the two poles of my brother's thinking, and the latter seemed to him the necessary means for interpreting the former.' In view of Iverach's criticisms of his own work it is interesting that Edward should further write of John, 'If he committed an error it was . . . that he followed Hegel in believing that the whole structure of dogma, as it had been developed by the Church, could be re-interpreted by philosophical reflection, without any essential change.' These remarks occur in the 'Memoir of Principal Caird' prefixed to John Caird's Gifford Lectures, *The Fundamental Ideas of Christianity* (1899 2nd edn; I, cxli, lxxvi). In this volume themes which are by now familiar reappear. The real is the rational; reason is organic in all things; the philosopher is in quest of absolute truth; and the God of religion is the absolute of philosophy. Although he is aware of the peril of pantheism Caird can nevertheless say that 'in one sense all philosophy is pantheistic. It rests on the presupposition that there is in the universe no absolute or irreconcilable division' (I, 105). But whereas man's individuality and responsibility, and the finite world's reality are sacrificed in pantheism, a true philosophy, wrote Caird in his *An Introduction to the Philosophy of Religion* (1880; new edn 1904, 221), 'gives us a principle in the light of which we can see that God is all in all, without denying reality to the finite world and to every individual human spirit, or without denying it except in so far as it involves a life apart from God — a spurious independence which is not the protection but the destruction of all spiritual life'. Caird never tired of asserting (the word is important) that we fully come into our own only when we are at one with God, the absolute spirit; and in Christianity, which takes up into itself the scattered rays of light to be found in other religions and transforms them, God is known as love. For all of which Caldecott praised him: Caird had shown that 'the principles of Transcendentalism are human, and can be separated from German clothing'.[3]

Josiah Royce

Many others contributed to the spread of absolutist ideas, not least the American Josiah Royce (1855-1916) of Harvard. Royce is a prime example of one who was by no means a slavish Hegelian. Indeed, this careful thinker's thought underwent a development which was to take him a considerable distance from his starting point. However, in his early book, *The Religious Aspect of Philosophy* (1885), he propounds a variety of absolutism which is the more interesting because of its difference of approach and tone from that of Bradley.

Where Bradley approached reality *via* the ontological path, viewing epistemological questions askance, Royce's point of departure is epistemological. His question is, 'How can we know the absolute?' His answer is reached through a consideration of error. The problem of error had been a standing objection against absolutism. Can reality embrace the errors of which we are undeniably aware? Royce replies that an error entails a failed intention: an erroneous idea does not convey what it was intended should be conveyed. But for an idea to be recognised as erroneous we must postulate an absolute mind 'to which all facts are known and for which all facts are subject to universal law'. Only such a mind can accommodate and see the resolution of all possible errors.

The upshot is that when we err we do not originate the error, we fall into eternally entertained errors. Similarly, the fact of evil which, as we have seen, made some theologians highly suspicious of the immanentist tendency to make evil simply a stage on the way to good, implies absolute goodness. By the time theologians objected to Royce's exclusively intellectualist absolute, and to his losing of the individual in the divine, Royce was already working his way towards a more ethical version of his theory.

Absolutism discussed

In a letter written to the Reverend J.P. Struthers on 15 February 1893 the theologian James Denney showed where he stood *vis-à-vis* absolute idealism. He referred to his reading of Edward Caird's Gifford Lectures as an 'unprofitable labour', and bemoaned the fact that the philosophers 'think themselves in a position to patronise heaven'.[4] But the philosophers were not to be deterred. In his *Christianity and Idealism* (1897) John Watson defended idealism, argued its compatibility with Christianity, and claimed that 'Idealism is in essential harmony with the Christian ideal of life, as held by the Founder of Christianity, however it may differ, at least in form, from popular Christian theology' (193). In the same year R.M. Wenley showed an acute appreciation of some of the difficulties attendant upon a too glib acceptance of Hegelianism. In his *Contemporary Theology and Theism* he wrote,

> if God be identified with the world in which his self-conscious revelation proceeds, then, not only is he degraded to a level where the spiritual characteristics, predominant in man, fail of universality, but the means whereby the interpretation of the divine self-disclosure may be read lose significance . . . Similarly, level everything up to God, and you run real danger of dissolving him, or, at least, of confounding him with some vague unity which is so crass that it cannot prove a well-spring in the experience of a spiritual being . . . Unity ejects content when identity comes in. And a God who is anything may, on closer inspection, turn out to be a suspiciously easy anagram for nothing. (169–70)

While welcoming Hegel's epoch-making discovery that experience must be its own judge, Wenley says that 'it requires to be extricated from the tangle of formal apparatus wherewith it was originally presented'. But any scruples he may have had about the presentation of idealistic philosophy were more than counterbalanced by his confidence in that type of philosophy as a whole: 'Idealist [man] is by nature, and idealist he, therefore, must remain . . . one hardly sees sufficient reason for giving up the priceless treasure of idealism, the rehabilitation of experience, because some idealists seek to show that deity is no more than the process of ideas' (190). T.W. Levin sought to deflate this somewhat optimistic view in his review of Wenley's book (*M* N.S. VI, 1897, 568), describing the last chapter on 'The Final Idealism' as being 'a little too rhapsodical for a philosophical treatise'.

It is important for us to observe that despite his hesitations concerning certain aspects of contemporary philosophy, Wenley felt it both possible and appropriate to state certain principles on which there was general agreement not only as between philosophers and theologians, but as between them and workers in other fields as well. He says, for example, that one might legitimately regard the notion of the unity of phenomena 'as a commonplace, a platitude, which philosophers, theologians, social reformers, and men of science agree to adopt' (131). Again, 'The truth is that latter-day science, theology, and philosophy have long been engaged upon a joint labor, and the larger confidence of many at present is a product of the equating of results' (159). In short the entire tone of Wenley's book serves to support his contention that 'Today theology is more closely connected with philosophy than ever' (128). Nor has he in mind the mere toleration of theology by philosophers, or *vice versa*; for in the prevailing climate he deems it opportune to suggest, and reasonable to expect, that the two disciplines will positively help each other: metaphysics performing its critical service upon philosophy and theology, and theology offering to philosophy its insights as to the nature of God, the divinity of Christ, and the problem of evil.

Iverach too saw no reasons why religion, philosophy and science should not render mutual assistance to each other, though he always insisted that religion, appealing as it does to the whole person, was more than a philosophy. Though he was, as we have seen, critical of idealism, he maintained a general optimism in his *Theism in the Light of Present Science and Philosophy* (1900): 'The conviction deepens with the ages that there is a thought greater than our thought, a system larger than we can yet grasp, and an ideal formed for man and not merely by man' (196). In religious terms this becomes:

God must be the ideal in whom all ideals meet. In Him must be the ideal of power, for from Him all power, as known to man, must flow. In Him is the ideal of reason, intelligence, wisdom; for all the arrangements of the universe are His appointments. Nothing exists beyond His power, nothing hidden from His omniscience. (249)

Once more, however, we observe that there is no unthinking alliance here between idealism and Christianity. Iverach can rejoice that 'Never in the history of human thought has the identification of the world-idea with the idea of God been presented in so alluring and persuasive a form as at the present hour' (292); he can acknowledge Hegel as 'one of the greatest, if not the greatest, of philosophic thinkers'; but he nevertheless concludes that 'we must sadly turn to our own path and take up the burden of our own work; for the idealist philosophy makes religion to be simply an aspect of itself, and does not leave us a God into whose fellowship we may enter, in whose service we may find perfect freedom' (292).

But if absolute idealism violates the Christian understanding of God, the Christian view of man fares no better; for individual personalities are regarded simply as reflections of one indwelling spirit:

In truth, we must arrive at a conception which leaves room for real individuality, that will recognise the uniqueness of every person, and yet place every person in relation to every other person and thing, that is, has been, or will be. It must allow reality to history, and permit a real progress and real events in it. It must recognise human activity as a factor in the world's history, and recognise somehow that good and evil, happiness and misery, righteousness and sin, are not appearance but stern realities which philosophy and theology must deal with. The cosmos is not appearance, man is real, and God is no abstraction. (305)

An unheeded warning

In view of Bradley's agnosticism theologians tended to give him a wide berth; and the same is true *a fortiori* of the atheistic and pluralistic absolutism of John McTaggart Ellis McTaggart (1866–1925), Fellow and Tutor of Trinity College, Cambridge. McTaggart's careful study of Hegel bore fruit in his *Studies in the*

Hegelian Dialectic (1896, 2nd edn 1922), *Studies in the Hegelian Cosmology* (1901, 2nd edn 1918), and *A Commentary on Hegel's Logic* (1910, 2nd edn 1931).

Like Bradley and unlike Royce, McTaggart followed the ontological path. He sought reality by a dialectical procedure — with this profound difference from his predecessors: his absolute idea, or final synthesis, is the determining factor of all the *preceding* categories. That is, he does not proceed from abstractions to still further abstractions, but from abstractions to the concrete reality which undergirds them all. Unlike Hegel's, his dialectical method is itself subject to development, and he allows that more than one line of development from one category to the next is logically possible.

McTaggart's commentaries on Hegel were but the prelude to the deductive *a priorism* of his *The Nature of Existence* (2 vols, 1921, 1927). Many have felt that notwithstanding the author's earlier declaration that 'All true philosophy must be mystical, not indeed in its methods, but in its final conclusions', this work more than merits Bradley's description of McTaggart's philosophy as 'an unearthly ballet of bloodless categories'. Critics were not slow to point to McTaggart's need to posit at least one empirical fact, namely, that something exists — and this they regarded as the Achilles' heel of his system. Undeterred, McTaggart argued that the whole of reality is composed of (metaphysical-Berkeleian) substance, and that the absolute is a pluralistic system of related selves. The self is changeless in essence and uncreated — hence to atheism. The absolute, which may be conceived not only pluralistically but also as one substance, is impersonal. Happily, selves are held together in the unifying bond of love. We are thus left with something in the nature of a spiritual vision in which love and, for good measure, immortality, are preserved — but all without the need of God. According to McTaggart, 'there can be no being who is a God, or who is anything so resembling a God that the name would not be very deceptive' (II, Sect. 500). Small wonder that McTaggart himself warned theologians that Hegelianism was 'an enemy in disguise — the least evident but the most dangerous'.[5]

However, not all theologians were duly warned. In his *Truth and Reality* (1901) John Smyth was content to reiterate conventional idealistic themes over against naturalism:

> Life is found to be one; and the only possibility of possessing

Truth at all lies in the acknowledgement of a Reality which
will give unity and harmony to all the various manifestations
of Life . . . The best condemnation of Naturalism is not only
its resolution of Life into that which is without form and void,
but also its resolution of itself into nothingness and eternal
silence. (3, 29)

I am not at present concerned to show how Smyth substantiates
his views, but I am interested in the reactions to them. One reviewer
(*ET*, VII, 1900-01, 261) said that this book 'shows quite conclusively how incapable is every form of naturalism of explaining
the things we see and know; it shows quite restfully how inevitable
is the entrance of the spiritual and how universal its application'.
A.J. Jenkinson was by no means so enchanted, and bearing the
words 'conclusively' and 'restfully' in mind it is instructive to attend
to his comments:

He deals cursorily with naturalism and erroneous or defective
idealistic theories. He disposes of the former 'in brief space,'
— not by meeting it upon its own ground, but by assailing
it with the abstract arguments of the class-room, an artillery
as noisy as it is ineffective . . . Its tone is bombastic; it abounds
in irrelevancies . . . (*M*, X, 1901, 415)

Jenkinson's judgement is to be taken the more seriously because
he confesses that he is *not* opposed to Smyth's aims. We thus see
that the ready association of idealistic philosophy with Christian
themes was too comforting in some quarters and increasingly suspect
in others. It hardly needs to be said that the versions of Christian
absolutism that were to appear during the early years of the 20th
century were more in the line of the Cairds than of any other
absolutist philosopher.

It does appear, then, that towards the close of the 19th century
there was a considerable amount of common ground between at
least some philosophers and theologians. There was a shared concern to discover, or at any rate to posit, that higher unity in which
all things were thought to cohere, and towards which they were held
to tend. While none swallowed neat Hegelianism, many felt that
Hegel had shown the unavoidable way forward in philosophy. Many
regarded philosophy, science and theology as partners in a quasi-
religious enterprise of truth-seeking, and no philosopher or
theologian had thought of questioning the place of metaphysics in

their respective disciplines. On the contrary, Wenley could claim that 'the perception grows stronger and stronger, affecting an ever widening circle of thoughtful men, that "everything physical is at the same time metaphysical" '.[6]

But the writing was on the wall. Or, to change the metaphor, the seeds were already being sown for the demise of absolute idealism as a philosophical force of the first order. We shall not be surprised to find that, in keeping with the fact that neat pigeon-holing is ruled out by the nature of the subjects under investigation here, the seeds of discord did not all come from the same packet. On the one hand we have a strain of philosophical and theological speculation fertilised by the concept of personality; on the other hand we have the resurgence of hardy perennial British empiricism; and, for good measure, there is also a dazzling profusion of hot-house pragmatism raised by F.C.S. Schiller which, if not widely popular in Britain, was unquestionably colourful.

General reflections

Before proceeding to the 20th century some general reflections are in order. To any who would construct a Christian philosophy by alliance with a philosophical 'ism' the story of the relations between absolute idealism and Christian theology must surely constitute a cautionary tale. There are in the first place tactical issues to be faced. Is it wise to nail one's colours to a mast which is capable of splitting in many directions, to the hurt of one's flag? What of the volatility of philosophical fashion? If Christianity is made to depend unduly upon a prevailing 'ism', what of the faith when that 'ism' is weighed and found wanting — or is just forgotten as if it had never been?

More important than tactics, however, is logic. It is interesting that despite their reservations concerning certain idealistic formulations, Watson, Wenley, Iverach and others were nevertheless willing to grant that some form of idealism provided the most suitable basis for a Christian philosophy. But there are ways of making this point which are tendentious in the extreme. Thus when, for example, Smyth says that 'This Reality, known in Philosophy by the title, "The Ultimate Ground of All That Is," is, in Religion, known as God',[7] we have a dogmatic assumption which begs the logical question: can terms be regarded as equivalent in the absence of a careful consideration of the world views within which they are used? To W.L. Davidson 'God' and 'absolute' are mutually transferable terms according to context: ' "God" is the term more properly designative of the Supreme Being when we are viewing Him as known by us or as revealed to us in our personal relations with Him, whereas "the Absolute" is more strictly applicable at moments when we are specially conscious to ourselves of the fact that God transcends our knowledge of Him . . .'[8] But this psychologising approach prompts Davidson to overlook the radical manner in which terms are re-baptised when they are transposed from one world view to another.

Bradley's absolute is *not* Smyth's or Davidson's. To take an example from another context: both Jesus and his religious opponents would have been able to issue the command, 'Love your neighbour'; but the point of the story of the Good Samaritan is that notwithstanding the literal identity of the words used they would not have *meant* the same thing in so speaking, since their understandings of 'neighbour' were so radically different. Iverach, once more. saw the point clearly: 'To speak of the absolute and unconditioned as synonymous with God, is simply to alter the conception of God.'[9] The upshot is that it is not the case that with more practice and experiment we shall be better able to transpose terms and their connotations from one world view to another. It is a question of logic. In utilising terms from other world views we are involved in an *analogical* procedure, and we must take seriously J.M. Keynes's distinction between positive and negative analogy. That is, we must be as concerned to see where our analogy breaks down as we are to show how well it fits the case in hand.

The very persistence of varieties of idealism through the centuries suggests that even if 'Reality-as-a-whole' as some idealists have conceived it is somewhat of a mare's nest, man's oft-expressed desire for some kind of synoptic vision — some account of 'what it all comes to' — is assuredly a phoenix. But the strength of the synoptic urge merely serves to underline the necessity that the philosopher of religion should beware of the peril of reductionism inherent in any attempt to construct a Christian philosophy on the foundations of, and in terms of, a prevailing philosophical 'ism'.

At its bluntest the question reduces to this: If we begin from 'alien' axioms how much of Christian truth can we subsequently work into our system? We have seen that as far as absolute idealism is concerned the shoe pinches at the following important points: Christ can be idealised off the stage of history; the self can be lost in the absolute; pantheising immanentism can blur the creator-creature distinction; and the radical nature of evil can be obscured by the emphasis upon the dynamic process towards perfection.

A reference to the interestingly ambivalent position of D. Miall Edwards will bring matters to a head. Although he favoured personal rather than absolute idealism, Edwards is typical of many Christian philosophers of the first half of the 20th century as far as method is concerned. On the one hand, and *theoretically*, he admits that there is no one generally accepted philosophy in terms of which the Christian faith might be presented. Accordingly,

> We shall be content with 'feeling our way about' amidst such philosophical systems and tendencies, ancient and modern, as are relevant to our purpose, with a view to discovering for ourselves, by the method of constructive criticism, the general outlines of a philosophy which will at once do justice to man's total experience of the world and serve as an intellectual framework for Christian convictions.

He aims to outline 'a philosophy which *culminates in* a Theism' (my italics), and having attempted this he treats of specifically theological matters: God, Christ and the Trinity. In other words, he seeks to arrive at a Christian philosophy by means of an examination of alien systems. He does not overtly consider the possibility that this is to put the cart before the horse, yet on his own admission he has an undisclosed criterion of relevance. What can this be?

That was the Edwards of *Christianity and Philosophy* (1932, 7, 8). On the other hand, and now in relation to *practice* we find that in his earlier book, *The Philosophy of Religion* (1924), he proceeds in what I am suggesting is the appropriate analogical way:

> Is God, then, identical with the Absolute? . . . If by the Absolute is meant the sum-total of reality, then, as Sorley says, God and the Absolute will not be identical, for there are real events and real beings which do not manifest the divine nature . . . If on the other hand the Absolute be defined as the Supreme Reality, in the sense of the original source, the ever-present sustaining power, and the ultimate goal of all things, then God is the Absolute Being . . . God, then, is the Supreme Reality of the universe, but to call Him the Absolute is misleading because ambiguous. As we understand Him, God is not the imperturbable, detached Absolute of some monistic philosophies . . . (302-3)

Here the notion of positive and negative analogy is properly utilised. What Edwards does not bring out is that it is the underlying clash in logic of different, and at least partially opposed, world views which creates the ambiguity to which he rightly points.

The most that idealism — or, for that matter, any other 'ism' can offer the Christian philosopher — and it is much, is a repository of analogies from which, in the interests of communication and construction, he may draw. Such analogies as he uses will need the most circumspect handling if the peril of reductionism is to be avoided. The Christian philosopher does not come empty-handed to other systems of thought; he comes as a Christian. Hence if he should decide for whatever reasons (e.g. in the interest of communication) to adopt the language of such systems, he would do well to reflect that his proper role *vis-à-vis* such language is not that of poacher, but rather that of anabaptist![10]

Notes

1. R. Flint, 'Theism', in *Encyclopaedia Britannica*, 9th edn (1888), vol. XXIII, p. 247.
2. T.H. Green, *Prolegomena to Ethics* (1883), ed. A.C. Bradley, (Oxford, Clarendon Press, 4th edn 1899), p. 98.
3. A. Caldecott, *The Philosophy of Religion in England and America*, (Methuen, London, 1901), p. 150.
4. See *Letters of Principal James Denney to his Family and Friends*, ed. James Moffatt (Hodder and Stoughton, London, 1922), p. 49.
5. J. McT.E. McTaggart, *Studies in the Hegelian Cosmology* (Macmillan, London, 1901), p. 250.
6. R.M. Wenley, *Contemporary Theology and Theism* (T. & T. Clark, Edinburgh, 1897), p. 162.
7. J. Smyth, *Truth and Reality* (T. & T. Clark, Edinburgh, 1901), p. 75.
8. W.L. Davidson, *Recent Theistic Discussion* (T. & T. Clark, Edinburgh, 1921), p. 153.
9. J. Iverach, *Theism in the Light of Present Science and Philosophy*, (Hodder & Stoughton, London, 1900), p. 307.
10. See further A.P.F. Sell, 'The peril of reductionism in Christian thought', *Scottish Journal of Theology*, XXVII (1974), pp. 48-64.

3
Approaches Old and New, 1900-20

By concentrating on absolute idealism for most of the last chapter the impression may have been given that philosophy at large was less varied than in fact it was. The truth is that although absolutism was dominant alternative approaches in philosophy were available. Prominent among these were personal idealism and realism, and in this chapter I shall take up their stories. But first, a bird's-eye view of the first decade of the present century.

Ferment and stock-taking in philosophy

Absolutism did not evaporate overnight. Until well into the 20th century John Stuart Mackenzie and others were ploughing the absolutist furrow. Mackenzie (1860-1935), Fellow of Trinity College, Cambridge, and from 1895 to 1915 Professor of Logic and Philosophy at Cardiff University College, propounded a version of the doctrine which showed itself increasingly hospitable to other, not always mutually compatible, lines of thought. His *Outlines of Metaphysics* appeared in 1902, in which he declared that 'the most important task for Metaphysics is that of sifting the ultimate conceptions that are left over by the special sciences, rather than that of directly attempting to bring the various special sciences together' (11). This is a somewhat less grandiose role than that envisaged for metaphysics by Wenley and others: but Mackenzie's programme is ambitious enough. He claims that metaphysics must be grounded in experience, and suggests that the real danger of psychologism may be avoided only if the metaphysician has constantly before him his goal of seeking to grasp reality as a whole.

Mackenzie criticises monistic idealism on the ground that if, as

Bradley holds, the absolute is completely coherent and self-consistent, it is 'difficult to see how any place is left for the incomplete, the incoherent, the contradictory, which yet in some sense exists' (151). As we have seen, Bradley sought to surmount this obstacle by resorting to the notion of degrees of truth, but Mackenzie questions the extent to which this can be done without modifying one's conception of the absolute. He criticises Leibniz's monism for failing adequately to account for the 'communion' of independent realities, and opts for Hegelian organism as standing the best chance of being made ultimately satisfactory and coherent. He grants that the human mind cannot conceive of the universe in a completely coherent way, but thinks that there is hope and encouragement in the real possibility that we may be able to conceive of it in a not completely *incoherent* way.

Whereas Mackenzie believed that the difficulties inherent in absolute idealism could be removed by idealists themselves, G.E. Moore was already trying to redress the philosophical balance by his appeal to common sense and his method of language analysis. For Moore, matter exists as well as spirit. He will not allow with the idealist that the only reality is spiritual. For him the only alternative to the belief that matter exists is the belief that nothing exists: 'All other suppositions — the Agnostic's, that something, at all events, does exist, as much as the Idealist's, that spirit does — are, if we have no reason for believing in matter, as baseless as the grossest superstitions.' Such was the heart of Moore's case in his celebrated paper, 'The Refutation of Idealism' (*M* N.S. XII, 1903, 453). We should, however, be cautioned that the idealism here refuted by Moore is Berkeley's idealism, according to which objects exist only in so far as they are perceived by a mind (human or divine); it is not the fashionable post-Hegelian absolutism of his own day.

A.E. Taylor's *Elements of Metaphysics* appeared during the same year as Moore's paper, and shows little concern at the latter's problem. On the contrary, Taylor was attempting to pave the way for a Christian absolutism — a quest which found a stringent critic in the pragmatist F.C.S. Schiller. In his article, 'Empiricism and the absolute' (*M* N.S. XIV, 1905, 348), Schiller inveighs against both Taylor and absolutism, and is particularly opposed to the idea that the absolute can be a postulated satisfaction of other desires. He finds it objectionable psychologically to suppose that imperfect parts should wish to become the whole; and from the standpoint of logic he cannot see how a combination of the imperfect could become the perfect. Taylor subsequently broadened his approach, as we shall see.

Schiller's *bête noir*, however, was no less a person than Bradley himself. According to Schiller Bradley had 'beguiled the fair maid, Philosophy' by his insistence upon the non-contradictory nature of ultimate reality, and by his refusal to provide an adequate account of human experience as it is. Schiller lamented the fact that Bradley had ascended from the sphere of appearances and had been received into the 'bosom of the Absolute' — all of which reminded the doughty critic 'of nothing so much as of the fabled "rope trick" of the Indian jugglers'.[1] Schiller pursued his quarry over the years with dogged persistence, and was jubilant on the publication of Bradley's *Essays in Truth and Reality* (1914), which he represented as a capitulation on Bradley's part to the position of William James and himself. He declared that the essays in question 'are as fine a sepulchral monument as the Absolute deserves, even though it be of necessity a cenotaph'.[2]

Some time before Schiller was conducting the last rites over absolutism (somewhat prematurely, as we shall see), experience, linked with the concept of personality, had come to the fore. As long ago as the 1880s A.S. Pringle-Pattison (then A. Seth) had protested against the Hegelian tendency to blur manifest distinctions in life and in the world by appealing to such blanket terms as the absolute. This line of thought was followed up by Clement C.J. Webb in an early article entitled, 'The personal element in philosophy' (*PAS*, V, 1904–5, 106). Webb argued that philosophy's concern was with experience as a whole, and that therefore the personal element was ineradicable from it: 'The whole personality of Plato or of Aristotle, of Spinoza or of Kant, is revealed in their systems . . .' (108). To a later philosopher this enthusiastic assertion would seem to make philosophy too much like psychological biography. But Webb never ceased to maintain the rights of personality in philosophy, and was to build upon his chosen foundation for many years to come. Among others who stood on the same foundation was Hastings Rashdall, who contributed an article entitled 'Personality: human and divine' to Henry Sturt's symposium, *Personal Idealism* (1902).

In view of the diversity of philosophical activity and method we are not surprised to find a number of stock-taking, 'recommendatory' articles appearing during the first decade of the 20th century. We find Shadworth H. Hodgson declaring that it is the task of philosophy to harmonise all facets of human experience, but also considering that the hope of our attaining to speculative knowledge of the absolute must be surrendered. He seeks to forestall opposition by suggesting that such a limitation of philosophy's scope will be liberating rather than the reverse; for once we have realised — and realised *via* philosophy itself — that the absolute is unattainable, we shall with the greater zeal apply philosophy's subjective method to the entire field of human thought and conduct. To none must this programme have been more disturbing than to religious philosophers of the Smyth variety. But Hodgson is not without some small comfort to offer them. He concludes his paper on 'Method in philosophy' (*PAS*, IV, 1903-4) by announcing his good news that there are signs that 'even Englishmen are coming to see the necessity of philosophy, as that line of thought which, from its independent investigation of human nature as a whole, can alone afford a theoretical justification of religion, as a certain kind of practical attitude towards the speculatively unknown and unknowable regions of the Universe' (15).

For Henry Sturt, however, in his article 'The line of advance in philosophy' (*PAS*, V, 1904-5, 29), the way forward consists in the philosopher's taking more account of the element of personal striving in life. Following the basic tenets of idealism and scientific development he advocates a form of voluntarism as against what he calls examples of the passive fallacy. These latter are intellectualism, culminating in panlogism; 'Absolutism, which denies that the world can change because it is divine and perfect, and merges human individuality and activity in the One-and-All, thus degrading all motion and activity to an unreal appearance of an essentially passive Absolute' (36); and subjectivism, culminating in solipsism. Sturt finds all these unhappy tendencies in Hegel, to whom is attributed the dominance of the passive fallacy. Sturt's concluding observation, 'A philosophy of striving is likely to be increasingly acceptable to a society in which striving for good objects is common and has no small chance of success' is not unimportant since it throws light upon one important aspect of the spirit of Sturt's age — a spirit of fairly widespread optimism, from which neither philosophers nor theologians were entirely immune. Not indeed that philosophers were verging upon the incautious. Höffding's opinion that 'It is the task of Philosophy to give us a standard to be used in the criticism of the spontaneously developed world-views' (*M* N.S. XIV, 1905, 207-8) was but one expression of a conviction that was to dominate large areas of philosophy until the 1930s, and which is not yet entirely dormant.

The year 1906 furnishes us with a good example of philosophical dogmatism. In *An Outline of the Idealistic Construction of Experience* J.B. Baillie claimed that 'The culmination of an Absolute Idealism is the justification of the idealistic position itself, as the ultimate form of knowledge' (344). The task of philosophy is not to create or to destroy modes of knowledge, but to explain all modes by demonstrating their inter-connections. For Baillie philosophy and religion are symbols which embody all that the other modes of experience aim at. He is convinced that 'For an idealism which takes Absolute Spirit to be the Unity of Experience, and which takes finite self-conscious Spirit to be at the point of view of the Whole, there can be only one philosophy and one method of interpretation' (43). The latter-day philosopher may be forgiven for thinking that an explosion of some dogmas of philosophy would have been salutary in 1906 and, in fairness to his contemporaries, it must be noted that not all were happy with Baillie's position. Iverach, for example (*ET*, XVIII, 1906–7, 422), was left with the unresolved difficulty of accounting adequately for the experience of other selves, without escaping the absolutist prison by the tunnel of the empirical. But in the event 1906 saw a critique of *Some Dogmas of Religion* by McTaggart. While not precluding thought of one absolute substance, McTaggart maintained his pluralistic stance which, as we saw earlier, was compatible with his atheistic version of the doctrine of immortality: if all reality is a harmonious system of selves, it is perhaps itself sufficiently godlike to dispense with a God' (250). Professor Macquarrie's verdict is just: 'This metaphysic of McTaggart, though atheistic, remains almost passionately religious. It might be compatible with some oriental religions, but it marks the furthest remove of Anglo-American idealism from Christian theology.'[3]

John Watson was soon to supply the lack felt by Iverach with respect to Baillie's position. In 1907 *The Philosophical Basis of Religion* appeared, and Watson felt it quite in order to begin his work with the anticipation that 'We shall probably all agree that a man's religion, as the expression of his total attitude to life, is that which gives meaning and direction to all that he thinks and feels and does; and that his philosophy . . . expresses his deepest and most cherished convictions.' He recognised, however, that the growth of earnest specialisation, resulting as it did in the ever-increasing difficulty specialists experienced in estimating the claims of pursuits other than their own, made for difficulty in the philosophico-religious debate. On the other hand, he considered that such debate was now easier to conduct in so far as 'by the inevitable progress of science and historical criticism, the dogmatic attitude of an earlier age has been superseded, or at least modified, and thus the combatants are in a better frame of mind for the construction of a more comprehensive doctrine' (2). From the point of view of attitude and aim the telling words here are 'inevitable progress', 'combatants, and 'the construction of a more comprehensive doctrine'. This last phrase notwithstanding, Watson was disturbed by certain aspects of both personal idealism and the new realism, though, as hinted above, he did make some effort to take account of the individual 'in terms of the spiritual medium within which he lives'. Further, he was convinced that no worthy results were to be gained by discussing the experience of the individual only. He regarded his system as one which combined the best elements of personal idealism and the new realism, labelled it speculative or constructive idealism, and sought to clear it of extreme absolutist adhesions.

By now some theologians, including J.S. Banks, were afraid that the pendulum would swing too far in the direction of experience. In 'The argument from experience' (*ET*, XIX, 1907-8-) he averred,

> A living experience is the common characteristic of all Christians, lettered or unlettered . . . But in our days it is set forth as the only trustworthy ground for all, superseding the evidences which have played so large a part in the past; historical and philosophical defences are discounted. Natural theology is discarded altogether, 'theoretic' reasoning is out of court . . . Far be it from us to undervalue the force of the argument, or to suggest doubt to minds at rest. Still, it is right to prove all things and to beware of building on too narrow a basis. (460)

Banks stoutly maintained that 'Faith, if it is to be worthy of God and man, must be rational' (461). Perhaps the philosophical equivalent of the theological subjectivism which Banks attacks is to be found in the work of Cook Wilson and H.A. Prichard. Their work, not to mention that of Moore and Russell, was no doubt among the prompters of Dr Scott Holland's plaintive cry:

> Metaphysics are in suspense. The five or six experts, who still hand on the good tradition can be heard crying in the night to one another. But no one listens; and they alone understand each other, and carry on faithfully, in a tiny knot,

the historic debate on the existence of the Absolute. Let them hold on to their high faith. Some day their cause will re-emerge. It cannot be that men will ever surrender the heritage won by the heroic endeavour that opened with Plato and closed with Hegel. But the Vision is not yet. And, in the meantime, we are engaged in a debate on a lower plane. We are scientific. We are psychological. We are empirical. We are pragmatic . . . Our entire thought is concentrated on Experience.[4]

By way of taking a sounding of the general situation towards the end of the first decade of this century, we may place side by side a further quotation from Banks's article (462) and one from a reviewer of R.M. Wenley's book *Modern Thought and the Crisis of Belief* (1909) (*ET*, XX, 1908-9, 547):

The modern aversion to the association of religion and philosophy is a strange phenomenon, reminding us of the fierce Montanist Tertullian, who cursed philosophy in the name of religion. The general mind of the Church was very different.

When we discover a believer among men of science we take him by the hand heartily. How much more when we discover a believer among men of philosophy. For is he not much rarer? And is not philosophy the real antagonist of our faith?

These statements are indicative of a mood of apprehension among certain theologians. They entertain the uncomfortable belief that all is not well in the theologico-philosophical world. As they stand, such statements as these are somewhat extreme in view of the tone of such philosophers as Baillie and Watson. On the other hand, the atheism of McTaggart and the humanism of Schiller, to say nothing of the work of Moore and Russell, can hardly have been comforting to those who still regarded Christianity and philosophy as inseparable allies. In view of all this the attitude of the *philosopher* J.S. Mackenzie is a little surprising. He agrees that the tendency among modern intellectuals (a term he encloses within inverted commas) is 'to think of religion as a sort of spiritual measles that some people catch at certain periods of their lives, or, at the best, as a help to the policeman; and of theology as a medieval form of sophistry which has only an antiquarian interest', but he is sure that this tendency will be reversed when the full flowering of idealistic cosmological construction (as distinct from epistemological ground-clearing) is seen.[5] But forces were hard at work which were to make Mackenzie's aspiration one which remains unfulfilled to this day.

Towards the dislodgement of absolutism

A number of factors contributed to the dislodgement of absolutism from the centre of the British philosophical stage. I have already referred to Schiller's pin pricks, but the combination of other forces was even more significant. There was opposition from psychologists such as William McDougall who, in his *An Introduction to Social Psychology* (1908), argued that absolutism was too 'intellectualist'; it did not take due account of those aspects of man's nature which were non, even anti-rational. Again, T.E. Hulme was among literary men who viewed absolutism askance on the ground that its quest for harmony, wholeness, all-embracing coherence flew in the face of the actual and irremediable *disharmony* between man and the material universe. To Hulme the absolute was invoked merely in order to paper over the cracks in a dubious theory. Then there was the tragedy of the First World War, which cast doubt upon the *bona fides* of Hegel himself. He was honoured by his own countrymen as a nationalist, and this could only damage his cause in the eyes of those Britons who were by now suspicious of all things German. It could seem *patriotic* to embrace realism; and the American philosopher Ralph Barton Perry was in no doubt that anti-idealist philosophy had 'gained great impetus from the war. There is a natural disposition to view with suspicion anything that came out of Germany.'[6] Certainly the catastrophe of war was more than sufficient to prompt the erstwhile proponent of absolutism, J.B. Baillie, to review his position radically. In his *Studies in Human Nature* (1921) he announced his conversion from idealism and his determination to develop a philosophy emphasising the concrete individuality of man, and based upon 'critical common-sense'.

Further erosion of absolutism followed upon the expression of insights damaging to it by those who were in general *sympathy* with it. Prominent in this connection are the philosopher Harold Henry Joachim (1868-1938) who, after lectureships at St Andrews and Oxford, became Wykeham Professor of Logic at Oxford; and the theologian John Richardson Illingworth (1848-1915), a pupil of Green and Rector of Longworth. Joachim, whose views were influenced by Nettleship and Wallace, but especially by Bradley, argued in *The Nature of Truth* (1906) that reality is one in the sense that we may not sever the experienced real from the experiencing of it. Truth is therefore systematic truth; that is, the coherence theory of truth is the most acceptable theory of truth. As he wrote, 'the truth itself is one, and whole, and complete', and 'all thinking and all experience moves within its recognition and subject to its manifest authority' (178). Herein lay the heart of his opposition to the realism of Russell and Moore. He could not hold that experiencing made no difference to the facts experienced, and he could not agree that relations are external to their terms. He did not, however, deny that our thought is of a reality other than itself, though he could not square this admission with his coherence theory of truth. Influenced by Bradley's distinction between appearance and reality, he ruefully concluded that in fact the coherence theory applies only to that ideal knowledge to which the human intelligence can never attain. That such truth is a reality at all we can only surmise. He thus concluded, 'I am ending with a confession of ignorance; but at least I have cleared my mind of much sham knowledge. And I am old-fashioned enough to believe that this achievement is the first requisite for any one who hopes to learn'(180).

Illingworth's hesitations concerning absolutism were theologically inspired in a way that those of Joachim were not. Like Joachim, however, he remained broadly within the absolutist tradition — he maintains, for example, that although matter and spirit are distinct, we know them only in their correlativity. But Illingworth's is an importantly qualified absolutism. In the first place, his immanentism owed at least as much to the Alexandrian incarnational-Logos theology as it did to post-Hegelian idealism. His view, as expressed in his essay on 'The incarnation and development' in *Lux Mundi* (1889), was that evolution, 'the category of the age', provided fertile soil for the re-planting of the cosmic aspects of the work of the ever-immanent Logos. Secondly, from the outset in his book *Personality, Human and Divine* (1894), he made it abundantly plain that he was not out to submerge the human personality within the absolute. As to the absolute itself, Illingworth did not follow Bradley and Bosanquet in denying personality to the absolute. For him the Christian Trinity is the archetype of the three-foldness of (ever incomplete) human personality, which comprises reason, will and love. Indeed, 'the actual Trinity of God explains the potential trinity of man; and our anthropomorphic language follows from our theomorphic minds' (214). In union with God incarnate 'our finite, imperfect personality, shall find, in the far eternity, its archetype and end' (216).

Although he was a slavish disciple of no-one, the influence of Lotze (whose *Microcosmos* appeared in English in 1887) is clear at certain points in Illingworth's exposition: supremely where he quotes Lotze with approval as saying that 'Perfect personality is in God only; to all finite minds there is allotted but a pale copy thereof' (53).

In 1902 Illingworth published his *Reason and Revelation*, and *The Doctrine of the Trinity* followed in 1907. If we were unaware of his understanding of the correlativity of the divine immanence and transcendence we might be surprised that whereas he published *Divine Immanence* in 1898, *Divine Transcendence* did not appear until 1911. But his work was all of a piece, and in the later volume he reaffirmed his earlier words to the effect that the conception of divine transcendence is 'from the Christian point of view, presupposed, and not precluded by that of immanence'. From this idea, in his later volume, he proceeded to draw that of a 'spiritual, and, in that sense, supernatural authority, which distinguished the organization, faith, and worship of the Church, and leads to a correlative element of obedience in the character of its members' (vi). *Divine Transcendence* was offered as a corrective to those pantheising immanentisms which blurred the creator-creature distinction.

Throughout his many books Illingworth sustained a remarkable consistency of vision. He believed that 'Christianity inevitably involves an intellectual view of the universe'; but if idealism was to him a theoretic necessity, the incarnation (in my view to the relative neglect of the atonement), with its implication of the sacramental nature of the universe, was Illingworth's motivating inspiration.

But if Joachim and Illingworth were, to a degree, fifth columnists in the absolutist camp, and if Baillie was a belated convert to a form of realism, who owed his conversion largely to non-philosophical factors, the personal idealists sought to remedy the deficiencies of absolutism by secession, whilst the realists endeavoured to expose the inadequacies of all idealisms. To these groups we now turn.

The personal idealists

The outstanding pioneer of personal idealism in Britain was Andrew

Seth Pringle-Pattison (1856–1931), who held chairs successively at Cardiff, St Andrews and Edinburgh.[7] In the case of Pringle-Pattison it is more than usually important to treat his works in chronological order, for his policy was 'construction through criticism', and his position evolved gradually *via* the careful analysis of the major available philosophical options.

In 1882 Pringle-Pattison's book *The Development from Kant to Hegel* was published. The second part of this work was reprinted, under the title 'Philosophy of religion in Kant and Hegel' in his collection, *The Philosophical Radicals* (1907), to which reference is here made. Beginning with Kant Pringle-Pattison avers that the foundations of Kant's philosophy are laid in his ethics. According to Kant we are immediately conscious of the moral law, and are required to postulate God, freedom and immortality as its necessary accompaniments. On this basis Kant allegorises Christian doctrines so that, for example, the individual's passage from corruption to purity of moral maxim is, in scriptual language, his becoming a new creature, his new birth. While Pringle-Pattison applauds Kant for regarding the Christian creeds more positively, and man less uncritically and optimistically than did the thinkers of the Enlightenment, he does find certain weaknesses in his position. The way in which Kant separates ethics from metaphysics is unconvincing, and results in excessive individualism. At this point Hegelianism has the advantage over Kant. Moreover, Kant's God is still postulated in the old, externalising, deistic manner: his God is a *deus ex machina*, invoked to ensure the final due adjustment of happiness and virtue. Strictly, the noumenal and self-legislative self leaves no room for a mechanistically conceived God. We are thus left with a dualism: with an unknowable God (for he belongs to the noumenal realm), and with knowable phenomena of whose nature we cannot make sense without postulating God, freedom and immortality.

For Hegel, by contrast, thought is the unity within which all opposites are reconciled. Thus, in connection with religion, Hegel claims that 'Thought justifies the content of religion, and recognises its forms, — that is to say, the determinateness of its historical appearance; but, in the very act of doing so, it recognises also the limitations of the forms' (287–8). In this way Kant's absolute distinction between God and man is done away, and we see this most clearly in Christianity.

The difficulty here is that if the degree of divine immanence is as great as Hegel supposes, how are we to account for the contingency, imperfection, suffering and evil which undoubtedly spoil the world? Pringle-Pattison rightly says that Hegel finds it much easier to show that, given blemishes, the world-spirit gradually wins its way by patience and struggle, than to show how the blemishes can be in the first place, given the divine perfection.

We see at the outset, then, that Pringle-Pattison attempts judiciously to weigh the pros and cons of Hegelianism. He adopts the same policy in his *Scottish Philosophy* (1885). It would take us too far afield to pursue his handling of his fellow countrymen in detail. What concerns us is the lesson he learned from them. He does not find that the older Scottish philosphers were opposed to system-building as such, though they did not employ themselves systematically. Rather, they saw their role as that of confronting the sceptic. They deal with particular issues, and their intuitionism leaves us with a number of isolated, allegedly self-evident propositions which are then dignified as first principles. On the other hand, Kant's system was deficient as an account of reality, for so much was said to be unknowable. Once again Hegel scores heavily: 'When we come to Hegel, we find a Method put into our hands, which professes to guarantee both the inner-connectedness of all the conceptions, and the self-completing integrity of the resulting scheme . . . [Hegel's analysis] is an indefinite advance on anything that had gone before it in modern philosophy' (197–8).

Pringle-Pattison admits that with 'the rank and file of the Hegelian army' Hegel's dialectical method became a fetish, and he insists that 'philosophical work cannot yet be done by machinery'. (By contrast, McTaggart maintained in his *Studies in the Hegelian Dialectic* that what is of supreme value in Hegel is not his general principle but his dialectic method, for the latter encouraged the detailed analysis of categories.) The method serves Hegel's over-arching immanentist principle, apart from which it is impotent. The method is directly derived from the nature of the self-consciousness and hence 'Hegel's results are so marvellously richer than those of Kant. Because the direct relation of all principles of explanation to the nature of the explaining self was not adequately grasped either by Kant or Reid, their enumerations of principles have unavoidably the appearance of being, as it were, in the air' (200–1). Absolute idealism gives due place to subject and object, denying reality to neither: 'Its sole thesis is, that the real is ultimately rational — *i.e.*, that its different elements constitute a system, in which, and in which alone, they can be understood (202). As for the absolute self-consciousness in which thought achieves a view of the systematic unity of all things, this is something in which we cannot but believe, though we cannot see it. Thus the element of faith cannot be excluded from philosophy. Whenever faith is pitted against reason 'mischief lurks not far distant'. The true antithesis is between faith and knowledge, and only by being God could we know in the strict sense. Denied such knowledge we must strive after *grounded* faith.

For all the advantages of Hegelianism as he saw it, Pringle-Pattison was alive to its deficiencies. In treating of humanity as a universal consciousness gazing at the spectacle of things it merges the individual with the universal to the detriment of the former. In his next book, *Hegelianism and Personality* (1887), Pringle-Pattison elaborates on the weaknesses of absolutism. Hegelianism's radical error is its identification of the human with the divine self-consciousness. Though it exists in relation to other selves and to the divine, he wishes to insist that each self is also a unique existent which is *impervious* (a word he later queried) to other selves, and resists invasion: 'though the self is . . . in knowledge, a principle of unification, it is, in existence or metaphysically, a principle of isolation . . . I have a centre of my own — a will of my own — which no one shares with me or can share — a centre which I maintain even in my dealings with God Himself' (217). Apart from this relative independence the religious approach to God, entailing as it does willed self-surrender, would be impossible. The Hegelian unification of the human and the divine subjects destroys the reality of both God and man.

Pringle-Pattison refined and reviewed his position over the years, and by common consent the first volume of his Gifford Lectures of 1912-13, *The Idea of God in the Light of Recent Philosophy* (1917), is his crowning achievement. On the basis of the general standpoint already sketched, he here passed in review the contribution of a number of his contemporaries, all the while seeking to avoid what he saw as the perils of Kantian dualism on the one hand and Hegelian monism on the other. His guide throughout, in steering between this Scylla and Charybdis, was the concept of personality. In a partial return to absolutism, and by way of balancing his earlier statement that all selves are *impervious*, he now places greater emphasis on the relation of intimacy in which selves stand to each other and to God. He has found no reason whatever to depart from idealism — 'the doctrine of the self-conscious life as organic to the world or of the world as finding completion and expression in that life, so that the universe, as a complete or self-existent fact, is statable only in terms of mind' (190); but nothing will persuade him to tolerate the unification of consciousness in a single self. This, he contends, would be 'fatal . . . to the real selfhood either of God or man' (390).

As Pringle-Pattison criticised the work of others, so his own efforts were subjected to criticism. Among the more religiously-inclined philosophers, for example, W.L. Davidson, in his *Recent Theistic Discussion* (1921), queried Pringle-Pattison's understanding of the relation of non-conscious nature to self-conscious finite being. How could nature emerge as the possessor of feeling and rationality? Again, does Pringle-Pattison not minimise the idea of transcendence? For his part Davidson does not wish to reinstate deism, but rather to preserve the idea of a creator God who is sovereign over all, and *hence* immanent. At this point, however, Davidson overstates his case; for Pringle-Pattison has, over against transcendence of the deistic kind, a highly suggestive comment in *The Idea of God*: 'the transcendence which must be retained, and which is intelligible, refers to a distinction of value or of quality, not to the ontological separateness of one being from another' (255).

Although applauded by some theologians for offering an idealist escape from the atheism of McTaggart and the agnosticism of Bradley, theologians of a more conservative kind were not satisfied that Pringle-Pattison had escaped pantheism. Such a remark as the following from his early work, 'Philosophy as criticism of categories' (reprinted in *The Philosophical Radicals*) would give them pause: 'So far is it from being a figure of speech that the self exists only *through* the world and *vice versa*, that we might say with equal truth the self *is* the world and the world is the self . . . it is only from the point of view of the self or subject that the identity can be grasped: this, therefore, is the ultimate point of view which unifies the whole' (333). Although, under the influence of the concept of personality, Pringle-Pattison came to construe this position epistemologically rather than ontologically, his doctrine of the organic unity of God, man and the world did give credence to a popular liberalism in Christian thought which was able to say too easily (according to its critics), and in a way damaging to the orthodox view of God's independence and man the sinner's dire need, that God needs us as much as we need Him. As Baron Friedrich von Hügel pointed out against Pringle-Pattison, 'God does not require finite beings nor the universe to attain to self-consciousness or self-articulation; whereas all finite beings and the universe strictly require God for their various degrees of reality and consciousness . . . The scholastic distinction between God's essential glory, as already attained by

His own unspeakably rich inner life, and God's accidental glory, as attained in and through finite spirits and their happiness as found by them in Him, may be clumsy, wooden, what not; but it stands for certain fundamental implications and intimations of religion.'[8] Similarly, to William Temple it seemed that Pringle-Pattison had made God into an adjective of the universe.[9]

Other Christian thinkers were less ill at ease with some of the implications of personal idealism. Hastings Rashdall (1858–1924), for example, proved to be a doughty advocate of a variety of personal idealism at Oxford, the citadel of absolutism. Rashdall was a Fellow of Hertford and of New Colleges, and, for the last seven years of his life, Dean of Carlisle. He contributed an article on 'Personality: human and divine' to the volume *Personal Idealism* (1902), edited by Henry Sturt, and elaborated the position there outlined in his two-volume work *The Theory of Good and Evil* (1907) and his *Philosophy and Religion* (1909). Suspicious of the impersonal absolutisms of Bradley and Bosanquet, Rashdall was much impressed by Lotze's emphasis upon the personality of God. He came to hold that our consciousness of ourselves as imperfectly thinking, feeling and willing gives us the ideal of a personal God who performs these functions to perfection. Where Rasdall's personal idealism differed methodologically from that of most other personal idealists was in his use of the Berkeleian principle that there can be no matter without a perceiving mind. There are finite minds, and there is the infinite mind of God which is the ultimate (because all-perceiving) ground of all things. Moreoever, *contra* monism, no one mind is absorbable by another; the distinction between subject and object is not to be effaced; and undue emphasis upon union and continuity would violate the integrity of the individual's personality. (C.C.J. Webb remarked that Rashdall's aversion to immanentism was 'perhaps . . . based upon, a mentality constitutionally devoid of the mystic's passion for union with the object of religious devotion'.[10])

There is, however, fellowship between the several individual selves, and God is the supreme personality. He is not the absolute, for the latter is an over-arching social, personal system within which all selves, including God's, are accommodated. In his *Philosophy and Religion* Rashdall summed up his philosophy thus:

> Inasmuch as it recognizes the existence — though not the separate and independent existence — of many persons; inasmuch as it regards both God and man as persons, without

attempting to merge the existence of either in one all-including, comprehensive consciousness, it may . . . be described as a form of 'personal Idealism.' But, if any one finds it easier to think of material Nature as having an existence which, though dependent upon and willed by the divine Mind, is not simply an existence in and for mind, such a view of the Universe will serve equally well as a basis of Religion (120-1).

Rashdall's position is to be distinguished on the one hand from that of McTaggart, who saw no reason to posit a supreme personality, and who held that every person, *qua* finite, is a 'primary part' of the absolute and *impersonal* unity. In an important footnote to his article in Sturt's volume, Rashdall accepts McTaggart's criticism of the idea that the supreme mind *is* the whole, but faults him for failing to recognise that the 'idea of a system which is not "for" any mind at all is not open to an Idealist; and the idea of a world each part of which is known to some mind but is not known as a whole to any one mind is almost equally difficult' (393). On the other hand, Rashdall's position differs from that of Pringle-Pattison. The latter, in common with many theologians, could not accept Rashdall's distinction between the absolute and God, or the declaration of God's limitation by the selves he creates. Rashdall sought to turn the finitude of God to advantage in connection with the problem of evil, but although he contended that the limitation of God was self-imposed, he had no satisfactory answer to James Ward who, in *The Realm of Ends* (1911), objected that 'self-limitation seems to imply a prior state in which it was absent' (243).

Clement Charles Julian Webb (1865-1954), Fellow and Tutor of Magdalen College, Oxford and, from 1920 to 1930 the first Oriel (later Nolloth) Professor of the Philosophy of the Christian Religion, was a personal idealist whose thought was influenced from many quarters. Kant's categorical imperative and Green's version of absolutism were in his case fertilised by Alexandrian Logos theology, by Lotze's personalism, by von Hügel's emphasis on the place of religious experience in Christian philosophy, by Rudolf Otto's analysis of the concept of the holy in his *The Idea of the Holy* (Eng. Trans. 1923), and by his own determination, in face of all a- or anti-historical idealisms, to assert the importance of Christianity's foundational historical *events*. In this last connection he went so far as to say that whilst 'there are those who would deny the historicity of Jesus . . . I regard this denial as the mere wantonness of doubt'

(*CQ*, VI, 1918, 447). Over a long life Webb developed his ideas — notably in his *Problems in the Relations of God and Man* (1911), and in his two series of Gifford Lectures: *God and Personality* (1918) and *Divine Personality and Human Life* (1920).

Webb approved of the way in which, as he understood it, the immanentism of idealistic thought had brought God close to man. He was concerned, however, that over-emphasis upon immanence could lead to a virtual denial of God's transcendence, and to the obliteration of human personality and individuality. At this point his appreciation of the worshipfulness of God came to his aid. Like Pringle-Pattison he understood transcendence in moral rather than in spatial terms. God is the holy absolute. At the same time God is supremely personal, and enters into personal relations with men. To this the incarnation is the paramount witness. Indeed, in his *God and Personality*, Webb can say that 'The success of Christianity in maintaining a doctrine of Divine Personality is due to its peculiar doctrine of Divine Incarnation' (82). Moreoever, it is our experience of encounter with the incarnate Christ which prevents the decline towards monism on the one hand or pantheism on the other. As for man, he is personally related to, but not identical with, God — just as Christ is both within the triune Godhead, yet distinct from the Father. Negatively, Webb objected to the way in which Bradley and Bosanquet separated God and the absolute, to the hurt of the former. For his part Bosanquet was quite appalled at Webb's insistence that humans *can* have personal dealings with the absolute. Webb also countered Rashdall's view of the self-limitation of God on the ground that having rejected the identification of God and the absolute, Rashdall had abandoned what was essential to religion.

Of Webb's friendliness towards, and sincere profession of, Christianity there can be no doubt. Indeed, the *Constructive Quarterly* article from which I quoted was entitled 'Christianity as the climax of religious development' — which is exactly what Webb took it to be. Not surprisingly, the reviewer in *The Expository Times* greeted Webb's *God and Personality* with jubilation: 'Is the reunion of philosophy and religion to come to pass even before the reunion of the Churches? The signs are all around us' (*ET*, XXX, 1918-19, 399-400). This was a much more hopeful view of philosophico-theological relations than that expressed in the same journal ten years earlier. Even so, some theologians wondered how determinative history really was in Webb's thought. True, he made much of the incarnation, but he could also say that we are to appraise history in the light of an ideal we entertain in our own minds; and he could also say that the supreme importance of Christ as redeemer is that in him the needs of the religious consciousness are met. This last opinion could not but seem tame to those who advocated objective doctrines of the atonement. They were uneasy lest the door be opened to those subjectivist theological liberalisms for which the worth of Christ was that (never mind who he is, or what he has done) somehow he appeals to, or suits the individual.

Before leaving the personalists I must advert to one writer who was much more the theologian than the philosopher: John Wood Oman (1860-1939). His position as Professor from 1907 and, from 1925 to 1935, as Principal of Westminster College, Cambridge, enabled him to influence the thought of many Presbyterian ministers and others. His outstanding book in the period with which this chapter deals is *Grace and Personality* (1917).

Oman's master-thought is that personhood is the highest category, and that the personal God is the highest being. This God has created a universe in which moral persons are nurtured. But this nurturing may be done only by moral means — hence Oman's critique of authoritarianisms whether biblicist, theological or ecclesiastical. A pretended authority may not coerce; a true authority does not coerce, but elicits a free, obediential response which itself enhances rather than diminishes the human person, and enables him to express his selfhood. As with Webb, so with Oman: Jesus is the paradigm, though Oman does not concentrate on the incarnation to the extent that Webb does. For both, however, personality is the key to their thought.

Without question the earlier absolutism of Green and Caird, and the personal idealism of Pringle-Pattison, Rashdall and Webb, was more congenial to Christian thinkers than the absolutism of Bradley or the pluralism of McTaggart. But, as we have seen, the personal idealists were not free from attack from various theological points of view. We must now turn to that more radical attack upon idealism of all kinds which, from the late years of the 19th century, was being mounted by the realists.

The realists

That not all were bowled over by idealism — even in the somewhat heady early years of its influence in Britain — is clear from Henry Sidgwick's remark in 1866 that Hegelian idealism was 'a monstrous mistake', and that we must return to Kant. In 1888 Thomas Case proposed an Aristotelian alternative to idealism in his *Physical Realism*. Of still greater importance as a teacher-critic of idealism was John Cook Wilson (1849-1915), Professor of Logic at Oxford, whose miscellany, *Statement and Inference*, was posthumously published in 1926.

Taught by Green but influenced even more by Lotze, Wilson came to attack idealist logic in the name of logic. Idealist logic turned upon the 'judgement'; that is, it presupposed that every statement derives from a specific mental act. Against this Wilson urged that statements can fulfil many purposes: they can express knowledge, opinion, supposition, or inference; and each of these is a distinct mental act, not a species of judgement. Furthermore, a judgement is not (*pace* the idealists) an assertion, but an inference. He thus came by stages towards a tentatively embraced realism which gave expression to his conviction that there can be no apprehension of an object unless the object enjoys an existence independently of the apprehending subject.

Among those in Wilson's line were H.A. Prichard and H.W.B. Joseph; and at least one budding theologian, Leonard Hodgson, appreciated their efforts. Recalling his pre-1914 student days in Oxford he said that 'Cook Wilson and Prichard were recalling us to the pre-Cartesian sanity of the assumption that knowledge means knowing a thing as it is, not altering it'.[11] Meanwhile in Cambridge, George Edward Moore (1873-1958), Fellow of Trinity College and later Professor of Philosophy, was patiently probing idealist arguments with a view to bringing philosophy down to earth. Bertrand Arthur William Russell (1872-1970) was at the same College, and the formative experiences of these two men who shared realism but differed within it, and whose objectives even in the early days were significantly different, are interestingly interwoven. It was Russell the mathematician who drew Moore away from Classics towards philosophy. At the time Russell was an Hegelian, having been influenced in this direction by McTaggart and Bradley. In his 'Autobiography' in *The Philosophy of Bertrand Russell* (1944, ed. P.A. Schlipp) he records the moment of his conversion thus: 'I remember the precise moment, one day in 1894, as I was walking along Trinity Lane, when I saw in a flash (or thought I saw) that the ontological argument is valid. I had gone out to buy a tin of tobacco; on my way back, I suddenly threw it up in the air, and exclaimed as I caught it: "Great Scott, the ontological argument is sound." I read Bradley at this time with avidity, and admired him more than any other recent philosopher.' (10)

But Russell's Hegelian sojourn was to be short lived. By 1897-8 Moore had been prompted by a passage in Bradley's *Principles of Logic* to think that the meaning of an idea was something wholly independent of mind. From this point, Moore tells us in his 'Autobiography' in *The Philosophy of G.E. Moore* (1942, ed. P.A. Schlipp), tendencies developed in his thought which were to lead people to designate him a realist. Russell was much impressed by Moore's discovery, and wrote in connection with his second conversion that Moore 'took the lead in rebellion, and I followed, with a sense of emancipation. Bradley argued that everything common sense believes in is mere appearance; we reverted to the opposite extreme, and thought that *everything* is real that common sense, uninfluenced by philosophy or theology, supposes real. With a sense of escaping from prison we allowed ourselves to think that grass is green, that the sun and stars would exist if no-one was aware of them, and also that there is a pluralistic timeless world of Platonic ideas (12).' This is a highly important passage, for it reminds us that for all their down-to-earthness *vis-à-vis* Hegelianism, many of the new realists were Platonists who were quite happy to contemplate eternal, unperceivable realities whose replicas (now known as sense data) are the objects of our sense perception. Unlike Locke's 'ideas' which were said to be 'in the mind' the realists accorded phenomenal existence to their sense data. In other words, in a common sense way the realists held against the idealists that reality is independent of mind; but they also held that we do not actually perceive objects as such, but sense data which are *appearances* of the objects. In this latter doctrine the realists were influenced by such continental thinkers as Brentano, Meinong and Frege.

Moore's penchant was for the common sense analysis of the statements of others. As he said in his 'Autobiography', 'I do not think that the world or the sciences would ever have suggested to me any philosophical problems. What has suggested problems to me is things which other philosophers have said about the world or the sciences' (14). It by no means follows that Moore was opposed to the metaphysical enterprise as such — nor was Russell. Indeed, the latter, much more systematically inclined than his friend, positively sought an alternative metaphysical system to idealism, which would take account of the real world as it was. As for Moore, it should be noted that it is a mistake to regard him as simply an analyst of ordinary language in the sense of ordinary usage. Some have forged too direct a link between Moore and Wittgenstein and the later analysts in this matter. The question whether ordinary language is more important to Moore than the appeal to common sense is one which has exercised Moore's critics. A.R. White, for example, argues in his book *G.E. Moore: A Critical Exposition* (1958) that the appeal to ordinary language is for the most part subsidiary to the appeal to common sense, and that Norman Malcolm 'and those who agree with him have reversed the correct relative positions of the two' (7). The truth would seem to be with White, and this is consonant both with the fact that although he had broken with idealism, Moore had not broken with metaphysics; and, more importantly, with Moore's own claim in his 'Reply to my critics' (in *The Philosophy of G.E. Moore*) that his concern was primarily with ordinary *beliefs*. Thus if a McTaggart told him that time was not real, Moore was immediately interested as a philosopher in an assertion which seemed to contradict the common sense belief of the mass of mankind.

On similar grounds it seemed to Moore that the proposition 'To be is to be perceived' lay at the heart of all idealist metaphysics, and that this proposition was false. This was the burden of his celebrated article, 'The refutation of idealism' (*M* N.S. XII, 1903, 433). Although when this article was reprinted in his *Philosophical Studies* (1922) Moore declared that it contained some 'downright mistakes', it did cause a profound stir in 1903 and the years immediately following because of its principal argument that if being perceived follows from being, then being and perception cannot be identical. On his own admission Moore is not here attacking the fundamental idealist doctrine that reality is spiritual; and it is quite clear that, thin as the line was between some varieties of idealism, Moore's strictures apply more to Berkeleian than to pure immanentist Hegelian idealism. Nevertheless, his conclusion troubled the waters of idealism at large: 'The only *reasonable* alternative to the admission that matter exists *as well as* spirit, is absolute Scepticism — that, as likely as not, *nothing* exists at all' (453).

Moore's major early work, *Principia Ethica* (1903), provides a good example of his method. He there writes that 'in Ethics, as in all other philosophical studies, the difficulties and disagreements, of which its history is full, are mainly due to a very simple cause: namely to the attempt to answer questions, without first discovering precisely *what* question it is which you desire to answer' (vii). He considered that if a resolute attempt to analyse statements were made many of the difficulties and disagreements would disappear, and he lamented the fact that few philosophers honoured their analytical responsibility. In the prosecution of his own analytical mission Moore appealed to common sense. He was persuaded that there are many common sense beliefs which we may legitimately hold despite the fact that we can neither prove nor disprove them. Among these beliefs are: that a great many material objects exist; that there are minds; that we are sometimes conscious of certain material objects, but that we are certain that they continue to exist when we are not conscious of them. Moore enumerated these and other common sense beliefs in the first lecture of a course he gave in the winter of 1910–11. This lecture, 'What is philosophy?' was reprinted in his book, *Some Main Problems of Philosophy* (1953). Even when taken all together, however, these common sense beliefs did not, he thought, constitute a description of the universe as a whole; and it was philosophy's task to provide this. Over against the beliefs of common sense he placed those of scepticism. He defended belief in God and belief in life after death against the charge that these two commonly held beliefs were contradictory of common sense. In the course of his work Moore subjected many words in common use — 'good', 'real', and others — to close analysis, and he did not set out, like the early Russell, to construct an ideal language.

It was no doubt Russell's love of the precision of logic and mathematics that encouraged him to seek an ideal, puzzle-free language. This apart, there was a marked similarity between himself and Moore in the emphasis both placed upon the importance of analysis. In his *A Critical Exposition of the Philosophy of Leibniz* (1900) Russell roundly declared: 'That all sound philosophy should begin with an analysis of propositions, is a truth too evident, perhaps, to demand a proof' (8). A Bradley or a Mackenzie might have accompanied him thus far, but it soon became clear that Russell's principles entailed destructive onslaughts upon many of the early 20th century citadels of both religious and secular philosophy. He advocated 'the substitution of piecemeal, detailed and verifiable results for large untested generalities recommended only by a certain appeal to the imagination' in his book *Our Knowledge of the External World* (1914, p. 4); and in his Herbert Spencer Lecture for 1914, *On Scientific Method in Philosophy*, he went still further, arguing that whereas ethico-religious and scientific motives had hitherto been the mainsprings of philosophical investigation, now the only sensible course was to thrust these motives aside since they constituted a grave hindrance to progress (3–4). Philosophy must concentrate on scientific methods; its propositions must be general and *a priori*; it will appear as indistinguishable from logic; and 'the essence of philosophy as thus conceived is analysis, not synthesis' (19). Russell grants that this approach entails our abandoning the hope of solving many of the more ambitious and humanly interesting problems of traditional philosophy; and he claims that of these problems those that are not for ever incapable of solution will be taken under the wings of the several special sciences.

We might have expected that the writings of Moore and Russell would have caused a fairly immediate stir in philosophico-theological circles; but, in fact, detailed contemporary evaluation from this quarter is almost entirely non-existent. But the subsequent influence of Moore and Russell's analytical activities was great upon secular philosophers who, far from being converts from a metaphysic, were not particularly interested in metaphysics, as we shall see; and some of this influence was felt also within less dogmatically minded philosophico-religious circles.

Unrepentant idealists and others

By no means all idealists were to be deflected from their course by the criticisms of the realists. Bernard Bosanquet (1848-1923), Professor of Moral Philosophy at St Andrews, to whom passing reference has already been made, wrote a series of books culminating in *The Principle of Individuality and Value* (1912), in which he advocated a version of absolutism similar in many respects to that of Bradley, but applied more widely to social, religious and aesthetic questions. He maintained that the freestanding individual, the 'concrete universal' which is itself a harmony of opposites, finds expression in the social, religious and aesthetic spheres; and that all these spheres are united in the absolute, which most clearly expresses the nature of individuality. Like Bradley, Bosanquet regarded religion as but a prelude to metaphysics, but on the question of God *vis-à-vis* the absolute, Webb correctly noticed a distinction between the two in his *God and Personality*: 'on the whole Mr. Bosanquet, though holding that to think of a God with whom we could be in personal relations is to think of a merely finite being and not of the Absolute, yet finds in the contemplation of the Absolute the satisfaction of his religious aspirations, while Mr. Bradley dwells rather on the thought that philosophy must recognize the God to whom religious devotion is directed to be not the Absolute but, like all else in our experience, an appearance of the Absolute' (132-3).

Much more consciously Christian (if not altogether orthodox) was Sir Henry Jones (1852-1922), Professor successively at Bangor,

St Andrews and Glasgow. Jones was a pupil of Edward Caird at Glasgow, and he carried the tradition of his teacher more surely into the 20th century than anyone else. Jones is not the patient expositor, the determined analyst. Rather, he is the impassioned advocate, pleading — even preaching — his cause. He adverted to world affairs; he drew on the romantic poets and on Browning (his Chair at St Andrews was in what would nowadays be regarded as the unlikely combination of Logic and Literature); he regarded idealism not simply as a theory, but as a practical creed. Indeed, some lectures he gave in Australia were published under the title, *Idealism as a Practical Creed* (1909). He here urged the self-defeating nature of pessimism and scepticism; claimed that the ideal is the real and the real the ideal; that man is in the making and that God is the perfect in process; and that it would be well for the Australians to try the experiment and see how far the idealist faith 'will stand the strain of a nation's practice'.

Unlike Bradley and Bosanquet, Jones had no difficulty in concluding that the absolute is God. Precisely because of their difficulties in this matter Jones charged his Oxford colleagues, and all advocates of the finitude of God, with an unresolved dualism. He called himself a realistic idealist. By this he meant that he was not a Berkeleian subjectivist; he agreed with the realists that the phenomenal world has an existence independently of its being perceived, but he maintained that the 'real' world of experience is no more than an aspect of reality as a whole. Into this wholeness religious experience gives us a glimpse which is veridical but not exhaustive. In the light of this truth we must set to work in the work-a-day world, for this is the sphere within which character is developed. As Jones rather disarmingly confessed in his Gifford Lectures, *A Faith That Enquires* (1922), he assumed rather than justified his central conviction that 'the moral life has a value which is final, unlimited and absolute' (350). Upheld by this conviction, and even after the bestiality of the First World War, he could optimistically aver that we live in a friendly and helpful world. This, he felt, was consistent with his view that evil, though real, is a necessary condition of moral progress, and *that* is good.

But if Bosanquet and Jones were not themselves in mortal combat with realists, the battle between idealists and empiricists of all kinds was not to be postponed. In 1913 G.T. Ladd lamented in an article entitled 'Rationalism and Empiricism' that 'What philosophy has been accustomed to regard as the most clearly established conclusions of the world's reflective thinking, on a basis of experience, is now assailed in the name of experience' (*M* N.S. XXII, 1913, 2). In the following year, in an article in the same journal entitled 'A defence of idealism', he adopted the role of adjudicator in the dogmatic struggle and, by way of awarding points to both sides, he claimed that the extreme opposition of an absolute or monistic idealism to a mechanical and materialistic philosophy results in a *reductio ad absurdum*. For the more complete and absolute the monism, the greater the effort to idealise the real universe. The more complete the mechanism, the more it is endowed with the most distinctive characteristics of human ideals. He concluded that 'no attempt at a system of idealism can be made which does not take its point of departure from that which is actual in human experience' (476).

Even as Ladd was seeking to pour oil on the troubled waters of dogmatic strife, C.D. Broad was saying that he did not wish to be dogmatic at all, thereby adding his weight to that of other philosophers who were revising the terms of reference of their subject. In his *Perception, Physics and Reality* (1914) Broad said,

> I have constantly put my conclusions in terms of probability and not of certainty. *This will perhaps seem peculiar in a work which claims to be philosophical.* It seems to me that one of the most unfortunate of Kant's *obiter dicta* is that philosophy only deals with certainty, and not with probability. So far is this from being the case that to many philosophical questions about the nature of reality no answer except one in terms of probability can be offered; whilst to some there seems no prospect of an answer even in these terms (ix, my italics).

Almost as interesting as the changing attitude here represented is the reaction of the reviewer in *The Expository Times*: Broad's approach, he said, was 'heretical' (*ET*, XXV, 1913-14, 552). One shouts 'Traitor!' when one's country is being betrayed, but 'Heretic!' when one's *dogmas* are being assailed.

We are on more familiar ground when we turn to George Galloway's *The Philosophy of Religion* (1914), for so long a standard text book. Galloway defines philosophy as reflection upon experience in order to apprehend its ultimate meaning, and says that the problem of the philosophy of religion is, in part, 'to exhibit those constitutive principles which underlie all religions' (8). For his method Galloway turns to Hegel, holding that philosophy will purify those ideas which in religion are presented to us in the form of imaginative or figurative thinking, and raise them to the speculative form of truth. He proceeds to describe the various forms of absolutism and personalism, and thinks that Rashdall, in his *Philosophy and Religion*, is especially fruitful concerning the latter. Whilst recognising the difficulties inherent in Rashdall's view that God is limited by minds other than himself, Galloway contends that the difficulties are fewer than in absolutism. He was content with the view that God and the absolute are not identical and later, in a review of Webb's *God and Personality* (*M* N.S. XXIX, 478), he urged this view against that author's assimilation of God and the absolute. Galloway passes empiricism and pragmatism in review, but is not deflected from his view that 'Idealism is the form of philosophical thinking which leads most readily to a philosophy of religion, inasmuch as mind or spirit is of primary value both for idealism and religion' (44). Not indeed that philosophy and theology can ever be combined; for theology is the exposition of the doctrines of an historic religion, and must be pursued under authority, whereas the philosophy of religion demands a wider and a freer vision.

In 1915 Canon Oliver Chase Quick published *Modern Philosophy and the Incarnation*. True to its title this book has a more modern ring about it than some of the philosophico-theological works of the first two decades of the century. It is difficult to give precisely the grounds for this impression, but perhaps they are to be found firstly in Quick's refusal to grind a dogmatic axe — indeed, he does not hesitate to criticise philosophical dogmas that were once held sacrosanct; and secondly, in his honest attempt to admit the difficulties of his own position and to face the challenge of recent philosophy, Russell not excluded. It is not without significance that, although when he reviewed Quick's book Schiller had to state that its 'main appeal is necessarily to the small section of philosophers who are interested in theology and the still smaller section of theologians who are interested in philosophy', he welcomed the book and composed as restrained and balanced a review as I have seen from his rather combative hand (*M* N.S. XXV, 1916, 124).

Quick regrets that 'Philosophy is divided against itself, and more so today than ever before' (19); and that, since the subject is too much the province of the expert it is unable to take a sufficiently comprehensive view of life: 'The metaphysician fails to sympathise with the grocer' (20). As for the theologian, he must make general statements about the nature of the universe, but he would do well to avoid linking his thought too closely to any one school of philosophy. The medieval mind was 'grievously mistaken' in permitting its theology to be so closely associated with its philosophy, for the former is now open to attack by all the opponents of the latter. There can be no reconciliation of theologians with philosophers until the latter give due place in their constructions to faith — and absolute idealism, pragmatism, Bergson and Russell are all criticised for falling short at this point. Faith is not blind trust. The claim that it *is* would be a valid charge only if we had no clear understanding of faith's goal. But the Christian has perceived that goal in Christ. Hence, 'In the historic Incarnation faith finds a revelation which is fully external and objective, and yet is given completely through the faculties of a common humanity' (92).

Not all philosophers, however — even those who displayed some interest in religion — were as positive as Quick hoped they might become. For example, the apparent support for religion offered by R.G. Collingwood in his *Religion and Philosophy* (1916) was not of a kind universally to commend itself to theologians. By defining 'God' in terms of the philosophical absolute Collingwood left himself open to the criticism of Galloway who says, 'For him, as for an old Apologist, Christianity is simply true philosophy' (*M* N.S. XXVIII, 1919, 365). Against this Galloway maintains the distinction between philosophy and philosophy of religion, for religion is grounded in a distinct experience. In a word, 'Mr. Collingwood's method of bringing speculative principles from without and applying them to Christianity is unsatisfactory and apt to mislead. It would be fairer if he developed his own theology in independence of the forms and language of Christian theology' (367).

In 1917 James Lindsay's *A Philosophical System of Theistic Idealism* was published. Lindsay is aware of, and quite undeterred by, the prevailing mood in philosophy: ' "A philosophical system" ! That sounds audacious enough in days when we are being constantly told that philosophers have ceased to frame systems and now merely write essays' (v). While recognising that the perfect system of theistic idealism had yet to be written, and that it would not appear for some time to come, Lindsay enthusiastically presented his interim statement. We need not follow him now, but it is pertinent to our study to mark the effect of his work in those very theological circles which were so dejected nine years earlier:

> It used to take a theologian to write the Philosophy of the Christian Religion; now any philosopher can do it. For there is so rapid an approach from philosophy to theology that the

time seems at hand when no distinction will be found between them. The theologian will interpret Christianity philosophically, the philosopher will be its theological expositor . . . [Lindsay] is a philosopher first. And he only accentuates a movement that is at the present moment sweeping every philosopher along with it (*ET*, XXVIII, 1916–17, 543).

Every philosopher? Not quite; but theologians were entitled to take some comfort from the work of many of their philosophical counterparts, as we have seen. William Ritchie Sorley (1855–1935), Professor successively at Cardiff, Aberdeen and Cambridge, whose Gifford Lectures entitled *Moral Values and the Idea of God* appeared in 1918, gave further encouragement to some theologians. He set out systematically to investigate the often-assumed link, Kantian in inspiration, between morality and theism. How far, he asked, are we justified in using ethical and axiological ideas in philosophical construction?

Clearly influenced by personal idealism, with its emphasis upon man's individuality, and upon the individuality of reality itself, Sorley developed an ethical theism which was to be but the first of a number of contributions of this kind, including those to be noted later by A.E. Taylor and W.G. deBurgh. Sorley argues that intrinsic moral values belong to persons only, and that they are as objective as the qualities or the causal connections which we ascribe to things and persons. Moreover, the value of goodness actually achieved in personal life implies as its ground or condition a standard or ideal of goodness. With Lotze Sorley begins from moral experience; we may not legitimately exclude moral considerations until the rest of our metaphysics is worked out. On the contrary, 'moral experience, and the moral order of which we are conscious, are part of the material which we have to take into account before we have a right to accept any philosophical theory or to adopt it as an adequate point of view for the interpretation of reality as a whole' (501). Furthermore, this 'recognition of the moral order, and of its relation to nature and man, involves the acknowledgement of the Supreme Mind or God as the ground of all reality' (504).

Sorley does not deny that men may rise to God from the contemplation of nature, art, knowledge; but these other avenues neglect moral considerations at their peril. Attention to moral values brings us to the threshold of religious values: indeed, our moral *dis*content urges us to ask whether final absorption — even in God — or the endurance of free minds is the goal of all. We cannot tell, but 'if free minds endure, it must surely be for a range of activity suited to the capacities and values which they have acquired in their mundane experience' (516).

In all of this we see Sorley's main themes at work: God as the absolute, the unity of the ontlogical and the axiological; the freedom of man; the purposeful process of all things. Sorley is challenged and inspired throughout by his view — already regarded as over-ambitious by many of his philosophical colleagues, as we have seen — that 'If we are unable to reach a view of [reality] as a whole, then we have attained no philosophy' (500).

Summary

We have seen that during the first 20 years of this century absolutism continued to be propounded, though its ascendency was over. Personal idealists challenged absolutism, thereby appealing to many theologians and philosophers of religion, whilst the realists attacked idealisms of either kind. The movement towards understanding philosophy as a matter of careful analysis rather than of dogmatic construction gained ground, though it scarcely influenced the practice of philosophers of religion until a later period, by which time most analysts had become avowedly anti-metaphysical in a way that the early Moore and Russell were not. On the contrary, there was something of a resurgence of the older type of alliance between philosophy and religion in the years following 1912. As late as the end of the second decade of the century men like Lindsay and Webb could prompt a somewhat premature optimism on the part of some theologians that as regards the philosophico-theological alliance the best was yet to be. With hindsight we may be forgiven for wondering whether such theologians were not like those who, as darkness approaches, sing loudly in order to keep their spirits up.

Notes

1. F.C.S. Schiller, 'On preserving appearances', *M* N.S. XII (1903), p. 346.
2. F.C.S. Schiller, 'The new developments in Mr. Bradley's philosophy', *M* N.S. XXIV (1915), p. 366.
3. J. Macquarrie, *Twentieth-Century Religious Thought* (SCM, London, 1963), p. 53.
4. Dr. Scott Holland in his Romanes Lecture. Quoted by W.H. Moberly,

'God and the absolute', in B.H. Streeter (ed.) *Foundations* (Macmillan, London, 1912), p. 483 n. 2.

5. J.S. Mackenzie, 'Edward Caird as a philosophical teacher', *M* N.S. XVIII (1909), pp. 533, 536.

6. R.B. Perry, *The Present Conflict of Ideals: A Study of the Philosophical Background of the World War* (Longmans, New York, 1918), p. 199.

7. In 1898 Andrew Seth was required to add 'Pringle-Pattison' to his name in order to secure an inheritance.

8. F. von Hügel, *Essays and Addresses*, Second Series (Dent, London, 1926), pp. 151, 154.

9. W. Temple in *Contemporary British Philosophy*, ed. J.H. Muirhead, First Series (Allen & Unwin, London, 1924), pp. 415 ff.

10. C.C.J. Webb, *A Study of Religious Thought in England from 1850* (Clarendon Press, Oxford, 1933), p. 139.

11. L. Hodgson, *Towards a Christian Philosophy* (Nisbet, London, 1943), p. 7.

4
Systems, Silence and Scholasticism, 1920–35

The first three years of the 1920s present us with as wide a variety of philosophical views as we have yet encountered within so short a period of time. We have Alexander and Whitehead with their realist metaphysics; the reiteration of idealistic themes in the work of Hoernlé, and in Jones's Gifford Lectures, to which reference has already been made; the elaboration by McTaggart of his earlier positions in his grand-scale system of deductive metaphysics, *The Nature of Existence* (I, 1921; II, 1927); and in Wittgenstein's *Tractatus* (Eng. Trans. 1922) we have one of the primary inspirations of that philosophy of language by which so many British and other philosophers have been influenced.

Samuel Alexander

The Australian Samuel Alexander (1859–1938), Fellow of Lincoln College, Oxford (1882–93) and Professor of Philosophy at Manchester University (1893–1924), was nurtured under the influence of Green and Bradley, but came to be much impressed by Moore's refutation of idealism. Alexander's thought developed over the years, and his mature conclusions were published in the two volumes of his Gifford Lectures (delivered in 1915), *Space, Time and Deity* (1920).

In the preface to the first edition of *Space, Time and Deity*, Alexander nailed his colours to the mast, announcing that his work 'is part of the widely-spread movement towards some form of realism in philosophy, which began in this country with Messrs. Moore and Russell, and in America with the authors of *The New Realism*' (vi). At the same time he was not unaware of the dangers to which the labelling of philosophers can lead: 'As to the terms idealism and realism, I should be heartily glad if we might get rid of them altogether: they have such shifting senses and carry with them so much prejudice' (I, 7-8). His own view was that

> The real difference between idealism and realism lies in their starting-point or the spirit of their method. For the one, in some form or other, however much disguised, mind is the measure of things and the starting-point of inquiry. The sting of absolute idealism lies in its assertion that the parts of the world are not ultimately real or *true* but only the whole is *true*. For realism mind has no privileged place except in its perfection. The real issue is between these two spirits of inquiry; and it is in this sense that the following inquiry is realistic. But no sane philosophy has ever been exclusively the one or the other . . . (I, 8)

On the question of the nature of philosophy in general, Alexander supports the view that the metaphysician is one who attempts to 'describe the ultimate nature of existence if it has any' (I, 2). Unlike the special scientist he is not free to leave any notion, such as 'relation' or 'limit', unexplained; and his mode of explanation must be to indicate what corresponds to them in experience. This is not to say that Alexander believes that an empirical philosophy is in some prerogative manner concerned with sense experience: 'The senses have no privilege in experience, but they are the means by which our minds through our bodies are affected by external objects' (4). Hence, 'A philosophy which pursues an empirical method is not necessarily a sensationalist one. It deals with the actual world, but the parts of it with which it deals empirically are non-empirical parts of that actual world' (I, 5).

Biological evolution, testifying as it was supposed to do to the struggle towards higher forms of life *via* ever more complex organisms, is Alexander's model; and he develops his version of the theory of emergent evolution propounded by the zoologist-philosopher Conwy Lloyd Morgan.[1] To Alexander space-time is the primal stuff out of which everything evolves. Though an empirical phenomenon, space-time also becomes in his hands the *a priori* presupposition of his metaphysical system. He recognised that space-time is to his system as the absolute is to idealistic systems. There is, however, this signal difference: whereas Alexander *sets out from* space time, most idealists *progressed towards* the absolute as the linchpin of their systems.

Evolution, according to Alexander, is a continuous process, and at any given stage the stage next to be reached constitutes deity. But deity is also the goal of the entire process. 'God' is a term which comprehends both the whole of space-time and the quality of deity which is so far actualised within it. Since, however, the quality of deity is ever in process of realisation, God must somehow be incomplete also: 'As actual, God does not possess the quality of deity but is the universe as tending to that quality' (II, 361). Were matters otherwise polytheism would result, for an actual substance is the product of the union of universal with particular, and any universal is open to numerous instantiations.

In a manner reminiscent of the phenomenological approach of Husserl (1858-1938) Alexander determines to be empirical in the widest sense of the word. He believes, for example, that the mutual interdependence of space-time is disclosed in man's experience. He further declares that though infinite in extension, deity is an empirical quality located within the universe; for man as such has religious aspirations, and the presumption must be that there exists an object in which these aspirations find fulfilment. Alexander would have felt that he had failed in his task of describing things as they are had he omitted the religious dimension from his system; but for him the religious sentiment is directed towards the next higher level of development, not to an existing divine object. Consistently with this he denies that we have exhaustively accounted for the universe when we have taken note of space-time; for the universe is more than spatio-temporal:

> It exhibits materiality and life and mind. It compels us to forecast the next empirical quality or deity. On the one hand we have the totality of the world, which in the end is spatio-temporal; on the other the quality of deity engendered, or rather being engendered, with that whole. These two features are united in the conception of the whole world as expressing itself in the character of deity, and it is this and not bare Space-Time which for speculation is the ideal conception of God. (II, 353-4)

Thus for all his empiricism, and unlike the American philosopher Edgar Sheffield Brightman (1884-1953),[2] Alexander does not wish to maintain the finitude of God as such. His view is rather that while there is a sense in which all finite things partake of infinity, deity is infinitely finite. For this reason (and this is the point at which his realism comes to the fore) although God exceeds our experience he is yet an object to whom we may respond. He is not, as with the idealists, *in* the mind, but is 'comprenent' with it. To Alexander the idealist contention that we are able to contemplate a mental act is indefensible. Equally, he goes far beyond Hume's view that ideas are psychic phenomena located 'in' the mind. On the contrary, they exist independently of the mind.

Here then is no sceptical naturalism, but a religiously impregnated naturalism. Alexander seeks to accord due place to value and to deity. Moreover, although the developing God himself originates in space-time — he is not the creator of the world or the ground of values — Alexander will not have his position mistaken for pantheism. He does not equate space-time with God — not least because space-time is not an adequate object of worship or the appropriate recipient of our religious emotions. Rather, 'God is immanent in respect of his body, but transcendent in respect of his deity' (II, 396). Here, in fact, is a harbinger of that pan*en*theism of which later process theologians were to make so much: all things are within God, though he is not to be exhaustively identified with the totality of things.

It would be a gross exaggeration to say that Alexander was immediately surrounded by eager disciples, though many philosophers admired the boldness and range of his vision. C.D. Broad, for example, wondered how seriously Alexander intended his view of God to be taken:

> Prof. Alexander's candidate for the position of God has the two merits of being necessarily mysterious to us, and being in a definite sense higher than ourselves. The vaulted roof of St. Pancras station seen at midnight has been known to evoke the religious emotion in one eminent mathematician returning to Cambridge from a dinner in town; and what the sight of St. Pancras has done for one man, the thought of the next stage in the hierarchy of qualities may do for others. It might indeed seem difficult to feel much enthusiasm about a God who does not yet exist, and who will cease to be divine as soon as he begins to be actual. Still the merit of faith is commonly held to increase with its difficulty, and the merit of religious adoration may vary according to a similar law.
> (*M* N.S. XXX, 1921, 148)

In his reply, 'Some explanations', Alexander made it clear that he *does* intend his theology seriously, and sought to clarify the point thus: 'God as actually possessing deity does not exist but is an ideal, is always becoming; but God as the whole Universe tending towards deity does exist' (*M* N.S. XXX, 1921, 428).

Among others who were less than fully satisfied by Alexander were G. Dawes Hicks and Clement Webb. The former felt (*HJ*, XIX, 1920-1, 581) that Alexander's system fell if one enquired how the 'imposing unity' space-time enters upon the stage in the first place, or makes for itself a stage (a question, surely, which Alexander's acceptance of the given in nature would hardly permit him to ask); the latter (*CQR*, XCIII, 1921-2, 342 ff.), owning little patience with the God of becoming who is simply a 'tendency', was, notwithstanding the admitted difficulties attaching to the concept, most concerned by the absence of personality in Alexander's God. For his part McTaggart is reported by John Passmore (*A Hundred Years of Philosophy*, 268) to have complained that 'in every chapter we come across some view which no philosopher, except Professor Alexander, has ever maintained'. We recall, of course, that at the time of writing McTaggart was in the midst of preparing his *The Nature of Existence* — *the* deductive system of metaphysics of this century, compared with which Alexander's work is at best visionary and at worst opaque.

From theologians there was relatively little *direct* comment upon Alexander's work, though the general position which they would have opposed to both Alexander and Whitehead had been well stated by James Orr in his *The Progress of Dogma* (1901):

> A God in process is of necessity an incomplete God — can never be a true, personal God. His being is merged in that of the universe; sin, even, is an element of His life. I hold it to be indubitable that God, in order truly to be God, must possess Himself in the eternal fulness and completeness of His own personal life; must possess Himself for Himself, and be raised entirely above the transiency, the incompleteness, and the contingency of the world-process. We are then enabled to think of the world and history, not as the necessary unfolding of a logical process, but as the revelation of a free and holy purpose; and inconsistency is no longer felt in the idea of an action of God along supernatural lines — above the plane of mere nature, as wisdom and love may dictate — for the benefit of His creature man. (323-4 n.)

On the same point, in *Positive Preaching and the Modern Mind* (1907), P.T. Forsyth was his forceful self:

> Any theology that places us in a spiritual *process*, or native movement between the finite and the infinite, depreciates the value of spiritual *act*, and thus makes us independent of the grace of God. Its movement is processional spectacular, aesthetic, it is not historic, dramatic, tragic or ethical . . . Mere process ends in mechanism, coarse or fine, and extinguishes a soul (1964, reprint, 146, 229).

A more direct challenge was issued by W.R. Matthews in his *The Purpose of God* (1935). He could not understand how the 'marvellous potentialities' of the evolving universe should reside in the simplest 'stuff'; and he lamented the fact that because of the failure to push the cosmological enquiry to its end we are left with description rather than explanation; whereas the business of philosophy is the search for explanation, 'which means the discovery of sufficient reason' (37-8).

It may be that the general silence on the part of theologians was prompted by the fact that Alexander's process-involved God was too much for them to stomach. Or perhaps Alexander's physico-biological background was so far removed from that of the majority of philosophical theologians that they felt ill at ease in his company, or at a loss to comprehend his meaning. Certainly many of them were still otherwise engaged — attempting to come to terms with Barth, or reworking the idealist mines. But however we may try to excuse them, the fact remains that if philosophers of religion refuse to converse with their secular colleagues — especially when the latter raise specifically religious questions — they tend to give the impression that they have nothing to contribute, thereby undermining any interest philosophers may have in *their* concerns. Even Hoernlé, with whose thought many theologians might have found themselves in some sympathy, roundly declared that

> From Professor A. Seth Pringle-Pattison's *The Idea of God in the Light of Recent Philosophy*, to H.G. Wells's *God the Invisible King* and *The Undying Fire*, these experiments, as varied as they are sincere, in re-thinking and reformulating are going on. But, with rare exceptions, the representatives of the churches are holding aloof, and continue to speak, if not to think, of God in terms which may be not unfairly described

as a fusion of the primitive monarchical idea with Aristotle's conception of the Eternal Thinker.³

In his *Religious Perplexities* (1922) L.P. Jacks reported, 'I have even heard it suggested, by extremists, that there would be more believers in God if all the theologians would take themselves off' (41).

A.N. Whitehead

It is probably true to say that more notice was taken of Alfred North Whitehead (1861-1947) by theologians contemporary with him than of Alexander. Certainly Whitehead has provided ample resources for latter-day process theologians. He is the supreme example in this century of a *philosopher* with a compelling religious vision, who thought that in important ways traditional theology had failed to do justice to its subject matter. Whitehead and Alexander were mutual admirers of each other's work, though Whitehead did not exploit the concept of emergence — any newly emergent *stage* might well be insufficiently plastic, and Whitehead set his face against all varieties of staticism. His is a philosophy of organism built along realist lines.

Whitehead's thought defies the would-be summariser, but something must be said about it. He is literally fascinating: he puzzles and perplexes — almost terrifies at times; he coins terminology which he does not always define or consistently employ; he uses common terms, notably 'feeling', in most uncommon ways; yet because of his haunting epigrams and paradoxes we cannot altogether avert our gaze. He invites us to share a vision — or, if not to share it, to see what we can make of it; and to any critical philosophers who might suppose that synoptic visions are things far too messy for philosophers to become entangled with Whitehead has his characteristic reply: 'If men cannot live on bread alone, still less can they do so on disinfectants.'⁴ This is more than a mere retort, however. Confronted by the complexity of things Whitehead is alive to the danger that 'clarity' may entail the falsification, or neglect, of evidence. As he put it in *Religion in the Making* (1926):

> It is characteristic of the learned mind to exalt words. Yet mothers can ponder many things in their hearts which their lips cannot express. These many things, which are thus known, constitute the ultimate religious evidence, beyond which there is no appeal. (67)

Consistently with this Whitehead inveighed against what he called 'the fallacy of misplaced concreteness', whereby a theoretical conception is mistakenly construed as a self-subsisting entity. Our human experience is not, he insists, as neat and tidy as this, but is of mutually related entities in a process which can be evaluated. For the same reason Whitehead was critical of the way in which Hegelianism *imposed* its dialectical system upon reality.

Whitehead had more right than most to vie for the attention of scientists and philosophers alike. A distinguished mathematician, he was a Fellow of Trinity College, Cambridge (1884–1910), and a Lecturer and later a Professor in Mathematics in London (1910–24). In 1924 he accepted an invitation to become a Professor of Philosophy at Harvard University, where he remained (as Professor Emeritus from 1937) until his death in 1947.

Whitehead published *A Treatise on Universal Algebra* (1898), and then began his fruitful collaboration with Russell his pupil, the culmination of which was the *Principia Mathematica* (1910–13). Prompted in part by the need, as he saw it, to provide a theoretical philosophical basis for Einstein's theory of relativity, Whitehead began to diverge from Russellian realism in the direction of an organismic cosmology. This period was marked by his works *An Enquiry Concerning the Principles of Natural Knowledge* (1919), *The Concept of Nature* (1920) and *The Principle of Relativity* (1922). Here Whitehead turned from static conceptions of space and time to the view that space and time accompany rather than originate events. He accords primacy to events, which are themselves not static, and which are mutually related to, though not absorbed by, other events. Echoing Heraclitus, Whitehead contends that there is continuous movement. But nature is not composed solely of events. There are objects too. We perceive events, but we recognise objects, for unlike ever-moving events objects are characterised by recurring features; and whereas an event depends for its being upon its relations, an object does not.

The 'mind-bending' nature of the summary just given is not the result of abbreviation, but is a function of Whitehead's predilection for using familiar terms in unfamiliar ways. We can, however, begin to detect the direction in which he would move us. There is first the idea of the relatedness of one thing to another within the world. To this relatedness, in which all entities are unavoidably implicated, Whitehead gives the name 'prehension'. These prehensions are not blank fiats; they are redolent of value, and in relationship they constitute webs of togetherness. Secondly, we note the importance attached to the perceiver's response to the world — not least in the matter of the recognition of objects. Thirdly, there is the emphasis upon process as against staticism. Whitehead tells us in *Adventures of Ideas* (1933) of his excitement when, as a young graduate, he heard Sir J.J. Thompson expound his theory that 'energy has recognizable paths through space and time. Energy passes from particular occasion to particular occasion. At each point there is a flux with a quantitative flow and a definite direction' (238). Lastly we note the all-embracing empiricism which was to lead Whitehead to protest against that 'bifurcation of nature' encouraged by Galileo and Locke, according to which the world of so-called scientific entities is to be distinguished from the world of immediate experience. To Whitehead science must deal with *all* that we experience — the aesthetic and religious no less than the physical and chemical. Indeed, his frequently misunderstood slogan, 'Nature is closed to Mind', means precisely that nature presents something to be reckoned with which may not legitimately be pared down to fit the mental prejudices of its investigators. Rather, as Whitehead contended in *The Function of Reason* (1929), 'The rejection of any source of evidence is always treason to that ultimate rationalism, which urges forward science and philosophy alike' (50).

Whitehead cannot conceive of 'vacuous actuality' — that is, of existence apart from subjective experience. 'The whole universe,' he says, 'consists of elements disclosed in the experience of subjects.' Apart from this experience there is nothingness. To understand any fact we must 'propose the general character of the universe required for that fact'. (At this point Whitehead is at his furthest remove from Russell, who had no interest in proposing the general character of the universe.) Further, every entity, from God to the merest 'puff of existence', is dipolar: it has both a mental and a physical pole, though (and this is not easy to grasp) this does not entail that every entity enjoys consciousness. To Whitehead consciousness arises within experience; it is not, as with the idealists, the presupposition of experience. To the integration and appropriation of the objective data of experience by a subjective entity he gives the name 'feeling' an unusual linguistic usage, and a further difficult idea prompted by his resolute opposition to any dualism (Cartesian or other) of body and mind. Everything, in its mutual relations, is part of the on-going process.

These ideas reached their fullest expression in Whitehead's Gifford Lectures, *Process and Reality: An Essay in Cosmology* (1929), and partly because of these Lectures Whitehead was extolled (in

The Times obituary of 31 December 1947) as 'the last and greatest of the Cambridge Platonists'. True, he was impressed by Platonic thought — and notably, as he admitted, by the *Timaeus*. But as Professor Dorothy Emmet has pointed out[5] although Whitehead did in a broad sense seek to 'find the forms in the facts', he did not elevate abstract forms or 'eternal objects' above the concrete processes of becoming. The process was his great concern — the process as pertaining to our 'cosmic epoch'. For Whitehead regarded metaphysics as treating of the formal qualities of all facts, but cosmology — his present concern as witness the subtitle of *Process and Reality* — as describing our present world order. Moreover the present world order is subject to change such that, for example, other kinds of facts would become apparent and other 'natural laws' obtain. In our epoch as it is, organisms *in concert* (and not as isolated Darwinian units) are in process of becoming; they mutually influence each other and shape their futures as they are urged towards the final synthesis. Such, Whitehead believes, is the underlying structure which we find if we attend to our experience.

Where in all of this is God? As we saw at the outset, Whitehead maintained that theologians had taken a wrong turn. Plato had provided a potent clue in his doctrine that the divine is persuasive, not coercive; that love, not power, has primacy. Sadly, however, Plato weakened this insight by having recourse to the concept of force. Next, in the incarnation of Christ we have the revelation of God's character and activity in the world — themes worked over by the Christian Fathers, with their proper emphasis upon the divine immanence. The Holy Spirit doctrine ought readily to have been worked out in terms of the divine persuasiveness, but unfortunately it was not. God the absolute despot was brought to the fore. (Space forbids the noting of numerous qualifications which might be made concerning Whitehead's reading of the history of Christian doctrine.) Negatively, Whitehead regards talk of God as potentate or 'ruthless moralist' as a 'scandalous failure'. By the same token the traditional theistic arguments fail. It is not so much that they fail as proofs (though they do so fail), as that they are not about *God* at all. They deal in abstractions. Positively, Whitehead seeks to restore the idea of the immanent, persuasive God, and he does so by resolutely placing God *within* the process. Now this entails the frank recognition that (*pace* much traditional theology) the world is as necessary to God as God is to the world: the unacceptable alternative, as far as Whitehead is concerned, is the reintroduction of a God-world dualism. There is thus *indirect* evidence for the existence of God — namely, that there is a non-contingent power apart from whom there would be no contingency. This is not the old argument from contingency all over again, for the God of whom Whitehead speaks is not in all respects a necessary being. He is in process and, as we shall see, he is subject to limitation.

Far from invoking God in order to save metaphysical principles from collapse, Whitehead boldy regards God as the chief exemplification of those principles. His nature, like that of all else, is dipolar. He has a primordial nature and a consequent nature. To say that he has a primordial nature is not to say that he exists *before* all creation; rather, he exists *with* all creation. This primordial nature is conceptual: God's mind conceives all that could possibly be. In his conceptual nature God is changeless; but in his consequent nature, which is 'the weaving of God's physical feelings upon his primordial concepts' God 'shares with every creature its actual world; and the concrescent creature is objectified in God as a novel element in God's objectification of that actual world' (488). In other words, God's primordial nature is constituted by his conceptual experience: it is 'free, complete, primordial, eternal, actually deficient [that is, as yet unrealised in the world] and unconscious'. His consequent nature 'originates with physical experience derived from the temporal world, and then acquires integration with the primordial side' (489).

God is not temporal, but he is an actual entity, present in each creative phase not as originator but as saviour of what is good in it. He is good, and his goodness imposes limitation upon him. For example, he cannot be evil and does not create evil. Evil is far more than a privation of good; it is a positive power in its own right. Happily, as Whitehead pointed out in *Religion in the Making*, evil is unstable: 'The fact of the instability of evil is the moral order of the world' (95). God, implicated as he is in the on-going process, cannot but be affected by evil: it limits him. He is, however, engaged in the struggle with it, and he is the companion of all who suffer in this life. The divine persuasion lures needy people to the goal of harmony in which the diverse elements in the world and in humanity are united. Both God and humanity, then, are characterised by becoming, not by being conceived statically. They are engaged in the work of self-creation, but the impetus comes from God. In the course of this development both God and humanity are challenged to respond to the novel. God is ever-renewing the world and ever-attracting people to join him in the task.

In all of which there was more than L. Susan Stebbing could

take: she wondered how Whitehead could on the one hand make so much of God's non-temporal actuality and then, on the other hand, speak of him as 'the poet of the world, with tender patience leading it by his vision of truth, beauty and goodness'. She regarded this 'indefensible' use of language as 'nothing short of scandalous' (*M* N.S. XXXIX, 1930, 475). It is difficult not to feel some sympathy with this comment; and I am at times more than a little inclined to endorse Professor Stebbing's conclusion: 'Whether it is the product of thinking that is essentially unclear but capable of brief flashes of penetrating insight; or whether it is too profound in its thought to be judged by this generation, I do not know. Reluctantly I am inclined to accept the first alternative.'

However we may judge him, Whitehead's over-all aim was clear. He is in quest of synthesis. He will brook neither dualism, nor the oft-attempted policy of obliterating one or other of the poles — good-evil, time-eternity. His dipolar exposition is his way of seeking to hold all things together. Small wonder that he leaves us in *Process and Reality* with paradoxes which are as tantalising as they are haunting:

> It is as true to say that God is permanent and the World fluent, as that the World is permanent and God is fluent.
> It is as true to say that God is one and the World many, as that the World is one and God many.
> It is as true to say that, in comparison with the World, God is actual eminently, as that, in comparison with God, the World is actual eminently.
> It is as true to say that the world is immanent in God, as that God is immanent in the World.
> It is as true to say that God transcends the World, as that the World transcends God.
> It is as true to say that God creates the World, as that the world creates God. (1978 edn, 348)

At the beginning of *Process and Reality* Whitehead stated that the task of speculative philosophy is to fuse science and religion into one rational scheme of thought. It is 'the welding of imagination and common sense into a restraint upon specialists, and also into an enlargement of their imaginations' (17). Many who would be quite unable to swallow Whitehead's system whole would gratefully confess that he has enlarged (if at times he has boggled) their imagination.

Systems, Silence and Scholasticism, 1920-35

William Temple

Of all theologians the one who showed the greatest, if carefully guarded, interest in the new realism was William Temple (1881-1944), successively Fellow and Lecturer in Philosophy at The Queen's College, Oxford, Headmaster of Repton, Bishop of Manchester, and Archbishop of York and of Canterbury. Temple has sometimes been represented as having undergone a sea-change in his thinking between the publication of his earlier works, *Mens Creatrix* (1917) and *Christus Veritas* (1924), and the appearance of his Gifford Lectures, *Nature, Man and God* (1934). Even in this last work, however, he describes himself as 'a loyal pupil' of the absolute idealist Edward Caird and, indeed, he dedicated the book to his teacher's memory. Nor did Temple's loyalty to Plato wane. His maintenance of the hierarchy of value led him to the absolute being who is transcendent over all. His deity, unlike those of Alexander and Whitehead, is in no danger of becoming imprisoned within the process.

On the other hand, in his Gifford Lectures Temple intends to turn away from idealistic epistemology and to take full measure of the fact that there is a world of real objects which stands over against mind:

> We have completely repudiated the Cartesian separation of Mind and Extension, and have accordingly rejected by implication both Idealism (which starts with Mind and makes the extended world adjectival to it) and Materialism (which starts with the Extended World and makes Mind adjectival to, or epiphenomenal to, this) — though our starting-point is closer to Materialism than to Idealism. For we start with the picture which science gives us of a world undergoing modification through the interaction of its constituent parts while as yet there is, apparently, no mind within it to observe its process. At a certain stage in the development of certain organisms, consciousness appears; and it first appears as an aid towards making effective the reactions of the organism (198).

Temple advocates a dialectical realism according to which there is movement from mind to world and back. Whereas to the idealists mind had priority as the knowing subject, the precondition of the actuality of the objective world, in Temple's dialectical realism priority is still accorded to mind but to mind as the purposive and only condition of the intelligibility of the same objective world. Thus, 'Realism becomes a basis for a spiritual interpretation of the universe, and the Materialism of our empirical starting-point is balanced by the uncompromising Theism of our conclusion' (498).

At times, however, Temple appears to vacillate, as when he says, 'My contention is that in cognition the subject-object relation is ultimate, and neither term is in any degree reducible to the other' (126). Now, as Ralph E. Stedman pointed out, this 'comes suspiciously close to the denial of the radical distinction between sensing and thinking, which, I take it, is the mark of epistemological realism' (*HJ*, XXXIII, 1934-5, 302).

We may further bring out Temple's ambivalence *vis-à-vis* idealism and realism if we compare and contrast him with Whitehead. At a number of points Temple appears to be in sympathy with Whiteheadian realism. Thus, he seeks to give an account of *all* that is there in human experience; he insists that consciousness presupposes experience and not *vice versa*, and he twice quotes *Process and Reality* (1929, 72) with approval on this point (112, 217). Again, to Temple as to Whitehead the Authority in religion is non-coercive, and man's ethical problem is seen by both in terms of conversion and vocation. Above all there is Temple's 'Whiteheadian' conviction that 'Reality is first presented as Process' (219).

Important as these points of contact and agreement are, there are differences too. While admitting his debt to Whitehead Temple breaks sharply with him over the question of the nature of God. He cannot see by what right Whitehead, on his presuppositions, can say what he does say about God's nature. (We recall Miss Stebbing's kindred difficulty.) Of Whitehead Temple writes,

> One is glad to know that he has the consolation of believing that 'love in the world passes into the love in heaven, and floods back again into the world,' so that 'in this sense God is the great companion — the fellow-sufferer who understands.' This is very near the Christian Gospel, and if only Professor Whitehead would for creativity say Father, for 'primordial nature of God' say Eternal Word, and for 'consequent nature of God' say Holy Spirit, he would perhaps be able to show ground for his gratifying conclusions. But he cannot use those terms, precisely because each of them imports the notion of Personality as distinct from Organism. (259)

Grateful though he is to utilise the concept of process, Temple, unlike Whitehead, will not dispense with the idea of a God transcendent over the world. In *Christus Veritas* he spoke of God and said that 'we shall confidently affirm Him as the sole self-subsistent Being, existing in absolute independence of all else, for whose pleasure and by whose creative activity all things are and were created' (22); and that confident affirmation remained his to the end. The world is thus in its natural processes sacramentally expressive of the divine will and purpose, and all is summed up in the Christian doctrine of the incarnation of Christ.

Temple's work displays the *theological* ambivalence to which any process-orientated theology is inclined. There is first the temptation at times so to blur the creator-creature distinction, and this despite the emphasis upon the divine transcendence to which attention has just been paid. The idea intrudes that God is somehow developed with the world, and this idea is to be found in both earlier and later works. Thus in *Christus Veritas* we are informed that 'God eternally is what we see in Christ; but temporally the Incarnation, the taking of Manhood into God, was a real enrichment of the Divine Life' (280). In *Nature, Man and God* Temple reaffirms the point argued in the earlier work that 'there was no Kenosis at all. The Second Person of the Trinity laid aside nothing, but added to His divine attributes the experience of a strictly human life' (326).

Secondly, there is Temple's less than *consistently* satisfactory account of evil. Like other idealists before him he finds it hard not almost to *require* evil as a stage on the way to good — especially given his optimistic ethical postulate of perfect goodness. Thus he can say that although human sin was not a 'necessary episode in the divine plan', it was 'always so closely implicated with the divine plan that it must be held to fall within the divine purpose'. I do not, however, find Temple as lacking in *hope* as does Professor Rogerson, who writes: 'I would see the Cross as a ray of hope in an inexplicable world, whereas Temple seemed to understand the Cross as the inevitable outcome in a world which was the expression of self-sacrificial love.'[6] But Temple avoided this disjunction and, in *Nature, Man and God*, says 'both — and' where Rogerson says 'either — or':

> the crucifixion of Jesus of Nazareth, interpreted as Christians have interpreted it, was for a moment the worst of all manifestations of evil; but throughout the ages it is the best of all manifestations of good; and the Christian scheme of

redemption affirms, not only a preponderance of good over evil, so that the temporary victory of evil is wiped out by a more decisive victory of good, but the conversion of defeat itself into triumph. (210)

Ludwig Wittgenstein

Of all 20th century philosophers the influence of Ludwig Josef Johann Wittgenstein (1889-1951) has probably been the most pervasive. It is not unkind to say further that of all 20th century philosophers he has most resembled, and behaved like, a cult figure. It is said that his assiduous pupils both drank in the teaching and copied the facial mannerisms of this open-neck-shirted professor who never graced the high table of his College with his presence, and whose room was furnished with deck chairs.

An Austrian by birth, Wittgenstein studied engineering in Berlin and aeronautical engineering in Manchester. His interest in engineering mathematics led him to Cambridge to become first Russell's pupil, and then his co-worker. The mathematical logic of Russell and Frege was to become the model for the clarity he was shortly to seek in language.

Towards the end of the First World War Wittgenstein, who was serving in the Austrian army, was captured in Italy. Meanwhile he had written the text of his *Tractatus Logico-Philosophicus*, and had reached the conclusion that he had nothing further to offer as a philosopher. Accordingly, on his release from detention in 1918 he returned to Austria and became an elementary schoolmaster. The *Tractatus* was published in Germany in 1921, and its English translation (complete with German text) appeared in the following year.

In his Introduction to the *Tractatus* Russell described the work as 'an important event in the philosophical world', and said that since Wittgenstein had constructed 'a theory of logic which is not at any point obviously wrong' he had 'achieved a work of extraordinary difficulty and importance'. For this reason the book 'is one which no serious philosopher can afford to neglect'. The distinguished historian of philosophy, Rudolf Metz, was not so cordial. To him the *Tractatus* 'embodies a very peculiar combination of rigorous mathematical and logical thought and obscure mysticism'.[7] For his part Broad declared in the preface to his *The Mind and Its Place in Nature* (1925), 'I shall watch with a fatherly eye the philosophical gambols of my younger friends as they dance to the highly syncopated pipings of Herr Wittgenstein's flute' (vii). Well, the piping has ended, but the dance lingers on! Indeed, as we shall see, it does more than linger, and over the years the piper has been lauded as the philosophical genius of all time, and denounced as the arch-trivialiser of philosophy.

We may best present the gist of Wittgenstein's intentions and suggest the flavour of his work by placing a number of his aphorisms in sequence thus:

> Most questions and propositions of the philosophers result from the fact that we do not understand the logic of our language. (4.003)
>
> The object of philosophy is the logical clarification of thought . . . The result of philosophy is not a number of 'philosophical propositions,' but to make propositions clear. (4.112)
>
> There is indeed the inexpressible. This *shows* itself; it is the mystical. (6.522)
>
> The right method of philosophy would be this. To say nothing except what can be said, *i.e.* the propositions of natural science, *i.e.* something that has nothing to do with philosophy: and then always, when someone else wished to say something metaphysical, to demonstrate to him that he had given no meaning to certain signs in his propositions. This method would be unsatisfying to the other — he would not have the feeling that we were teaching him philosophy — but it would be the only strictly correct method. (6.53)
>
> Whereof one cannot speak, thereof one must be silent. (7)

The importance for the early Wittgenstein of the model of empirical science, and his sympathy with those who were at that time attempting to construct the ideal language, emerge clearly from these extracts. What is equally clear is that Wittgenstein regarded it as the philosopher's task to show that the metaphysical puzzles which tantalise and perplex man are wrongly so-called; there would be no puzzles were there clarity of language. This is not to say that Wittgenstein was opposed to metaphysics as such; it is simply to say that he regarded many so-called metaphysical problems as pseudo-problems which were not candidates for solution but for dissolution.

For evidence of Wittgenstein's interest in metaphysics we need look no farther than his picture theory of meaning. From this it becomes clear that he is concerned not only with the meaningfulness or otherwise of discourse, but also with the ontological status of language. That is, he is all the time asking what *reality* must be like if language is appropriately used in such and such ways. He writes:

The total of reality is the world. (2.063)

The picture presents a situation in logical space, the existence and non-existence of states of affairs. (2.11)

A picture is a model of reality. (2.12)

It is like a scale applied to reality. (2.1512)

In other words, the real world consists of an infinite number of atomic facts which it is the task of language to picture. For every fact, or possible state of affairs, there is a proposition which pictures it. As the theory develops it becomes clear that those propositions only are meaningful which are employed by natural scientists in their work. They are concerned with the world as it is, and their language properly pictures it. All other propositions are either tautologous (as in mathematics and logic) or, strictly, non-sensical.

In the conclusion just reached we have the kernel of that community of interest which developed from the mid-1920s between Wittgenstein and the logical positivists of the Vienna Circle. The Circle included among others Moritz Schlick, Rudolf Carnap, Friedrich Waismann and Otto Neurath. All profoundly interested in the presuppositions of science and mathematics, they sought to apply to the anti-metaphysical empiricist tradition associated with the names of Hume, Comte and Mach the rigour of modern mathematical logic. They held that truth is either formal (logical) or factual (empirical). Any proposition which did not fall into either of these categories could not be true or false; it was literally meaningless. Although Wittgenstein was associated with this group, though never a full member of it, logical positivism did not make its full impact in Britain until the publication of A.J. Ayer's 'manifesto', *Language, Truth and Logic*, in 1936. We shall return to this book in the next chapter. Meanwhile we should note that testimony to Wittgenstein's refusal to adopt the anti-metaphysical stance comes from the heart of the positivist camp itself. Carnap writes,

His intellect, working with great intensity and penetrating

power, had recognised that many statements in the field of religion and metaphysics did not, strictly speaking, say anything. In his characteristic absolute honesty with himself, he did not try to shut his eyes to this insight. But the result was extremely painful for him . . . Schlick, and I, by contrast, had no love for metaphysics or metaphysical theology, and therefore could abandon them without inner conflict or regret. Earlier, when we were reading Wittgenstein's book in the Circle, I had erroneously believed that his attitude towards metaphysics was similar to ours. I had not paid sufficient attention to the statements in his book about the mystical, because his feelings and thoughts in this area were too divergent from mine. Only personal contact with him helped me to see more clearly his attitude at this point.[8]

What, then, of Wittgenstein's statements concerning the mystical? As we have seen, he holds that 'There is indeed the inexpressible. This *shows* itself; it is the mystical.' Wittgenstein himself was conversant with such feelings as wonder, guilt, adoration and dedication; he had himself undergone a mystical experience on the Eastern front during the War. Nothing, however, may properly be *said* about such things. Thus the fact that the Wittgenstein of the *Tractatus* is no dogmatic positivist of the more intransigent kind offers no comfort to those who wish to engage in theological discourse. I say 'the Wittgenstein of the *Tractatus*' because, as we shall see, his later philosophical work (for he did return to philosophy) has proved immensely stimulating, not least to those who have engaged in the more informal varieties of religious language analysis.

Taking stock

In view of the variety of philosophical aims and styles in the early 1920s it is not surprising that a number of philosophers felt the need to take stock of their discipline and to reassess its role. Some did this with special reference to religious questions. Thus, for example, Hoernlé declared in his *Studies in Contemporary Metaphysics* (1920) that 'To philosophise is to seek an attitude towards the universe as a whole, or, in so far as the search at all succeeds, to have such an attitude' (11). Furthermore, 'no philosopher who deals with fundamentals, or tries to get beyond piecemeal problems to an understanding of the whole, can avoid dealing with religion as one of the central experiences' (8).

The reaction of one philosopher to certain of his colleagues comes out clearly in Hoernlé's chapter entitled, 'The idol of scientific method in philosophy'. It is said that advance in the sciences has resulted from the application of a truly scientific method; and from this it is inferred that philosophy must find a new method if there is to be advance there. But Hoernlé doubts whether there is but one scientific method; and he does not think that the question of the manner of philosophising is as important as that concerning the appropriate problems for philosophical investigation. He suggests that if the method of the pure scientist be adopted one set of problems will emerge, while if the method of the experimental scientist be adopted a different range of problems will be presented. He illustrates this contention by reference to Russell who, following the first alternative, is led into instrumentalism. In Hoernlé's view Russell does not so much offer an improved method of philosophising, as give philosophy a new task altogether. It is not merely that what was once known as philosophy must now be known as something else, for in offering his method Russell is making a judgement embodying a world view — a 'view of a world of abstract logical entities and relations'. The weakness of instrumentalism lies in its failure to appreciate the intrinsic value of thinking. Hoernlé's continuing conviction is that 'a reasoned and reasonable theory (or, if the word be preferred, 'faith,') is not unattainable and has rewarded the venture of philosophising again and again' (48).

Webb was among others who sought to take stock. In his Inaugural Lecture, *Philosophy and the Christian Religion* (1920), he outlines his conception of the relation of the former to the latter:

> Philosophy and Religion have always been closely associated, though their relations have not always been amicable. Philosophy springs out of Religion, because it is in Religion first that man expresses his concern with the Whole . . . This concern distinguishes him, as we suppose, from the other animals, and Philosophy is nothing but the deliberate and disinterested investigation of the object of this characteristically human interest. Religion and Philosophy are thus concerned from the first — and Religion earlier than Philosophy — with the same object. (11-12)

None of which blinded Webb to the fact that from certain points of view Christianity more than some other religions seems to resist reconciliation with philosophy. He attributes this to the fact that Christianity is more, not less, philosophical than other religions in so far as in Christianity we are presented with a series of concrete facts which have to be related to abstractions of universal significance. 'Religions which remain in the region of the universal and treat the individual and the historical as something illusory may seem to afford the philosopher a greater shelter than Christianity; but only at the cost of abandoning the supreme venture to which, as a philosopher, he is committed — that of understanding not merely universal principles . . . but the real world of historical individuals, in which alone these principles can live and move and have a genuine existence' (17).

Despite all apparent difficulties and occasional animosities, Christianity has, according to Webb, rendered invaluable service to the philosophic cause during its long history. It has sometimes provided a refuge to certain aspects of the truth which were endangered by the prevailing fashion in philosophy — as when in face of nominalism or positivism Christianity has borne witness to the unity that is in the manifold; and as when, over against pantheism, Christianity has reminded the world of a particular providence, of personal immortality. Yet again, Christianity has afforded the highest and fullest conception of spiritual being, and has provided greater stimulus to the development of the notion of personality than any other system.

In the two volumes of *Contemporary British Philosophy* edited by J.H. Muirhead (1924, 1925) a number of philosophers considered what they were about. Broad contributed an influential article entitled 'Critical and speculative philosophy'. He sought to show that although the two types of philosophy may be distinguished they can never entirely be divorced from each other. They represent different approaches to the subject matter of philosophy. Critical philosophy seeks to analyse and define the concepts which are used in daily life and in the special sciences; it examines our fundamental presuppositions. Speculative philosophy, on the other hand, treats of the nature of reality as a whole. Broad realises that even the practice of critical philosophy presupposes a certain view of the latter question: 'It assumes that our minds are so far in accord with the rest of Reality that by using them carefully and critically we approach nearer the truth. But it is still clearer that Speculative Philosophy presupposes a considerable amount of Critical Philosophy' (I, 96).

Broad considers that the main value of speculative philosophy lies in the fact that in the practice of it the philosopher is compelled to take a synoptic view of the world; 'and anyone who does not do this at some time in his life is bound to hold a very narrow and inadequate idea of Reality' (I, 98). Nor must religious and mystical experience be left out of the reckoning; for apart from the consideration of the possibility which they place before us, namely, that we may be brought into contact with an aspect of reality which is not revealed in ordinary sense-perception, any speculative philosophy will be extremely one-sided.

Dean Inge went further, maintaining not merely that it is advisable to take account of things religious in any speculative system, but that 'I am unable to distinguish between philosophy and religion. If the perfectly real can alone be perfectly known, and if to know God, the perfectly real Being, is eternal life, the goal of philosophy is the same as the goal of religion — perfect knowledge of the Perfect' (I, 191). Webb was able to distinguish between philosophy and religion while both were *in via*, so to speak: 'Philosophy is consciously from the first engaged in the quest of that which is truly and ultimately real; but Religion is concerned with this same object, yet not at first consciously' (II, 349-50). *Le Sacré* or *das Heilige* comes first in religion.

In view of the opinions expressed by Broad, Inge and Webb — to which might be added those of Hoernlé — and in the wake of the more extended works of Webb, Jones, Alexander and Whitehead, W.G. de Burgh was not without justification when he wrote, 'Half a century ago, the pretensions of religion to give speculative truth would hardly have aroused serious attention in a gathering of philosophers. Today the case is otherwise; though many, perhaps a majority, still share in the traditional aloofness towards theology and its dogmas' ('Metaphysical and religious knowledge', *PASSV*, IV, 1924, 1-18). At the same time he was not in favour of installing philosophers as high priests of religion, implying that certain types of philosophical *gnosis* could lead only to widespread popular befuddlement. He illustrates his concern to keep philosophy in its proper place by referring to McTaggart, who had said that no-one had a right to religion who had not studied metaphysics.[9] De Burgh prefers to agree with his teacher William Wallace who, in his *Lectures and Essays on Natural Theology and Ethics* (1898, 163) had said that God, 'If he come at all, he comes altogether, . . . sooner perhaps to the day labourer than to the speculative thinker . . . The modern world can only gain religion, and have such vision of God as man can have, when it realizes to the intensest that the wise and foolish equally enjoy his sunlight, and that to him nothing is common or unclean.'

No doubt an extreme version of the fear here implied lies behind T.E. Jessop's remark in his article, 'The philosophic approach to religion': 'For many religious people philosophy is the mother of heresy, the champion of impiety, and the refrigerator of the soul' (*MC*, XIV, 1924–5, 565). Jessop sets out to indicate the ways in which religion may benefit from philosophy. He reiterates the contention of many of his contemporaries that religious questions may not be omitted from any discipline which claims, as philosophy does, to be all-embracing. More positively, he suggests that philosophy provides religion with a weapon of defence, with an aid to spiritual stability, and with an instrument of evangelical persuasion. But there are limitations too: philosophising is a long and slow process, whereas life is short and swift; and philosophy cannot take the seeker all the way. 'It can help to put us in the position to see, but it cannot make us see' (574). He concludes that 'The final vision of religious truth is inevitably mystical, and the living out of it essentially practical. Philosophy, being only a theoretical activity, here stops short, but not without having led many pilgrims along sure paths to the outer court of the Temple' (574).

We may reasonably claim to have taken a fair sample of assessments of the relations between philosophy and religion in the early 1920s. Religious philosophers had some grounds for their general optimism, though this might have been tempered somewhat had they explored the implications of the *Tractatus* more closely. But they cannot be deemed unduly blameworthy when so few of their secular contemporaries had studied the new teaching in depth. Nor did the latter yet have the excuse that exotic influences had to some extent diverted their attention from things at home. In theology, on the other hand, Barth had spoken.

Neo-Thomism

As we enter the second quarter of the century we find that we can no longer delay reference to the revival of Thomism; but first some general remarks.

The customary bracketing of Aquinas with Aristotle implies no absence of Platonism in the Angelic Doctor's thought. For example, the Platonic doctrine that Aquinas inherited from Dionysius the

Areopagite and John of Damascus to the effect that God is to be reached by a process of subtraction entailing the reduction of limitations, constituted a profound stimulus to Aquinas's construction of the *via negativa* — the negative way of saying what God is *not*. Again, the fourth of Thomas's Five Ways — his arguments for the existence of God — is the argument from value, a peculiarly Platonic argument: there must be something 'which is to all beings the cause of their being, goodness, and every other perfection'. We may indeed go so far as to say that Aquinas's free use of Aristotle and Plato, not to mention Avicenna and Maimonides, is indicative of a far greater degree of openness than is displayed by some of his more recent followers. Furthermore, as E.L. Mascall has pointed out in his *Existence and Analogy*, 'the fundamental principles of St. Thomas's metaphysics — his existentialism — while it completely revolutionized Aristotelianism, did not come from Aristotle at all, however necessary it may have been if Aristotle was to be made really coherent' (xvii-xviii).

It was in his epistemology that Aquinas's Aristotelianism emerged most clearly, for he concurred with Aristotle in thinking that while sense experience is the fount of knowledge the mind is capable of drawing from that experience more-than-empirical knowledge. He thereby opposed both the Plantonic theory that the forms alone could be said to be knowable, and also the sensationalist theory of Democritus, according to which knowledge comes *via* our senses. As to the truth thus acquired, it is well known that Aquinas distinguished between truth attainable by the reason of man, and truth attainable only as it is revealed by God to man. It is sometimes wrongly supposed that Aquinas was insisting upon two different kinds of truth. In fact he held to the indivisibility of truth, emphasised the inability of a truth acquired by reason to conflict with one given in revelation, and, in face of that mystery which he sensed to be at the heart of things, merely held that human limitation requires more than the exercise of human reason if the deepest truths are to be apprehended at all.

Thus Aquinas held that truths concerning the Trinity, the Incarnation, the resurrection of the body, and others, could be known only by revelation. This in no way ruled out their rational, albeit incomplete, defence. On the other hand, truths concerning such matters as the existence of God could be discovered by the natural reason: 'The existence of God and other like truths about God which can be known by natural reason are not articles of faith, but are preambles to the articles' (*Summa Theologica*, I, Ques. II

2nd Art., Reply to Objection I). The idea comes right down to the Second Vatican Council: 'The same holy Mother Church holds and teaches that God, the beginning and end of all, can be certainly known by the natural light of human reason from the things of creation' (Session III, Cap. 2 *de fide*, DB 1785).

The impression is sometimes conveyed that the revival of Thomism began in the year 1879, with the proclamation of Pope Leo XIII's encyclical, *Aeterni Patris*. It is certainly the case that in this encyclical the Pope commended to the faithful both the study of Aquinas, and the study of ways in which Thomism might be developed so as to meet the challenge of contemporary thought. But in doing this the Pope was giving fresh impetus to a movement — whose pioneers included Vincenzo Buzzetti, Domenico and Serafino Sordi, Gaetano Sanseverino and the Pope's own brother, Guiseppe Pecci — whose objective was to raise philosophy in public esteem by showing its relevance to current thought. However, to deny the Pope the honour of being the sole originator of the movement is not to underestimate the far-reaching effects of his action. The works of Mercier, De Wulf, Gilson and Maritain constitute an impressive testimony to the extent and depth of Neo-Scholastic writing in the first quarter of the century.

Neither British nor Irish circles can claim an early representative of an outstandingly formative kind, though the diligence of such writers as Fr. P. Coffey of Maynooth did much to lay the foundation of modern Thomistic studies in the British Isles. Coffey's major works were *The Science of Logic* (1912), *Ontology* (1914) and *Epistemology* (1917). He proves to be no exception to the general rule that Thomists are anxious to preserve the independence of their philosophy; they wish to steer a course between theology on the one side and ecclesiastical authoritarianism on the other. Like many others Coffey seems to recognise the dangers of special pleading in philosophy, whilst at the same time finding it difficult not to ensnare himself in them. Thus in his *Epistemology* he writes:

> It is of the first importance for the catholic student to realise that among all peoples who have inherited Christian culture and civilisation the choice of ever-increasing multitudes of those whom we may describe as the leaders of thought — and consequently also of the masses influenced by them — is now no longer so much as formerly between Catholicism and some other form of Christianity, but rather between Catholicism and the rejection of supernatural religion

altogether. Nowadays the religious question in the main resolves itself into Catholicism *versus* Unbelief, Agnosticism, Monism, Naturalism. (I, 7-8)

He goes on to explain that the difficulties which impede the acceptance of Catholic truth arise out of false theories of knowledge; and then he reminds his readers (if not always himself) that

> our investigation, if it is to attain its object, must be wholly impartial and disinterested. A treatise on the Theory of Knowledge cannot possibly be apologetic or polemical in the religious sense. It must be purely philosophical; it must appeal to reason, not to authority; it must be grounded on universal human experience; it must assume nothing except on grounds of reason; in this sense it must be 'presuppositionless'. But only in this sense; for it will bring to light many presuppositions without which no rational investigation and no intelligent thought would be possible. (8)

Coffey is convinced that Christians are justified in entertaining the 'unwavering confidence' that the foundations of their faith will be justified by a purely rational and competent examination of human certitude.

It cannot be denied that Coffey, and those who thought like him, were, in the early years of this century, addressing almost exclusively the converted. Neo-Thomism had not as yet emerged into the arena of general philosophical debate in this country and, Coffey apart, was almost entirely at the textbook and manual stage of development. At last, however, tentative exercises in public relations were commenced from the Neo-Thomist side, and some desire was shown to launch out into the Anglo-Saxon philosophical deep. The earliest example of this that I have been able to trace is F. Aveling's paper on 'The Thomistic outloook in philosophy'. Aveling finds two reasons for the disrepute into which Scholastic philosophy has fallen. In the first place, 17th-century scholastics were ill advised to neglect, as they did, the science and philosophy of their day. Secondly there is the mistaken belief that scholastic philosophy is not only necessarily connected with, but is subordinate to, Christian dogma. Aveling's case is that

> Considered as a purely rational discipline, scholastic philosophy has a subject matter and a view point, a set of

> principles and a method, peculiarly its own . . . It can be
> disentangled from its theological implications, presented as
> a system, and judged on its own merits. (*PAS*, XXXIV,
> 1923-4,170)

We need to follow Aveling no further; suffice it to note the fact that the Aristotelian Society was open to receiving an address on Thomism at all.

The publication of *Present-Day Thinkers and the New Scholasticism* (1926, 2nd edn 1927), edited by John S. Zybura, was opportune. This is an invaluable survey from our point of view, for it provides comments of British philosophers, among others, on the brand of philosophy with which it deals. These comments are the more interesting first, because Scholasticism was only just beginning to emerge from its seminarian confines, and it is good to be informed of the reception it received; and secondly, because apart from Zybura's questionnaire we should have had no means of knowing the attitude of some of the philosophers in question towards the New Scholasticism, for they did not for the most part take it into consideration in their published work.

That Zybura is a man with a mission is clear:

> In our era of reappraisals and readjustments it is being
> increasingly realised that in order to secure the structure of
> civilisation, we must plan to build on the bedrock of perennial
> principles, of absolute and transcendental values: reliance on
> the shifting sands of scientism and sentimentalism, of
> relativism and romanticism has led but to disaster. It is this
> insight which inspires the present noteworthy trend of many
> of the best trained minds to that type of philosophical thinking
> whose very soul is absoluteness, objectivity, wholesome
> commonsense, the reign of intelligence. (viii)

Rhetoric of this kind must not blind us to the valuable service performed by Zybura in placing Neo-Scholastics and others on the same stage if not in the same play. Further, since the initiative lay with the former, they seem to have gone out of their way to be just to their guests, and frank in the recognition of their own warts.

The book falls into three parts: 'Opinions of Non-Scholastic philosophers on Scholasticism', 'The Neo-Scholastic movement explained by its representatives', and 'Scholasticism and the period of transition, — status and value of the New Scholasticism'. By

Systems, Silence and Scholasticism, 1920-35

way of providing material for part one Zybura sent a questionnaire to 65 professors of Philosophy in non-Roman Catholic universities in the USA, Britain and Canada. Thirty-three answers for publication were returned, the remainder who replied stating that they had insufficient knowledge of Scholasticism to enable them to pass comment upon it. In Zybura's own words:

> An expression of opinion was requested on the following points: present attitude of non-Scholastic thinkers towards Scholastic and Neo-Scholastic philosophy; reasons for the unfriendliness or indifference towards it, — whether they are to be found in the content, or method, or other aspects of that philosophy; the contributions which it can make towards the solution of contemporary problems; present prospects for a *rapprochement* between it and other currents of present-day thought; the means to be used for bringing about a better understanding and a closer co-operation in the domain of philosophy. (xi)

Clement Webb would have found no dissent among his philosophical colleagues from his statement that 'The notion which was prevelant 100 to 150 years ago and later, that their [i.e. the Schoolmen's] speculations were a solemn trifling or even that their submission to certain dogmas as revealed was such as to deprive their work of all claim to freedom and originality, is now rarely held by the instructed' (62-3). Webb feels that the revival of interest in Scholasticism has been fostered on the one hand by the tendency towards realism in philosophy generally — many of the Schoolmen having been Aristotelian in outlook — and, on the other hand, by the extreme idealism of Croce and Gentile, which has caused some to seek points of contact with such other illustrious Italians as Aquinas and Bonaventure. However, some idealists suspect the realist bias of Scholasticism, and the latter's hostility to immanentism; these would probably value the content rather than respect the method of Scholastic philosophy. Webb believes that *rapprochement* draws ever nearer with the increase of historical sympathy — a sympathy in which the 17th and 18th centuries were, by comparison with the 20th, deficient. A further factor auguring well for harmonious relations is the decrease in sectarian controversy. Meanwhile, the Scholastics can help the cause of mutual relations by removing the impression that they espouse their particular variety of philosophy because their ecclesiastical superiors instruct them so to do, rather than because they are convinced of its superior worth. For their part non-Scholastics should remember that the validity of reasoning is more important than the motives which incline individuals to attend to particular lines of argument.

A.E. Taylor confesses that Scholastic philosophy is, in general, little known because life is short, foreign languages are difficult, and texts are not readily accessible. Like Webb he feels that the method of the Scholastics goes against them: 'There is the feeling that to a very large extent they are spending their time in making subtle formal distinctions to which nothing empirically real corresponds' (68). However, Scholasticism can make a vital contribution towards the solution of contemporary problems, for it provides a corrective to the Kantian substitution of a theory of knowledge for a theory of being, supplies abundant excellent psychological analyses, advocates thorough objectivity in ethics, and insists that full justice be done to human individuality without, like Känt, reducing all that distinguished one man from another to the level of the merely 'phenomenal'. Finally, Scholastics may help relations forward by translating some of their terms into those used by 'moderns', and by trying to understand more deeply than they do the concerns of 'modern' philosophers. For his part the ' "modern" has to learn that there really is no such thing as a breach of continuity in the history of philosophy' (71), with which Taylor alluded to the custom widespread in British philosophical departments — then as now — to make a huge leap in the syllabus from Aristotle to Descartes.

We might note in passing that Taylor had already amplified his last point here in his Aquinas Sixcentenary Lecture, *Saint Thomas Aquinas as a Philosopher* (1924):

> the bad habit of beginning the study of so-called 'modern' philosophy with Descartes, in whom the epistemological problem is falsified from the first by 'representationist' assumptions [with which criticism the otherwise very different Whitehead was in thorough accord], is responsible for generations of mere fumbling in the dark which might have been escaped if the gentlemen of the eighteenth and nineteenth centuries had been willing to do less 'sneering at Aquinas' and more study of him. (32)

Taylor's mature conclusion on Thomism is that 'the Thomist philosophy is no mere Aristotelianism revised but a masterly synthesis of both Plato and Aristotle with one another and with

Augustine, effected by original insight of the first order' (24).

Reverting to Zybura's book we find that by contrast with Webb and Taylor, J.W. Scott and Aveling suggest that it is the content rather than the method of Scholasticism that prompts indifference on the part of non-Scholastic philosophers. Scott points out that to have a consistent attitude on many questions is not the same thing as being in possesssion of solutions that cut ice in the concrete setting of modern life. Muirhead and Alexander question whether Scholastic philosophers possess sufficient freedom of thought for *rapprochement* to be a genuine hope, though the latter acknowledges that his impression in this matter may be an erroneous one, deriving from inadequate knowledge of Scholasticism. For his part, John Laird observes that there cannot be a single attitude either to non-Scholasticism or to Neo-Scholasticism, for both are so varied. He feels that the most that can be said is that it is more readily agreed than hitherto that the Schoolmen made important contributions to human learning, and that the work of certain Neo-Scholastics, particularly that of Gilson, is 'of the greatest service to all historians of philosophy and to modern thinkers' (81). His recommendation is that ' "Scholastic" and "non-Scholastic" thinkers should cultivate good will, and at the same time dispute with the utmost vigour and pertinacity' (83).

What now of the Neo-Scholastic reactions to these comments? As if in answer to Laird, Switalski admits that within Neo-Scholasticism there are sharp differences on many points, though fundamentally there is unity. All Scholastics adhere to the belief that the human mind can grasp the order of reality, and subscribe to theocentric idealism — that is, 'that conception of the universe which holds that all the reality of being, order, and activity is ultimately grounded in one, self-subsisting, personal God, who is the last end to which all reality is ordained' (178). Gény, however, realises that this very unity can present an obstacle to modern minds, for the latter tend to distrust any system which purports to be fixed. Further, the modern conviction that we cannot know things as they are in themselves, but only the phenomena which our minds produce within themselves, constitutes a predisposition against Scholasticism, and one which, according to Gény, Scholastics have yet satisfactorily to remove. In his contribution Maritain tends to lay more of the blame for unhappy relations upon the non-Scholastics, claiming that their proneness to subjectivity, their hatred of Christianity, their belief that Scholasticism is merely 'a theological philosophy', and their faith in the continuance of progress — which causes them to suspect a philosophy from the past, are all factors which make *rapprochement* a distant goal. He does, however, see a hopeful sign in the contemporary longing for realism.

As we leave Neo-Scholasticism for the time being, we may refer to some remarks of the President Emeritus of Notre Dame University, John Cavanaugh, who contributes the Introduction to Zybura's symposium:

> Certainly if one may judge from the spirit manifested in the contributions of both Scholastics and moderns . . . a very comfortable *rapprochement*, if not a complete one, is easily within the horizon of hope. At the present time unquestionably the Scholastics are a thousand times more familiar with the so-called modern philosophies, than the moderns are with Scholasticism. (iii–iv)

My own feeling is that while the first sentence here was somewhat over-optimistic, the second contained more than a grain of truth.

1930–35

The years 1930–35 saw the appearance of a number of impressive works of religious philosophy, the advance of encounter theology, and some general surveys of the philosophy of religion.

In 1930 A.E. Taylor's Gifford Lectures, *The Faith of a Moralist* (2 vols) were published. By now Taylor, though not a traitor to Plato, had taken to himself much of value from Aquinas and others in the Aristotelian tradition. He can also speak with approval of the aims of such philosophers of organism as Alexander and Whitehead — however much he might dissent from some of the ways in which they present their cases. He stops short, however, of believing that it is possible to produce a logically coercive natural theology, and rather seeks to show that our ethical experience requires completion in religious experience. There is an eternal good which, however, cannot be attained unaided by sinful humanity. Happily, there is the 'initiative of the eternal' which comes redemptively to our aid.

Whereas Moore, Russell and Whitehead made the pilgrimage from idealism to realism, R.G. Collingwood, in his *An Essay on Philosophical Method* (1933) gave evidence of moving in the opposite direction. He is in no doubt that philosophy must reflect upon its own nature, for its task is to reflect upon all. What then is philosophy? Can we define it in terms of its object? No, because philosophy is a voyage of exploration, and it cannot be assumed that its object is fully known before the voyage commences. Again, it might be thought that philosophy may be defined in terms of the ends it desires to attain. But these vary from philosopher to philosopher, and even the individual philosopher's mind on this matter may undergo change. The only satisfactory approach is to consider philosophic method, for philosophy is an activity characterised by certain describable marks. Unlike mathematics and empirical science philosophy is not hypothetical; the philosopher's task is to enunciate propositions which are 'in essence and fundamental intention categorical' (121).

In one of the most interesting sections of his book Collingwood takes up cudgels against prevailing scepticism, warning that scepticism in philosophy can all too easily become a covert dogmatism, as for example in the contention that philosophy cannot establish positive or constructive positions. A second form of scepticism which Collingwood finds repulsive is that which avers that when philosophy fails, as it must, science and common sense can lead to constructive conclusions. Then, by way of a *tu quoque* argument, he asserts that 'analytic philosophy does indeed involve a constructive philosophical doctrine, but, true to its character as a form of scepticism, declines the task of stating it' (146).

It fell to A.C. Ewing to restate the permanent values of idealism, after taking due account of the various onslaughts that had recently been made upon it. This he did in *Idealism, A Critical Survey* (1934). Of the need of such a review Ewing was in no doubt:

> The need for such an evaluation of idealism is all the greater because so many prominent philosophers of other schools now seem to think that there is nothing to be learnt from it and despise and ignore it in a way which of itself suggests to a discreet observer that the reaction may have gone too far. (1)

Ewing grants that the realist attacks upon idealism have produced certain beneficial results. For example, realists have shown that the theory of a physical world existing independently of any experience, while incapable of strict proof and still open to many difficulties, is at least reasonably arguable; and they have insisted upon the need for clear statements of views and careful analyses of concepts. Even so, 'There is no reason why a philosopher might not have the clarity and precision of the logical analysts without their philosophy' (9). He is, however, honest enough to confess that he can see some justification for Broad's remark that 'the writings of too many eminent Absolutists seem to start from no discoverable premises; to proceed by means of puns, metaphors, and ambiguities; and to resemble in their literary style glue thickened with sawdust'. For the other side Ewing fastens upon this remark of the logician F.P. Ramsey: 'The chief danger to our philosophy, apart from laziness and wooliness, is *scholasticism*, the essense of which is treating what is vague as if it were precise and trying to fit it into an exact logical category'. Thus, by way of carefully balanced discussions Ewing seeks to breathe new life into idealistic bones; and that he was not alone among philosophers in not falling for the view that philosophy is nothing but language analysis is clear not only from the work of Taylor and Collingwood to which I have referred, but also from the following impressive list of works: C.A. Campbell, *Scepticism and Construction* (1931); G.F. Stout, *Mind and Matter* (1931); and A.D. Ritchie *Natural History of Mind* (1936).

The years which here concern us marked a period of heightened activity on the part of philosophical theologians and philosophers of religion. The theology of encounter received a considerable impetus from D.M. Baillie's book, *Faith in God and its Christian Consummation* (1927), and from H.H. Farmer's *Experience of God* (1929). Farmer owed a good deal to Oman and to Martin Buber, and Donald Baillie — and also his brother John, who was shortly to weigh in on the side of encounter theology — would have agreed with what Farmer wrote in a later book, *The World and God*: 'The essence of religion in all its forms is a response to the ultimate as personal' (28). We shall return to encounter theology (which in some ways marks a *via media* between Temple and Brunner) when philosophers of religion begin to analyse its presuppositions — that is, after analytical philosophy has made its impact upon the philosophy of religion.

In the field of more strictly religious *philosophy* we find B.H. Streeter's *Reality* (1926), in which it is argued that our best clue to the ultimate nature of reality resides in the noblest features of humanity as we know it; and, above all, Frederick Robert Tennant's *Philosophical Theology* in two volumes (1928, 1930). It is probably true to say that no philosophical theologian of the period received kinder or more respectful treatment from secular philosophers than Tennant (1866-1957), a pupil of Ward and a lecturer at Cambridge.

Tennant sets out to construct an empirically based theism. He rejects those theistic arguments which rest upon *a priori* premises, and those which appeal to ethical data or to mystical and religious experience. This done, there is but one way left: the cosmological. Not indeed that Tennant builds upon specific instances of causation or purpose: his is a cosmic teleology. That is, he seeks to show that when we consider the broad evidence of conformity to law within the universe, we are led, not unreasonably, to suppose that the theistic account of the cause of what we have discovered is most probably the correct one. Clearly, to any theism of this kind the problem of evil — its apparent inequitability and capriciousness — is a standing problem. Tennant fully appreciates this and concludes that 'The facts which suggest a theistic interpretation of the world also suggest that in this life our seeking rather than our finding is God's purpose for us: question and counter-question, intercourse and dialogue, rather than full light and certain knowledge. The risks attending faith are not fatal, while they are conditions of the ethico-religious status in the life that now is' (II, 208). All of which was a serious attenuation in the opinion of those theologians whose theodicy was more explicitly grounded in the Cross-Resurrection event. But to the philosopher, Broad, the thought came that 'If a system of speculative philosophy cannot be established by Dr. Tennant's method, I agree that it is still less likely to be established by any other' (*M* N.S. XXXIX, 1930, 483).

Turning now to some surveys of the philosophy of religion we find that in his *Studies in the Philosophy of Religion* (1930), Pringle-Pattison follows Plato in holding that philosophy is the synoptic view of things. It is an intellectual endeavour to organise one's experience of the world into a systematic whole. Hence, the philosophy of religion will consist in the attempt to analyse and interpret religious experience in its bearing upon our view of man and of the world in which we live. The philosopher of religion seeks principles common to all manifestations of religion, and this implies that it is not his purpose to perpetuate old distinctions as between 'true' and 'false' religions. While religion always has an intellectual element, 'we confound religion with philosophy if we make religion consist in intellectual assent to certain conclusions of the reflective reason' (4). Philosophy cannot, of itself, create a religious atmosphere, but it can encourage men to discard intellectually untenable, or morally unworthy, religious beliefs. Finally, the philosopher of religion has the task of harmonising our religious experience with the rest of our experience, and of effecting 'such restatement as is necessary in the interest of our world-view as a whole' (10).

That D. Miall Edwards was in general accord with Pringle-Pattison is clear from his *Christianity and Philosophy* (1932). In his view religion and philosophy are bound to react upon one another, for both are interested in truth, and truth is a self-consistent organism. At times, however, we find that religion and philosophy are at war with each other. Even then we must resist the temptation to over-simplify the matter; for

> There is never one homogeneous thing called 'religion' confronting another homogeneous thing called 'philosophy' . . . What generally happens is that a school of religious thought enters into a friendly alliance with a school of philosophic thought which it feels to be most akin to itself, borrowing its terms and categories as auxiliaries for the systematic interpretation of the truths for which it stands, in order both to satisfy its own intellectual conscience and to defend itself more effectively against rival theologies and opposing philosophies. (3)

Edwards does not deny that the Christian faith is a gospel before it is a philosophy, 'But implicit in its gospel are certain affirmations about the ultimate nature of reality behind and within the world's appearances, and in this way it enters into the same field as philosophy either as a rival or as an ally' (6-7). For Edwards the way forward lies in a form of personal idealism which allows room both for God as the ultimate reality, and for humanity as, or as capable of becoming, a spiritual personality, possessing real, though limited freedom; possessing too the capacity to worship. Philosophy aims at formulating a comprehensive and synthetic *Weltanschauung*, and in the process of so doing it must criticise all unwarranted assumptions. In so vast an enterprise the consideration of religious experience must have its place and, for its part, religion must be willing to allow its hypothesis to be scrutinised in the light of experience as a whole. For despite the affinities between religion and philosophy in so far as both are concerned with truth, there are clear differences between them. For whereas philosophy is concerned as a matter of intellectual curiosity with truth for its own sake, religion engages a man's entire personality, and involves intellect, feeling and action.

In his *The Philosophical Approach to Religion* (1933) E.S. Waterhouse gives his blessing to this general approach, and then proceeds to treat of God, the world and immortality. It cannot be said that these philosophers of religion give evidence that they are aware of the changing face of secular philosophy. Or, if that is too harsh a judgment (for Edwards, for example, refers to Alexander and Whitehead), they have not felt it necessary to adjust their views in the light of the challenge implicit in Wittgenstein's *Tractatus* or the advancing empiricism of their day. They seem content to reiterate ideas upon the relationship between religion and philosophy which were current in the first decade of the century. This they had a perfect right to do; but the fact that they did not make a case in relation to recent thought leaves one with the inevitable feeling that their victory was somewhat glib. No doubt they could, by invoking such names as those of Alexander, Whitehead, Hoernlé, and Ewing, claim sanctuary — if only by the skin of their teeth. But the times they were a-changing.

As if to prepare for the reception of new emphases — or, in some cases, with a view to bolstering ageing positions against them — we find a number of 'stock-taking' articles in the decade prior to 1935. As if gripped by a premonition of things to come, W.G. de Burgh wrote an article entitled 'Logic and faith' — the very conjunction of the two terms is significant — in which he spoke of the epistemological characteristics of religious faith, of verification, and of the philosopher's faith. 'In principle,' he declared, 'faith is an assurance of truth beyond, or at least in independence of inferential evidence. Its proper object is the unproven and the dubitable . . . faith, for all its certainty of conviction, fails to prove' (*P*, I, 1926, 424). Religious faith is not confined to belief in propositions, it includes trust in God; indeed the experience of this trustful relationship precedes the beliefs. The experience itself is 'an immediate awareness of the given reality'. This is not to deny that faith requires the reinforcement of logical thinking. As for the verification of the truth received by faith, de Burgh holds that the *onus probandi* lies with the doubter, while the final verdict lies with those qualified to judge of the matter. Neither in theology nor in philosophy is it a question of faith *or* logic; both disciplines require faith *and* logic for their fullest development.

De Burgh's contribution may be regarded as a preliminary, transitional skirmish. That is, while he appears to adhere to the notion of philosophy as being a body of dogma, he is not unaware of the challenge of verificational analysis. Here too we have an early example of what was to become an increasingly important weapon in the religious philosopher's armoury: the *tu quoque* argument employed to show that the positivist no less than the religious man has some sort of faith in certain basic presuppositions.

In an article entitled, 'The purpose of philosophy' F.B. Jevons argued that the business of philosophy is to produce by intuition a synoptic vision of reality. Philosophy's purpose is not to *make* the several parts of knowledge into a whole, for 'that implies that there was a time when knowledge was not a whole, yet had parts, and next that philosophy then obligingly came to the rescue and made the parts into a whole' (*P*, I, 1926, 75). Rather, philosophy's role is to make us *see* the whole. In 'Our present outlook in speculative philosophy' J.S. Mackenzie worked out the implications of this in his own way. He remains convinced that the search for coherence, and the attempt to bring the findings of the special sciences into systematic relation is the legitimate aim and function of speculative philosophy. The philosopher must still be concerned with appearance and reality, the universal and the particular, necessity and contingency, the idea of the absolute, and the problem of creation. These must all be viewed in relation to modern science and in terms of their bearing upon practical life. As for verification: 'The views to which we are led are simply the views that appear to us to be most intelligible. Very little can be done in the way of testing them, in the sense in which scientific hypotheses can be tested. Their internal coherence is the only ground that we have for believing them to be true' (*P*, V, 1930, 23).

Three years earlier Mackenzie had applied this general approach to specifically religious questions:

> Speculative conceptions of what is to be understood by God or the Absolute may, to some extent, be made intelligible; but, so far as I can see, they cannot be made completely comprehensible by us . . . Any perfect insight would probably involve some transcendence of the spatio-temporal conditions by which our definite thought, as well as our practical activities, are necessarily bounded . . . Religion, I believe, means mainly devotion to the best that we know . . . Our whole spiritual nature calls out for objects capable of meeting and satisfying its deepest demands. (*P*, II, 1927, 462)

The penultimate sentence here seems to manifest the influence of that liberal optimism upon which, in latter days, a considerable amount of theological scorn has, not altogether unjustifiably, been poured.

Systems, Silence and Scholasticism, 1920–35

A view which is at once more positive and more theologically orthodox is propounded by Temple who, in the wake of Jessop to whom I have already referred, writes of 'The value of philosophy to religion'. His thesis is that religion requires the support of philosophy; first, in order that its full significance may be realised in all departments of experience, for both religion and philosophy claim to be all-embracing and they must therefore stand or fall together. Second, philosophy can provide religion with arguments against hostile criticism. Third, philosophy can save exponents of religion from alienating those they would attract. In this last connection it is imperative that the theologian be conversant with the nature and limitations of that influential type of scientifically grounded philosophy which is having such an impact upon current thought (*P*, III, 1928, 345-8).

The articles we have considered make no attempt to rule religious questions out of the philosophic court. On the contrary, their authors in no way deny that in some sense philosophy, no less than religion, depends upon a kind of faith, and involves a vision of wholeness. Temple can go so far as to say,

> while it can by no means be said that the weight of philosophic authority is predominantly on the side of traditional orthodoxy, it can I think be claimed that it is on the side of a spiritual and religious interpretation of the universe, and that, broadly speaking, Religion has nothing to fear from the guides whom it will find today ready to assist it in its own philosophic enquiries. (347)

Perhaps not, but for how much longer would assistance be forthcoming? Positivism and analysis were on the march, and W.M. Urban, in his 'Modernism in science and philosophy', felt impelled to castigate certain philosophical elements which he considered to be undesirable in the extreme:

> My own belief is that we have suffered too gladly and too long the monstrous irresponsibility of certain individuals and groups of thinkers in philosophy. We have hung our heads in shame before these supermen who have assured us that only after we have changed all our modes of thinking can we hope to attain the heights of intelligence on which they have their being. We have taken some of these modernist movements of thought too seriously. I, for one, have at least a suspicion

that when we find it necessary to change all our modes of
thought there is something questionable in the alleged 'facts'
that compel us to make so drastic a change; when we require
an entirely new language and logic to apprehend and express
reality it is because there is something essentially unintelligible
in the concept of reality we are trying to express; and that,
finally, when we are brought to the brink of the unmeaning
there is something radically wrong with the thinking that
has brought us there . . . Perhaps, as Spengler somewhat
contemptuously asserts, he who tries to think outside the
presuppositions of his time is a fool. It may be. But he may
also be God's fool. (*P*, V, 1930, 241-2, 245)

I commend Urban's zeal, but I am bound to record the fact that
his peroration did little to stem the analytical tide, or to deliver his
opponents of their delusions. Had he succeeded we should not now
be on the point of turning to those successors of Moore, Russell
and Wittgenstein, about whom there is general agreement that they
set a trend in philosophising, and considerable disagreement as to
whether their efforts were for good or ill.

Just before proceeding, however, mention must be made of two
interesting Neo-Scholastic works which appeared during the years
with which this chapter deals. The first is Anstruther's translation
of *Foundations of Thomistic Philosophy* (1931) by A.D. Sertillanges —
a popular work not lacking in warnings, 'none can depart from
St. Thomas's teaching, especially in metaphysics, without danger';
and eulogies:

A philosopher's business is to expound this fulness in all
things, and not to be too taken up with just the large things.
St. Thomas succeeded. He stresses nothing unduly. He argues
quite simply, and betrays his interest quite naively; he calmly
applies far-reaching principles to small nothings, till he
persuades you that there *are* no nothings, that everything is
great and divine, and reflects its Author. (8)

At a more sophisticated level R.P. Phillips contributed his two-
volume work, *Modern Thomistic Philosophy* (1934) — still a standard
text book in many seminaries. To him philosophy is 'the scientific
knowledge of all things gained through consideration by the natural
light of reason, of their fundamental reasons or causes' (I, 19).

I cannot help but wonder what certain analytical philosophers would have made of some of these statements — and wonder is all I may do, for although Zybura had succeeded in eliciting the views of certain British philosophers upon Neo-Scholasticism almost ten years before Phillips's work was published, real attempts to engage in dialogue between philosophers of all schools had yet to be made in Britain.

Notes

1. See his *Instinct and Experience* (Methuen, London, 1912); *Emergent Evolution*, (Williams & Norgate, London, 1923).
2. See E.S. Brightman, *The Philosophy of Religion* (Skeffington, London, 1947).
3. R.F.A. Hoernlé, *Studies in Contemporary Metaphysics* (Kegan Paul, London, 1920), p. 299.
4. A.N. Whitehead, *Science and the Modern World* (Cambridge University Press, Cambridge, 1926), p. 30.
5. See D.M. Emmet, *Alfred North Whitehead*, reprinted from the *Proceedings of the British Academy*, XXXIII, p. 14.
6. J.W. Rogerson, 'William Temple as philosopher and theologian', *Theology*, LXXXIV (1981), p. 333.
7. R. Metz, *A Hundred Years of British Philosophy* (Allen & Unwin, London, 1938), p. 721.
8. *The Philosophy of Rudolf Carnap*, ed. P.A. Schlipp (Open Court, La Salle, Illinois, 1963), p. 27.
9. J.McT.E. McTaggart, *Some Dogmas of Religion* (Edward Arnold, London, 1906), pp. 292-3.

5
Advancing and Marking Time, 1935–45

In the decade with which this chapter is concerned, while there is advance on certain fronts there is not, owing to the disruptive effects of the Second World War, the proliferation of philosophical writing that might otherwise have been expected. Many philosophers were engaged in non-professional duties, and not all were able to do their philosophising *en passant* — as Dorothy Emmet is said to have done in drafting her book, *The Nature of Metaphysical Thinking*, whilst firewatching. For the same reason a far greater proportion of the writings that are available are in the non-analytical as opposed to the analytical style than we should have found had younger philosophers been left to their normal devices.

One of the most striking features of this decade is the amount and type of activity in the field of the philosophy of religion. Whereas in the 1920s philosophers of religion were still for the most part content to seek a reconciliation of their work with that of metaphysicians, we now find that although they have not become analytical exclusivists they are beginning to join more freely in the general investigation of philosophical aims and methods. In other words, their emphasis upon *philosophical* dogmas is considerably less than it was; and this, in turn, is a reflection of the fact that philosophers at large are not so dogmatically-minded as once they were. No doubt this has something to do with what Gilbert Ryle called the laicising of our culture and the professionalising of philosophy : philosophy is no longer almost exclusively the preserve of ministers of religion.

Before turning to the writers who immediately concern us, two further general points must be made. First, we shall increasingly find passing references to, and writing of an introductory kind upon, existentialism, together with detailed scholarly work on Kierkegaard in particular. Thus, for example, Miss Emmet wrote on 'Kierkegaard and the "existential" philosophy' (*P*, XVI, 1941, 257-71); and W. Lowrie published his *Kierkegaard* (1938), and devoted many years to the translation, exegesis and exposition of his subject.

As its name implies existentialism gives priority to questions of existence : the necessity and the problem (not the doctrine or the theory) of *my* being is paramount. Existentialists emphasise the contribution the individual can make to his own condition; or else, in despair, they conclude that he can do nothing except accept his lot. They devote considerable attention to man's fears, hopes, desires and will. Man is *here* and must respond to the world as it impinges, or forces itself, upon him. Furthermore, man is in a state of anxiety; for on the one hand he is under the necessity of willing and choosing, of deciding; on the other hand he does not see all of the picture, is liable to err, and is threatened by the unknown. Finitude is his peril, nothingness his greatest enemy. In face of this diagnosis some existentialists are more hopeful than others. Some believe that it is possible for man to transcend his plight and to achieve 'authentic existence'. Others deny this: man can but live with his condition. Christian existentialists such as Marcel tend to be found in the former category; atheists such as Heidegger (who disclaimed the designation 'existentialist' — and often sounds quite 'religious') and Sartre in the latter. All were, to a greater or lesser degree, inspired by Kierkegaard, to whom we shall return later.

In mood and style existentialist writing differs markedly from that of traditional philosophical writing; indeed many existentialists have poured scorn on the older metaphysics because of its disregard of man's true nature and position in the world. In view of the themes treated by existentialists it is not surprising that many of them have found expression through the drama and the novel rather than through the philosophical treatise. As for the impact of existentialism upon British philosophy (and in relation to the latter I adjust my sights in this book), it can only be said to have been slight. Existentialists may have reminded some philosophers of some themes to which they ought to turn their attention; but for the most part existentialist jargon and method — and, in some cases, its gleeful lack of method — have been shunned. Certainly there was ground for Walter Kaufmann's rhetorical adjudication between analytical and existentialist philosophers: 'Why must we either ignore anguish or treat it as man's central experience? Why must we spurn experience, either because it is too messy or because it is not messy enough?'[1]

Relatively more attention has been paid to existentialism by British theologians — not least in the interests of getting to grips with Bultmann and his successors. However, John Macquarrie's *An Existentialist Theology* (1955) remains one of the few substantial works of its kind from a British hand. In the 1950s the work of the philosophical theologian Paul Tillich, in which existentialist and idealist features coexist if they do not (according to some) blend together, aroused some interest among British scholars; and to this we shall come in due course.

The second general point is that during the years 1935-45 there is increased activity on the part of encounter theologians. H.H. Farmer's book, *The World and God*, published in 1935, revised and reprinted in 1936, and reprinted again in 1939 and 1942, has had a lasting effect upon generations of theological students and others. The work is a detailed exposition of the Christian awareness of God as personal. On his own admission Farmer does not stay to probe the difficulties (real or imagined) attaching to the ascription of personality to God, partly because other writers have already done this,

> but chiefly because incomparably more important than meeting abstract philosophical difficulties is the endeavour to open men's mind to that personal approach of God to the soul which, if there be any truth in our position at all, is already going on in the concrete actualities of their daily experience. The real difficulty with most people is not the conundrums which the philosophers ask . . . but their own inability to interpret the thought of God as personal in terms of the world as they know it, or seem to know it, in their personal dealing with it. (9-10)

Farmer singles out the concepts of prayer, miracle and providence for special treatment 'because in them are focused the fundamental factors of the Christian's life of personal fellowship with God'.

John Baillie's *Our Knowledge of God* (1939), which had attained its sixth impression by 1952, was a further significant example of encounter theology, though here the position was expounded in relation to Barthianism on the one hand and to the older natural theology on the other. Baillie's emphasis throughout is upon the personal encounter with God. Indeed, 'The great fact for which all religion stands is the confrontation of the human soul with the transcendent holiness of God' (3). Our experience of God is not inferential; it is a 'mediated immediacy'. That is, it is not reached by speculation; it is given, but given supremely through Christ. What Dorothy Emmet wrote of Farmer's book may also be said of Baillie's: it is 'exactly the sort of approach to the conception of God as personal which puts the basic Christian insights into a form in which contemporary philosophy must reckon with them' (*MC*, XXVI, 1936–7, 215). But it was to be some years before even a minority of British philosophers were to reckon with encounter theology in a serious way.

Religion and philosophy

In her *Philosophy and Faith* (1936) Miss Emmet provides fuller treatment of matter raised ten years earlier by de Burgh. She wishes to discover whether there is a faith underlying the pursuit of philosophy by asking what are the presuppositions of clear and effective thinking. She sees no reason to suppose that philosophers have some peculiar means of access to absolute truth, nor yet that philosophers must necessarily be somewhat inhuman persons. She is quite sure that if both philosophy and religion are concerned with truth, there cannot ultimately be any conflict of principle between them. At the same time, 'I do not believe that it is possible to give a definition of so elusive and many-sided an activity as philosophy. But we can follow Plato's example: on the one hand we can show philosophy in action; and on the other hand we can make a number of significant statements about it, each of which tells us something about the task of philosophy, but none of which is satisfactory if taken as a formal definition' (27).

As for the philosopher himself, he 'has to achieve the very difficult balance of keeping a sufficient detachment from the world to be able to develop his powers of sustained thought and reflection, and to be sufficiently in it for his reflection not to become unreal' (63). Like the religious person, the philosopher depends upon revelation in the sense that he relies upon the given; but the philosopher *qua* philosopher does not subscribe to a body of revealed truths. Nor are the results of the two men's activities the same; for whereas the philosopher's is an activity of intellectual interpretation, the religious person's is one which demands that he worship.

But what if the philosopher happens to be a Christian? Will the phenomena of credal definitions unduly constrict him? Will they undermine his intellectual integrity? Miss Emmet sees no reason why they should:

> If the philosopher may look to creeds as pointers, keeping before his mind the paradoxes of religious insight which are continually demanding interpretation, rather than as intellectual tests of personal belief, he may do his work within the fellowship of the Christian Church without violating his essential task. (152)

He may need to be somewhat detached in attitude, but his must be the detachment of vocation, not of indifference. After all, 'a complete scepticism is intellectually self-defeating, for how can we know that we cannot know anything?' (156)

In the following year Professor W.G. de Burgh (1866-1943), Professor of Philosophy in the University of Reading, followed up his earlier work with an article 'On the idea of a religious philosophy' (*PAS*, XXXVII, 1936-7, 1-22). He sought to show that religious experience can yield 'knowledge as verifiable and illuminative as that reached by any other line of approach' (2). Accordingly a religious philosophy is a real possibility. De Burgh concurs with Miss Emmet in thinking that all knowledge is revelational, but does not on this account believe that all is plain sailing for those who would too readily equate religious with philosophical concerns. No doubt 'If the human mind could know perfectly there would be no place for the distinction between religious knowledge and philosophy' (7), but human limitations make possible a variety of approaches towards a common goal. The situation now is that

> Philosophy has ceased to be theocentric and become centred either in the cosmic order or the human mind. That is why, in advocating its synthesis with religion, we must start from the distinction between religious knowledge and philosophy, as philosophy is now practised and understood.
>
> They differ, first, in their starting-points. Religious knowledge is from the outset directed towards God. Philosophy, on the other hand, like science, takes as its initial data ourselves, the selves of others, and the world revealed through sense . . . (8-9)

Moreover, philosophical knowledge moves forward by general thinking; religious knowledge by personal acquaintance. Nevertheless the latter may be synthesised with, and complete, the former.

Advancing and Marking Time, 1935-45

This is not to say that there will be no gaps left,

> But this at least will be achieved: religion will no longer stand over against metaphysics as an alien mode of apprehension, but will form the keystone of its synthesis. God will no longer be thought as super-rational, beyond the reach of human knowledge; He will be known, on the strength of His self-revelation, as the object of a reasonable faith. (22)

De Burgh's book *Towards a Religious Philosophy* appeared in 1937, and in it he developed his ideas further. He insists that reason includes intuition and faith as well as the process of logical inference, and advocates a return to a theocentric world view. His fondness for the Middle Ages is apparent at this point, though he is convinced that a theocentric world view for our times must be one that is freshly minted. In his Gifford Lectures, *From Morality to Religion* (1938), he sought to supply the need. He differentiates religion from morality thus: religion entails the acknowledgment and worship of God; religion is essentially *theoria* whereas morality is essentially *praxis*; and the highest motive for the religious man is the love of God. Acting in accordance with this motive the religious man's performance of his duties undergoes 'a subtle and significant transformation'. The fact of personal moral failure is an important stimulus to the completion of morality in religion. We see our need, and divine grace comes to our aid. Apart from religion terms like 'humanity' and 'personality' are vacuous. Only the vision of life in the kingdom of God gives life to these otherwise empty forms. That kingdom is eternal, and it is only beyond this world that what we see as the quest of the good life and the (sometimes conflicting) path of duty are harmonised in God the source of all good and our supreme end.

We breathe a slightly different, though still a religious air when we turn to *The Philosophical Bases of Theism* (1937). These Hibbert Lectures were given by G. Dawes Hicks (1862-1941), Professor of Philosophy at University College, London. Here Hicks was reflecting towards the end of a long and active philosophical life. With typical Unitarian fervour he proclaims that 'whoever refuses to accept an external warrant, such as an infallible church or divinely inspired scriptures, has no alternative but to turn to the method of free rational enquiry, which in its more developed stage is the method of philosophy' (10). Hicks does not deny that religion has to do with revelation, but to anyone who would suggest that because of this a philosophy of religion is out of the question, he replies (with half an eye to the continent?) that revelations are not communicated or imported 'ready made into the mind without the operation on the individual's part of any process of intellection' (46). The role of philosophy *vis-à-vis* religion is to criticise the contents of its experience, to analyse and determine the significance of its notions, and above all, to ask, 'Is a theistic conception consistent with such an interpretation of the whole of our experience, as philosophy is now in a position to offer?' (50)

Hicks contends that revelation is to be sought in the historical process, and that from man's side his intellectual, moral and religious experience is all relevant to its appropriation. Schleiermacher, with his recourse to feeling, is criticised (not altogether justly perhaps) for failing to see that a feeling of dependence could be discerned only by a cognitive act. Religious feelings are the fruit of religious ideas. This is so even in the case of the mystics, who in fact describe their experiences in terms learned from institutional religion, tradition and rational reflection. Thus, some mystics 'see' the Virgin Mary, but mystics of other faiths 'see' quite different things. Hicks is convinced that feeling and knowing are inseparable. In similar vein he criticised Otto on the ground that if the numinous *is* non-rational, as Otto says it is, it is incomprehensible and cannot therefore be 'clothed with the ideas of goodness, mercy and love' (140).

Hicks's book drew a number of respectful reviews, though some expressed reservations at certain points. Webb regretted Hicks's lack of sympathy with mysticism, and felt that he was too easily prone to construe the relation between the divine and human spirit in terms of the relation between one human spirit and another (*P*, XII, 1937, 487). De Burgh queried Hicks's teleological emphasis: 'How is this thorough-going teleology to be reconciled with the real individuality and freedom of finite human minds? Is it not as fatal to their (relative) independence as any naturalistic doctrine of mechanism?' (*M*, N.S. XLVII, 1938, 85). But Tennant was in general agreement with Hicks's conclusions and with the methods by which they are reached. In particular Hicks does well, against Taylor, to reject the notion of a timeless consciousness, 'and also the pantheistically inclined doctrine of the inclusion of finite minds in the absolute or universal Mind' (*MC*, XXVII, 1937-8, 684).

Almost certainly Hicks would have found the opening remarks of Ian Ramsey's article, 'The quest for a Christian philosophy', very much to his liking:

> We witness . . . a flight from Reason which leads to philosophical and theological panic of the most reprehensible kind: we witness an utter bankruptcy of philosophical and theological thought. Such is the deplorable state of affairs which confronts us today.
>
> And what is to be the remedy? For myself, I see only one hope: the setting forward of such a system of speculative and constructive philosophy as will be adequate not only for the philosopher, but for the Christian. (*MC*, XXX, 1940-41, 458)

Sadly, since the demise of Hegelianism both the relations between, and the value of, philosophy and religion have deteriorated:

> In philosophy, the admirable and justifiable movement of Moore and Russell in favour of clarification as a function of philosophy has been pushed to highly ingenious but ridiculous extremes in those varied doctrines of 'Logical Positivism' with which the names of the Vienna Circle (especially Schlick), Professor Wittgenstein and Mr Ayer are united in varying degrees of disgrace. (462)

Philosophy is not alone in being at fault, however:

> philosophy has never unfortunately had a monopoly of absurdity, and Barthianism, with its distaste for Reason, seems to be an admirable partner for our new brand of philosophical method. (462)

If this is 'young man's language' it will serve to balance that of Mr Ayer to whom we shall shortly come. But at least Ramsey did seek to tackle and not merely reprove, his foes, and this is what too few theologians seemed anxious to do. Laments came easier to them:

> In our own country Idealism still boasts illustrious representatives; it still wins fresh recruits. But whereas at the beginning of the century an Idealist epistemology was I suppose defended by a majority of philosophical teachers, by now the tide has for some time set in the direction of Realism. Some philosophers of note — especially in Cambridge — not only do not accept an Idealist metaphysic, but regard the whole attempt to frame a systematic theory of reality as a misunderstanding of the function of philosophy . . . It is

indeed hard to resist the impression that, valuable as has been the strict method of the new school as a corrective, the conception of philosophy, as understood by some at any rate of its adherents, has been gravely impoverished.[2]

Confronted by what he regarded as a dire situation, Ramsey wondered which way to turn. Will Neo-Thomism meet the need of the hour? He is doubtful of the wisdom of meddling with so systematic a philosophy as that of Thomas, and cannot see why we should expect it to suffice today. Thomism suffers from being bound up with an antiquated view of science, and breathes too much the *a priori* search for certainty. Certainly it has no right to a special claim upon our intelligence such as would preclude us from independent reflection. Ramsey's positive view is that philosophy needs an empirical foundation, and must work towards producing a reflective, ordered, and systematic life, together with a correlated language system which will render this life expressible. In particular a Christian philosophy will need to show clear links between the theory of the self and the doctrine of immortality. Finally, 'in reaching our idea of God we shall do well to take our cue from the relation of God to the world of sense-experience, analyzing that idea of God as far as possible in terms of our concept of personality' (465-6).

Ramsey has here raised many of the matters which were to come to the fore in post-War philosophy of religion — not least through his own instrumentality: the need to examine the structure of religious discourse; the place of empiricism in Christian philosophy; the renewed emphasis upon personality. In that it looks back in some ways to the personal idealists and forward to the analysts of religious language, and to latter-day Thomist-non-Thomist discussions, this article may truly be said to be transitional.

Leonard Hodgson (1889-1969) was as dismayed as Ramsey by certain of the directions philosophers were taking. In an interestingly autobiographical preface to his *Towards a Christian Philosophy* (1943) he informs us that after a period away from academic life he returned to Oxford to find that the happy marriage between philosophy and theology which he had expected to take place in his earlier days had not in fact occurred. On the contrary he found philosophy

> back in the morass of analysing its own procedure, fleeing from the contemplation of a terrifying universe to an escapist chasing of its own tail. And the younger theologians, unable

apparently to receive the revealed humility of a God who wills to give Himself intellectually as well as bodily into the hands of men, claim to be the mouthpiece of a revelation which is beyond human criticism. (9)

Hodgson's response to this situation was to react against it, and in words that were already sounding old-fashioned he said that philosophy is 'an attempt to find the key to unlock the secret of the unified system of reality' (19): and again, that philosophy 'is the constant endeavour to complete the work of science and relate the actual work of scientific investigation to the ideal world of self-consistent, self-justifying goodness' (43). As for Christian philosophy, this is 'the attempt to interpret the meaning of all things in the light of God's revelation in Christ' (25). In agreement with de Burgh and Miss Emmet, Hodgson asserts that in so far as the discovery of truth 'is due to God's provision of that which we learn about Him, it comes through divine revelation; in so far as it is apprehended by us through our human capacity for grasping it, it comes through the use of human reason' (62).

Ramsey's hesitations concerning Thomism were by no means shared by Felix Hope, whose article on 'Scholasticism' is a notable exercise in public relations. The following is Hope's concise statement of the distinctive features of scholastic philosophy:

Scholasticism defends against the idealists the existence of an external world; against the sceptics, the validity of the sense-perceptions by which we apprehend the external world and the validity of the intellectual processes by which we interpret things and reason about them. It teaches the essential difference between living and non-living matter, and from the nature of vital activities it concludes to the existence in living things of a vital principle or soul. It sees in man not merely the power of sense perception, but from the nature of his intellectual processes concludes that he is animated by a principle which is immaterial and spiritual — a rational soul which, by giving life to the body, constitutes the human personality, and yet does not depend upon the body for its existence. In that soul it recognises, from an examination of human actions, the faculty of free-will. It holds that the intelligence, by reasoning from the facts of experience, can establish the existence of a Supreme and Infinite Spiritual Being, who is the First Cause of things, the Creator of the universe, the Founder of the cosmic order, and the end of man. In the domain of human action, Scholasticism holds that there is a natural distinction between good and evil, and that our duty to do good and avoid evil is absolute. (*P*, XI, 1936, 447-8)

In the course of his article Hope provides evidence to remind us once more that Aquinas was studied in Britain long before the revival of scholasticism, and even during periods when Roman Catholic schools were neglecting him. Hume and F.D. Maurice are cited as students of the Angelic Doctor. It has to be said, however, that not even Hope's careful paper did much to increase the number of philosophers (many of whom were in the line of Hume in other respects) who paid professional attention to Aquinas in the first years of the decade with which we are presently concerned. The concentration of interest was upon analytical philosophy of various kinds. As we proceed to examine analytical philosophy we shall see precisely why some examples of it prompted such misgivings as we have noted on the part of theologians.

Analytical variety

If the incautious use of such descriptive terms as 'idealist' and 'realist' can hide more than it reveals, this is doubly the case with the term 'analysis'. The impression may all too readily be conveyed on the one hand that no pre-20th century philosopher ever stopped to consider the meaning of the terms he used; and on the other hand, that the successors of Moore, Russell and Wittgenstein share a common platform in all matters philosophical. It is perhaps best to speak in terms of general approach rather than of hard dogma. It is then not out of place to say that a considerable body of philosophers have come in this century to believe that the function of the philosopher is not to extend the borders of knowledge by the discovery of new facts, still less to attempt to draw together the findings of all the specialisms of the day and make a coherent whole out of them. Rather, his is the humbler task of analysing and clarifying what is already known (which does not, of course, preclude the possibility that in this as in other fields it is possible to perform a humble task in a decidedly arrogant manner!)

R.B. Braithwaite brings this out by reference to two of the progenitors of the attitude in question. He reminds us of Russell's view that the function of philosophy is to solve certain specific problems which are not problems of the special sciences; while Moore maintained that the business of philosophy is to accept the propositions of common sense and then to analyse their meanings. Braithwaite concludes, 'Implicitly in Russell and explicitly in Moore, philosophy demands the answers to the question, "What is the analysis of what we all agree to be true?"' [3]

On this basis (and at the risk of categorising philosophers falsely) we may say that some have given themselves to the analysis of propositions — even of metaphysical ones; that others have directed their attention towards the removal of confusions within ordinary language; and still others have concentrated upon the search for a criterion of meaning. Examples within each of these somewhat arbitrary classes are forthcoming in the 1930s and to some of these we now turn.

In the first category we may place L.S. Stebbing and A.J.T.D. (John) Wisdom. In 'The method of analysis in metaphysics' Miss Stebbing contends that 'Metaphysics is a systematic study concerned to show what is the structure of the facts in the world to which reference is made, with varying degrees of indirectness, whenever a true statement is made' (*PAS*, XXXIII, 1932-3, 65). The metaphysician does not discover new facts, but rather analyses those already known in order to show, for example, exactly what we are believing when we believe that there is a table in the room. How are our beliefs inter-related? Are they consistent? If they are inconsistent, how may they be adjusted, and which should be rejected? These are the questions to which the metaphysician should direct his attention. Miss Stebbing does not rule out the possibility of construction, but does not think the time is ripe for it. In the same year Miss Stebbing made more specific reference to logical positivism in her 'Logical positivism and analysis' (*PBA*, 1933, 53-87).

Wisdom agrees with Miss Stebbing and with Wittgenstein in declining to believe that the metaphysician has to do with certain transcendental entities; and in his paper, 'Is analysis a useful method in philosophy?' (*PASSV*, XIII, 1934, 65-89), and in his series of articles on 'Logical constructions' (*M*, 1931-3), he seeks to show how analytical techniques can delineate the ultimate logical structure of ordinary propositions.

For Gilbert Ryle, who falls into our second category, philosophy has the task of displaying the logical structure of facts with which we are familiar; and also the therapeutic mission of eradicating puzzlement caused by the ill-advised use of ordinary language. He ends his celebrated article, 'Systematically misleading expressions' as follows:

> I conclude, then, that there is, after all, a sense in which we can properly enquire and even say 'what it really means to say so and so.' For we can ask what is the real form of the fact recorded when this is concealed or disguised and not duly exhibited by the expression in question. And we can often succeed in stating this fact in a new form of words which does exhibit what the other failed to exhibit. And I am for the present inclined to believe that this is what philosophical analysis is, and that this is the sole and whole function of philosophy. But I do not want to argue this point now. (*PAS*, XXXII, 1931-2)

Though Ryle's major works were to come later, this article already shows his affinities with Moore (whose notes on 'The justification of analysis' appeared in *Anal.*, I, 1934, 28-30) and with the later Wittgenstein. From this point of view we may say that Ryle, of Oxford University, spans both the years and the ancient universities.

So, in a more doctrinaire way, does A.J. Ayer, who exemplifies our third category. He was instrumental in causing the more positivistic implications of Cambridge philosophy to receive attention at Oxford. In the preface to the first edition of his *Language, Truth and Logic* (1936), he acknowledges his debt to Russell and Wittgenstein. Cambridge, however, was not the only source of his inspiration, for he had personal contact with members of the Vienna Circle. In an article entitled, 'Demonstration of the impossibility of metaphysics' Ayer throws down the gauntlet with characteristic verve:

> My purpose is to prove that any attempt to describe the nature or even to assert the existence of something lying beyond the reach of empirical observation must consist in the enunciation of pseudo-propositions, a pseudo-proposition being a series of words that may seem to have the structure of a sentence, but is in fact meaningless. I call this a demonstration of the impossibility of metaphysics because I define a metaphysical enquiry as an enquiry into the nature of reality underlying or transcending the phenomena which the special sciences are content to study . . . it will be shown in this paper not that

the metaphysician ought to use scientific methods to attain his end, but that the end itself is vain. Whatever form of reasoning he employs, he succeeds in saying nothing. (*M*, XLIII, 1934, 335-6)

Ayer invokes the principle of verification in order to show that propositions that are neither empirically verifiable (at least in principle) nor analytic are *ipso facto* meaningless.

This was too much for some to take. C.A. Mace, in his article, 'Representation and expression', had already expressed surprise that a man should write nonsense without recognising it as such (*Anal.*, I, 1934, 33-8); but Ayer, with reference to no less a person than Heidegger, showed in 'The genesis of metaphysics' that this was not only possible, but all too frequent (*Anal.*, I, 1934, 55-8).

In *Language, Truth and Logic*, the 'manifesto' of British positivism, Ayer set out his position in greater detail. He did not simply repeat the views of others, as Miss Stebbing was quick to realise: 'on the contrary, he is concerned with stating views so thoroughly his own, so natural to his mode of thinking, that he cannot realize the possibility that any competent philosopher might differ from him' (*M* N.S. XLV, 1936, 355). In the second edition of his book (1946) Ayer acknowledged, with becoming humility, that the work was 'in every sense a young man's book'. But he still believed that the point of view expressed in it was 'substantially correct'. He does not opt for conclusive verifiability, for this would make such a general proposition as 'Arsenic is poisonous' nonsensical; and he does not agree with Popper that a factually significant proposition is one which can be definitely confuted by experience, for this hypothesis can be neither conclusively confuted nor verified. He therefore advocates the adoption of a 'weak' criterion of meaning: a proposition is verifiable if it is possible for experience to make it probable. We are thus enabled to utter meaningful propositions about matters which are in principle verifiable, or might one day be verifiable.

Ayer relates his position to religious questions, and we are not surprised to discover that the possibility of knowledge of God is ruled out by Ayer's demolition of metaphysics. According to his criterion the propositions of the theist are not really propositions at all. Going further than Wittgenstein, who held that there is something which cannot be expressed, he holds that there is nothing, and that attempts to express it cannot but be meaningless: 'to say that "God exists" is to make a metaphysical utterance which cannot be either true or false' (115).

The traditional moves in natural theology are ruled out. For example, Ayer will not allow us to proceed from nature to nature's God; for

> if the sentence 'God exists' entails no more than that certain types of phenomena occur in certain sequences, then to assert the existence of a god will be simply equivalent to asserting that there is the requisite regularity in nature; and no religious man would admit that this was all he intended to assert in asserting the existence of a god. (115)

Religious experience fares no better, for while we may not deny that a person is experiencing a certain emotion, this in itself gives us no ground for asserting the existence of a transcendent being who is the object of the emotion in question. Thus the somewhat cold comfort offered to the theist is that 'His assertions cannot possibly be valid, but they cannot be invalid either' (116). On all of which Miss Stebbing remarked, 'The plain man would not find it easy to see the difference between Mr Ayer's non-atheism and the fool's atheism' (*M* N.S. XLV, 1936, 364); and J.D. Mabbott wrote that

> It may indeed be difficult to analyse the statement that God exists or impossible to prove that the soul is immortal, yet if a principle requires us to maintain that proof and analysis are not needed because both statements are nonsense, we shall say, 'So much the worse for the principle'. (*P*, XI, 1936, 351)

If the theist requires further warm comfort we may advert to a television programme in which Ayer confessed that after 40 years of work upon the principle of verification he had not yet found a trouble-free way of stating it. Indeed as early as 1959, in his *Logical Positivism*, Ayer recognised that the Vienna Circle in fact regarded the verification principle as a convention. But the implicit defensiveness here only reinforces the charge levelled by Miss Stebbing when *Language, Truth and Logic* first appeared: 'I must confess that I find it very difficult to see how the principles of logic can be wholly an affair of convention, and consist wholly of definitions.' And in his review Mabbott said that a hard critic would say that Ayer has adhered firmly to his stipulative definition that 'meaningful' means 'verifiable (at least in principle) or tautologous' and has thus, on his own theory, presented us with a string of tautologies.

Advancing and Marking Time, 1935–45

It was not long before the principle of verification came under attack (a) because it was not itself either open to empirical verification or tautologous; and (b) because those who propounded it were covert *metaphysicians*, for the principle of verification rested upon a tacitly held view of the nature of *reality*: reality was such that certain types of propositions only could be meaningful.

In his 'Logical positivism and theology' H.H. Price, though not himself a positivist, appreciated the force of the positivist argument, but sought to indicate a way forward for the theist — even if he was not over-confident that the way could be successfully pursued:

> If we wish to defend Theism . . . we must try to show that in ordinary perception and introspection we meet with events which give evidence of the existence and activities of a non-human intelligence: evidence similar in kind to that which each of us uses to justify his belief in the existence and activities of other human intelligences like himself. But whether there really are such events, and whether (if there are) the intelligence whose existence they give evidence of has the characteristics which Theists would wish to attribute to God, I do not know. (*P*, X; 1935, 331)

Setting out from a similar recognition of the unscientific nature of religious propositions, Karl Britton made his response to the positivistic challenge in a far more positive way. In 'The truth of religious propositions' he begins by affirming that religious propositions have a value for the believer irrespective of their truth or falsity. He admits that such propositions cannot properly be called 'true' or 'false' in the sense proper to scientific propositions, and takes this to indicate that criticism of religious language misses the point if it be levelled from the standpoint of the scientist *qua* scientist. But the challenge to demonstrate how a religious proposition acquires meaning remains; and Britton claims that such a statement as 'The Lord is my shepherd' is true if the feelings and actions it arouses in me, and perhaps in others, are accompanied by feelings of moral approval:

> I hold a pragmatic view of the nature of religious truth. 'R [e.g. 'The Lord is my shepherd'] is true' says something about the consequences of believing R — that they are good, and hence that it is useful to believe in R. (*Anal.* III 1935–6, 26–7)

The moral feelings of a given group, he continues, determine the meaning of 'useful'; religious truth is relative to a given group; and conversions — which are not changes of opinion, but of heart — from one group to another may be expected.

Stock-taking

As far as I have been able to discover, such philosophical discussions as those offered by Price and Britton earned neither acclaim nor reproof from theologians (at any rate in print). Among philosophers who would not normally be described as analysts in any party sense the reaction to the changing fashion in philosophy was mixed. Whereas, as we have seen, Jevons and Mackenzie did not enter the lists, both W.T. Stace and A.C. Ewing did take stock of the new situation. Stace did not believe that the positivists had justly or successfully banished metaphysics from the field, though in his 'Metaphysics and meaning' (*M* N.S. XLIV, 1935, 417-38) he did express gratitude to them for having brought the question of meaning out into the open. For his part, in 'Two kinds of analysis' (*Anal.*, II, 1935, 60-4), Ewing investigated the concept of analysis itself. He argued that in one sense analysis entails the investigation of what a speaker intends to assert, while in another sense the purpose of analysis is to examine the qualities, relations and species of continuants mentioned in statements. In the former sense analysis is a useful means to an end; in the latter sense it must always be the concern of all philosophy.

H.F. Hallett wrote 'On being a philosopher'; and in contrast with an increasing number of his colleagues he declared that the philosopher's task is 'rightly to recognise the nature of the finite and temporal and its relation to the infinite and eternal; rightly to distinguish the eternal finite from the transitory, and to understand the precise degree of the temporality of the temporal' (*P*, XII, 1937, 9). I am not at all sure what this means, nor whence the appropriate instruments for the task might be obtained. We breathe a more familiar air when we return to Stace, for whom philosophy remains 'the knowledge of ultimate principles' (*P*, XII, 1937, 307); but in the same issue of *Philosophy* Ryle, in his article, 'Taking sides in philosophy', rebukes the dogmatically-minded. He claims that 'There is no place for "isms" in philosophy . . . to be affiliated to a recognisable party is to be the slave of a non-philosophic prejudice in favour of a (usually non-philosophic) article of belief' (317).

His basic objection to 'isms' is that since philosophy is a species of discovery the philosopher should be circumscribed by no false limits: 'My whole case is that there is a schismatic tradition in philosophy, and that "schismatic philosopher" is a contradiction in terms' (322). He admits that allegiance to a school may engender zeal, promote combativeness, and foster team spirit, and he does not deny that he himself has an 'ism' — 'But it is not a banner so much as a susceptibility.'

Ryle's programme of undogmatic analysis probably appeared too remote from life as it is lived to some. 'Where is philosophy going?' asked J.H. Muirhead; and to the extent that the answer was 'In a positivistic direction' he was none too happy, for,

> To accept such a limitation of it would be equivalent to offering as the only alternatives to the pure naturalism, against which the best minds of our times are in revolt, either a return to tradition and authority, a region in which we have to accept what we are told and to think for ourselves at our peril, or a mystical appeal to an inner light, a region in which anything can be thought and nothing can be either proved or disproved. (*P*, XII, 1937, 394)

Muirhead is convinced that there is a more excellent way, and he urges philosophers to seek it.

Perhaps R.E. Stedman's 'A defence of speculative philosophy' was more to Muirhead's liking. It exemplifies an attempt to argue with, rather than to shout at, certain philosophical trend-setters. Thus, for example, Stedman points out that it can be said against Ayer's 'Demonstration of the impossibility of metaphysics' that most, and the most recent, metaphysicians have denied that their purpose is to describe a reality lying beyond experience. Again, even if it be true, as Ayer alleged in 'The genesis of metaphysics', that metaphysicians have allowed themselves to be caught in linguistic traps, this is no proof that all of them must always be so trapped. Against Ryle Stedman argues that the question of the validity or otherwise of arguments is not the only thing that causes philosophers to differ: 'I submit that the premises, what is being argued about, and the weight of the evidence, are almost always in question' (*PAS*, XXXVIII, 1937-8, 135). To many philosophers of latter days Stedman's assertions will appear as truisms: 'Analysis is *essential* to philosophy, [but is not] its *essence*' (121); 'It is misleading to speak of a systematic philosophy as being true or false *as a whole*' (131);

and, in answer to the question, 'Why bother with metaphysics if it is not probative, gives no knowledge, and never ends?' — 'The obvious answer is that men will continue to wonder and will continue to need a relatively stable "ideological" structure within which to carry on their lives' (141). No doubt to some in the heat of battle over philosophical aims these appeared as the utterances of one who wishes to eat his cake and have it; but there was wisdom in Stedman's remarks, and to many today his is the received wisdom.

From the numerous surveys of analytical philosophy by those who were more or less sympathetic with it I take those of Russell and Miss Stebbing.[4] In his article 'On verification' Russell contends that we know a good deal more about facts as distinct from sentences than some philosophers are disposed to think: 'The view that we only know sentences avoids, no doubt, many difficulties, but it fails to explain how, since sentences are facts, we can know even them' (*PAS*, XXXVIII, 1937-8, 20). He suggests that if facts become known to us through language then a relation is implied between the structure of the sentences and the structure of the facts, and this 'may possibly justify, in some degree, the traditional attempt to use logic as a clue to metaphysics'. Professor Stebbing sought to solve 'Some puzzles about analysis', arguing that although common sense requires no defence, it is not the purpose of the philosopher merely to tell us what we mean by what we say. Rather, 'the purpose of analysis as practised by philosophers is to enable us to learn how to avoid asking misleading questions — to which we are only too likely to find senseless answers — and to encourage us to ask sensible questions' (*PAS*, XXXIX, 1938-9, 84).

At the outbreak of the Second World War C.E.M. Joad addressed an urgent 'Appeal to philosophers' (*PAS*, XL, 1939-40, 27-48), in which he charged them to devote their attention once more to what he conceived to be their proper task, namely, that of revealing truth and increasing virtue. He ascribed their reluctance in these matters to their professionalistic contentment with their narrow specialisation, and to their fear of taking a stand on major issues. As if in partial answer to this plea, though doubtless they did not go as far as Joad would have wished, some philosophers did reconsider metaphysical questions at this time. This is not to say that they all approached these questions in the traditional manner. Least of all could this be said of Collingwood, whose book *An Essay on Metaphysics* was published in 1940. Whereas Collingwood had earlier held that the philosopher is entitled to produce a constructive system of categorical assertions, he now adopts a more historical approach to the matter of the discovery of absolute presuppositions, and a more sceptical attitude to the question whether or not these can be defended. He urges that absolute presuppositions are not susceptible to verification; they are not propositions, and therefore the true/false distinction does not apply to them. Pseudo-metaphysics has its origin in the belief that absolute presuppositions are relative presuppositions, and that they are therefore verifiable propositions towards which we adopt one attitude or another. Genuine metaphysics, on the other hand, is simply 'the attempt to find out what absolute presuppositions have been made by this or that person or group of persons, on this or that occasion or group of occasions, in the course of this or that piece of thinking' (47). Like Ryle, Collingwood distrusts doctrines, schools, and parties — though this is not, as with Ryle, because 'isms' are unduly restrictive, but because they trade in the abhorred pseudo-metaphysics. Collingwood treats the positivists to detailed criticism. He warns them that for all their exaltation of science they endanger science if they attack metaphysics — if by metaphysics we mean the absolute presuppositions of science, or the attempt to discover what those presuppositions are at any given time. Without absolute presuppositions there would be no science and no argument; they cannot be changed or proved by argument; proof depends on them, not they on proof. In his final chapter Collingwood indicates the peril to both civilisation and science that lies in the anti-metaphysical protest, and concludes: 'When Rome was in danger, it was the cackling of the sacred geese that saved the Capitol. I am only a professional goose, consecrated with cap and gown and fed at a college table; but cackling is my job, and cackle I will' (343).

D.M. MacKinnon was concerned with tradition in quite a different way. In his paper, 'What is a metaphysical statement?' he wrote, 'It seems to me increasingly plausible that the debates of traditional metaphysics do concern genuine questions' (*PAS*, XLI, 1940-1, 15); and he points out that metaphysical thinking is always analogical thinking, 'except for the idealist metaphysician for whom one might say its character resides in the unfettered pursuit and willing acceptance of the goal which thought qua-thought proposes to itself' (21). The important concept here is that of analogy, for we shall soon begin to find that after the positivistic 'purge' of metaphysics, metaphysicians begin to pay more attention to the analysis of concepts and, more importantly, they do not simply revert to the concepts of earlier British idealism; they take a broader view, and are even prepared to reappraise much older varieties of metaphysics. Which is but another way of saying that the voice of neo-scholasticism is beginning to be heard in certain non-Roman Catholic philosophical circles. Conceptual analysis begins to provide the platform on which, for the first time, there can take place genuine and mutual dialogue between non- and neo-scholastic philosophers. There is thus ushered in a period of fresh metaphysical variety.

Metaphysical variety

John Laird (1887-1946), Professor of Moral Philosophy in the University of Aberdeen, upheld a version of realism throughout his many works. Influenced by the common sense approach of Moore, and by the determination of Alexander and others to deal with what is there, he stood consciously — even proudly — in the line of Thomas Reid, the founder of the Scottish common sense philosophy. Knowledge is not a matter of the mind only. Knowing involves the immediate apprehension of realities that are over against us. Of all the Gifford Lecturers Laird is literally the most down to earth. From his two Gifford volumes we see quite clearly that he is not given to vain speculation, and that he will not resort to apologetics — wherein 'the goalkeeper is also the referee'.

In *Theism and Cosmology* (1940) he sets out from a provisionally held realism to discover how far the fact and nature of the world will take us in the direction of theism. He rejects the cosmological and teleological arguments for the existence of God but (to Webb's delight) does not reduce theology to a kind of poetry. Webb does, however, regret Laird's abandonment of

> what is perhaps Kant's most important contribution to the philosophy of religion, namely the proof of the inconclusiveness of 'rational theology' as a theoretical justification of religion, apart from a specifically religious experience; a proof which is not vitiated by what I take to be a mistake on Kant's own part, his identification of religious experience with the consciousness of moral obligation. (*P*, XV, 1940, 430)

In his second volume, *Mind and Deity* (1941) we find that Laird will not build upon either religious experience or revelation. All transcendentalism excluded, we are left with a deity-tinged pantheism.

While Miss Emmet rightly felt that Laird had shown the relative philosophical strength of a type of theism which to many makes little appeal (*T*, XLIII, 1941, 312-14), most were inclined to agree with Broad: 'The impression which I get from the two Series is that, unless Theism can derive support from the facts of specifically religious and mystical experience which Professor Laird has deliberately excluded from his purview, there is nothing to entitle it to serious consideration' (*M* N.S., LI, 1942, 188).

If Laird seemed to many to exclude too much, others were, no doubt, inclined to include too much for the liking of some secular philosophers. I refer in particular to the Anglo-Catholic neo-Thomists, whose two most important early representatives were Austin Farrer (1904-68) and E.L. Mascall. The former's *Finite and Infinite* and the latter's *He Who Is* both appeared in 1943. Farrer argues that in expressing themselves finite substances (including man) express the creativity of God. By the employment of our natural reason we may attain this limited knowledge of a creator God. On this foundation revelation builds. With Oxford analytical philosophy swirling around him Farrer invokes the concept of analogy, arguing that God makes himself known, *via* analogies, as the God of providence and grace; and as Farrer expounds his analogies their links with metaphysical and poetic symbolism become plain.

Both Farrer and Mascall adopt the cosmological approach in natural theology, and both shun the ontological argument for the existence of God. But whereas Farrer was concerned to undertake his study with half an eye to recent philosophical analysis, Mascall, though by no means unaware of Ayer and others, was as concerned to relate his position to, and at points carefully distinguish it from, other recent Thomist philosophers and such contemporary theists as Whitehead and Tennant. Whitehead's God is too dependent upon the world. He is 'not needed by Whitehead as the self-existent infinite Being upon whose love and power the world depends for all that it is and has; he is needed merely as the locus of the eternal objects without which actual occasions would not be able to effect their own self-creation' (1966 reprint, 157). Above all (and in endorsement of A.E. Taylor's view), 'By taking as his fundamental category a concept of "Creativity" which is essentially *becoming*, rather than a concept of *being* which, in its analogical fecundity, bridges the gulf between the finite and the infinite, he has condemned his cosmology to imprisonment within the realm of finite existence, and has thrown away the only key which could release it' (160). As for Tennant, his cosmic teleology 'affirms the existence of a God who is less than the God of traditional theism in that, while the universe is dependent upon him for its existence, nevertheless he is bound to create it and once he has created it is limited by it' (177). We cannot reach the notion of a genuinely transcendent cause from a consideration of the way in which the beings which compose the world behave. For himself Mascall believes that philosophy is still the handmaid to theology; that grace completes and does not destroy nature; and that when philosophy, like the Queen of Sheba, brings her treasures to theology, she finds 'a greater than Solomon'.

Two years later a further contribution to theism came from the pen of A.E. Taylor: *Does God Exist?* In his preface Taylor makes his position quite clear. He grants that no man 'has ever been led to a living faith in God simply by a chain of syllogisms'. His purpose therefore is the more appropriate one of seeking to remove certain objections to theistic belief, and to show that unbelief, not belief, is the unreasonable attitude to adopt. Nor does he deny the necessity of God's self-disclosure, of revelation;

> But a man cannot be expected to receive anything as such a communication from God until he is at least satisfied that it is reasonable to believe that there is Some One to make the communiction. *That* is the point on which I am trying to offer some reassurance (7).

Taylor builds upon the factuality and reality of our moral convictions concerning right and wrong. Moral considerations are primary, and when we turn from them to view the natural order it is not unreasonable to see therein the outworking of a moral purpose which has the development of moral personalities as its supreme objective. We could then come to believe in the *creator* of an order so designed, though this conviction would be reached by faith-commitment, and not as the last step in a logical argument. But what of disorder, of evil? Here we can but posit — again by faith — a realm in which such matters are remedied and the purpose of all is not finally frustrated.

Few did as much to keep the metaphysical flag flying during the dark days of the Second World War as Dorothy Emmet. In 'The use of analogy in metaphysics' she sets out to enquire whether what we call a metaphysical system is not a *Weltanschauung* based on analogy with something which has seemed significant in the experience of the metaphysician. She believes that in addition to logical argument and criticism there is a particular kind of spiritual or intellectual experience which excites a philosopher, and from the standpoint of which he constructs his *Weltanschauung*. This implies no reduction of the scope of metaphysics — it does not become merely a study of the psychological and temperamental idiosyncrasies of its practitioners, 'For it is at least possible that metaphysicians who are capable of particularly vivid, though different, forms of intellectual experience, may in effect be able to appreciate certain aspects of reality to which those forms of intellectual experience are responsive' (*PAS*, XLI, 1940-1, 31). Miss Emmet discusses the Thomist doctrine of analogy at some length, and then provides her own account of the metaphysician's role. The metaphysician must make as careful an analysis as possible of forms of thought and experience, and then he must somehow convey his impression of what it all comes to in the form of a 'total assertion': 'A partial assertion is either a proposition stating matter of fact or a logical proposition which can be brought into a coherent system with other propositions of the same type. A total assertion cannot be verified; it expresses a judgment concerning the nature of something as a whole' (39). These total assertions may not be made in defiance of the deliverances of empirical science, and the metaphysical analogies by means of which they are expressed will serve so long as they throw light upon the partial assertions which are accumulated empirically, and so long as they prompt further thought. The most positive ground of all is gained 'in our better understanding, through its conscious articulation, of the experience from which the analogy has been drawn' (46).

These themes, among others, receive fuller treatment in Miss Emmet's *The Nature of Metaphysical Thinking* (1945). She here pays particular attention to religious symbolism, pointing out that the religious symbol has to direct the gaze both to a relation within experience, and to something qualitatively other which stands beyond experience — 'Hence the ambivalent and ambiguous character of religious imagery' (105). On the question of metaphysical theory she holds that such a theory develops an outlook on the world in terms of some co-ordinating relation which is judged to be important. The validity of this judgement cannot be directly demonstrated, but it may be tested and checked by the tests of coherence and comprehensiveness. It is thereby saved from mere subjectivity. This is not to deny that in the last resort, although 'A metaphysical thinker may try to see life steadily, he cannot see it as a whole. He can only express what he grasps in the perspective of his experience' (227).

Our final reference in this section may be to H.H. Price. In an article entitled 'Clarity is not enough' he sought to adjudicate between philosophical analysts and some of their more vociferous opponents. Some, says Price, question the importance of philosophy conceived as analysis — to which he replies that since the time of Socrates philosophy has, 'with the possible exception of the darkest part of the Dark Ages', been concerned with clarification. Others accuse the analysts of being deficient in moral earnestness, and of trivialising their subject. Price counters by saying that the principles which the allegedly trivial examples illustrate are by no means trivial.

At this point I digress, and present one quotation and two summary statements:

> What is philosophy? Once again this has become a burning question for philosophers . . . Philosophy, we are told, especially in its academic form, nay because of its academic form, has become barren; it has lost touch with the vital problems and perplexities of our age.

> The plain man often regards philosophy as an idle luxury: the philosopher's questions are not his questions.

> The social reformer charges the philosopher with having abandoned his position as leader for that of onlooker.

Whence come such statements as these? Are they the laments of one who, in the midst of war, looks to the clarifiers for bread and is given a stone? No; as it happens they are the observations of R.F.A. Hoernlé in his *Studies in Contemporary Metaphysics* (1920, 3-6). The moral is plain: he is grossly misguided who thinks that British philosophy never appeared remote and esoteric to anyone prior to the advent upon the scene of Ayer, Ryle and Wisdom.

We return to Price, whose opinion is that

> the most we can fairly say against our modern clarifiers on this head, is that they have sometimes paid too little attention to pre-verbal or non-verbal thinking. For we do also think in images as well as in words, and there is even a sense (I believe) in which we may be said to think 'in' actions and motor attitudes . . . Of course you may refuse to call it thinking if you like, but it does seem to be a very

important kind of symbolic cognition. (*PASSV*, XIX, 1945, 20)

Price himself feels that the modern man has the right to expect some kind of help from philosophers towards achieving a systematic approach to the world. He agrees with those who point out that a metaphysical system cannot be said to be simply true or false, and that what the metaphysician has to show is that his scheme is a possible arrangement of the body of empirical data. Price would say that there is such a thing as *synoptic* clarity as well as analytical clarity, and that philosophers ought to strive to attain both. The extent to which philosophers heeded this advice after the cruel days of war will become apparent in what follows.[5]

Notes

1. W. Kaufman, *A Critique of Religion and Philosophy* (Faber & Faber, London, 1959), p. 27.
2. J.M. Creed, *The Divinity of Jesus Christ* (1938); quotation from Collins Fontana 2nd edn 1964, pp. 17–18.
3. R.B. Braithwaite, 'Philosophy' in H. Wright, (ed.), *University Studies* (Nicholson & Watson, London, 1933), p. 4.
4. Related articles include, A. Duncan-Jones and A.J. Ayer, 'Does philosophy analyse common sense?' *PASSV* XVI (1937); J. Wisdom, 'Metaphysics and verification', *M* N.S. XLVII (1938); M. Black, 'The "paradox of analysis"', *M* N.S. LIII (1944); and 'The "paradox of analysis" again', *M* N.S. LIV (1945).
5. For some reactions to British philosophy on the part of those beyond our shores see e.g., E. Nagel, 'Impressions and appraisals of analytic philosophy in Europe', *JP*, XXXIII (1936); J.N. Findlay, 'Some reactions to Cambridge philosophy', *AJP*, XVIII (1940), and XIX (1941); S.S. Orr, 'Some reflections on the Cambridge approach to philosophy', *AJP*, XXIV (1946).

6
Languages, Standpoints and Attitudes, 1945-55

In 1929 Wittgenstein returned to Cambridge and to philosophy. He at once began to import a new dimension to analytical philosophy. In his *Blue Book*, which was circulated from 1933 and published with his *Brown Book* in 1958, we find him repudiating the view he had advanced in the *Tractatus* to the effect that there is in principle one flawless scientific language by the employment of which everything that it is possible to express may be said; and that it is the philosopher's task to discover this language. Language is now seen by Wittgenstein to be an activity performed at various levels, and for a variety of purposes. It is used for making statements, expressing hopes, issuing commands, and so on. Thus he now brings to the fore the question of the uses to which language is put, and considers the question of linguistic propriety in the light of the purpose of the several 'language-games'.

We may do many things with language, and each sort of doing has its rules — rather as a game does. The analyst must explicate the rules, and this can be satisfactorily done only if the analyst attends to the 'form of life' in which the language he is investigating is located. These forms of life are given. Wittgenstein goes on to claim that metaphysical perplexities arise when the various language-games are confused — as they would be, for example, if we thought that 'wishing' is the *name* of a psychic process and not a human activity. Further, if we suppose that there is a feature held in common by all things called by the same name, we open ourselves to yet more delusions. In fact there need be no common feature at all, but only a certain 'family resemblance' — such as we find between games of various kinds. As he wrote in *Philosophical Investigations* (1953), 'We remain unconscious of the prodigious diversity of all the everyday language-games because the clothing of our language makes everything alike' (224e). In all of this we have one of the most important stimuli to the so-called 'therapeutic analysis' — that is, to the view of philosophy which claims that the philosopher's task is to 'heal' unwarrantably puzzled minds by removing sources of perplexity which result from incorrectly used language.

The application of this revised approach, in which the objective is no longer the quest of criteria of meaningfulness but the analysis of linguistic usage with a view to 'therapy', has been widespread. Wittgenstein himself related the technique to his understanding of religious belief. Religious belief is an activity which is logically distinct from all others, and when believers express their convictions they are 'using a picture'. This picture is logically located within the religious language-game, and the difference between believers and unbelievers is that the former do, and the latter do not, use the relevant pictures with the appropriate references.

It appeared from all of this that religious language was being granted a reprieve: if religion counts as a form of life, then religious language is meaningful within that form. But those who drew this conclusion were perhaps somewhat premature. For I do not think that a gulf may be fixed between the 'early' and the 'late' Wittgensteins. His ontological interest remained throughout — and so did the strictly unutterable mystery. Hence God-talk still cannot *refer* to anything, and a form of life is by no means the same thing as a way of life — it is simply a language-game, as is clear from *Philosophical Investigations*: 'the term "language-*game*" is meant to bring into prominence the fact that the *speaking* of language is part of an activity, or of a form of life' (11e). In Chapter 7 we shall consider the approach of D.Z. Phillips to religious language. He is generally regarded as one of the more faithful followers of Wittgenstein — something for which he has been commended by some and trounced by others. We simply note here that the ground was being prepared in the years 1945-55 for a radical, and some would say a reductionist, approach to religious language.

That J.L. Austin (1911-60) sought to remove sources of perplexity by the means of acute and detailed analysis none will deny. Austin does not stay to relate his activities to the general course of philosophical debate, and he does not spend time in discussing the methods of, or policies for, philosophy. He analyses; and in his contribution to the symposium 'Other minds' (*PASSV*, 1946) he introduces a concept of which much was subsequently to be heard: that of the performative utterance. A performative utterance is one which involves a commitment. Thus, 'I know x' does not mean that I am engaged in a special act called 'knowing x'. Rather, it means 'I am taking my stand on this.' Austin is opposed to 'the scandal of inconclusiveness', and believes that we can reach firm conclusions only if we are not premature or impatient in system-building. In his contribution to the symposium, 'Are all philosophical questions questions of language?' Stuart Hampshire points out that no criterion has yet been suggested by which we can distinguish between a question of language and a question which is not one of language. Furthermore, by saying that all philosophical questions are questions of language, some philosophers wish to imply that 'no philosophical questions are empirical questions', or 'all philosophical questions are questions of definition'. But 'Probably no philosophical questions are *purely* empirical questions, and some philosophical questions are *purely* questions of definition, but certainly some philosophical questions are partly one, and partly the other' (*PASSV*, XXII, 1948, 47).[1]

That C.D. Broad's view of the scope of philosophy was not narrowly analytical is clear from his paper, 'Some methods of speculative philosophy'. He argues that analysis and synopsis are constantly present features in philosophical writing, while synthesis may be present 'in a vanishingly small degree'. He considers that it is generally the case that synopsis provides the stimulus to analysis. In various areas of thought, considered separately, we find an internally coherent set of concepts and principles; but when we contemplate these various departments together these principles appear to be in conflict. This causes intellectual discomfort and prompts analysis. The synthetic task is that of supplying a set of concepts and principles which shall cover satisfactorily all the various regions of fact which are being viewed synoptically. Broad does not think that there are any clearly defined rules for the discovery of the principles of synthesis. What often happens is that a philosopher is strongly impressed by some feature which is characteristic of an important region of fact. He then seeks analogues between that region and others in which the feature is at first sight not so prominent, and is perhaps not even noticeable (*PASSV*, XXI, 1947, 20-1).

Miss D.M. Emmet by no means despaired of the possibility of synthesis in philosophy, and in two articles published at this time she raised once again the question of the role of metaphysics *vis-à-vis* world views. In her contribution to the symposium, 'Can philosophical theories transcend experience?' (*PASSV*, XX, 1946) she dissents from the view that metaphysics has to do with the attempt to describe the nature of non-phenomenal things-in-themselves. Indeed, she says 'I . . . suspect that it is the belief that this is what metaphysics must be that largely serves to bring it into disrepute' (202). More positively she asserts that

> Metaphysics may also be taken to mean the attempt to arrive at some co-ordinated world view. This may be an endeavour to systematise experience, but it may also mean going beyond experience, which is partial and fragmentary, in an attempt to construct some kind of speculative theory about the nature of 'reality'. I suggest that this is done by taking certain logical relations or concepts expressing relations found within certain ranges of experience, and generalising these so as to form some kind of analogical model of 'reality' by the help of which further ranges of actual and possible experience may be co-ordinated. (203)

Her conclusion is that

> speculative metaphysics is likely to consist in the construction of models based on analogical extensions, on the one hand from logical concepts, and on the other hand from concepts formulating intra-experiential relations of a selected kind. Such theories must obviously transcend experience. Their fruitfulness is likely to depend on the number and variety of contacts with experience which can be shown in their development. (209)

In 'The choice of a world outlook' (*P*, XXIII, 1948) Miss Emmet probes more directly the alternatives faced by those who would affirm a world view. If we content ourselves with investigating matters of fact we shall never be able to state a world view; but if we try to state our ultimate presuppositions we shall run the risk of falling foul of an ideology that is merely socially and psychologically conditioned. Alternatively if we make a commitment of an existential kind, how shall we appraise our presuppositions objectively? Is there a way out of this *impasse*? The Neo-Thomists are among those who answer in the affirmative. Their solution does not, however, appear entirely to satisfy Miss Emmet, for she has reservations concerning the general and undifferentiated notion of 'pure being'. Further, she does not feel that the Thomistic employment of the causal argument for the existence of God is legitimate; for it is not easy to see how a notion of inductive explanation applicable to sequences of events within the world can be made to apply to the world as a whole.

The upshot is that world views are better regarded as interpretations rather than as explanations or hypotheses — despite the big concession to relativism inherent in this. As to the appraisal of world views, the following are among the tests whch Miss Emmet deems appropriate: Do they respect empirical facts so far as these can be established by experiment and research? Do they realise the existence of a reality beyond ourselves? Do they recognise that since they are based upon interpretations of experience they must necessarily be incomplete? Are they held critically, and do they conduce to the recognition of obligation on the part of those who hold them? Do they sustain the sense of the importance of life?

Of all those who, at this time, sought to reinstate a broad conception of the philosopher's task none was more polemical than W.H.F. Barnes whose book *The Philosophical Predicament* was published in 1950. The logical positivists, with their dogma 'All clear language is scientific language' are 'the dogmatic theologians and heresiologists of the Orthodox Church of Natural Science' (101). The attempt to eradicate metaphysics is quite misguided, and if we commit ourselves to philosophising at all we shall find that 'there is no valid distinction between critical and speculative philosophy, no rationally defensible halting-place short of a complete and comprehensive philosophical system' (183). The Thomists, of course, had never thought otherwise, and to them we now return.

Emergent scholasticism

In the post-War period the voice of scholasticism has been increasingly heard in general philosophical debate. The pioneering sallies of Aveling and Hope caused little stir in the philosophic current; but now, with post-textbook confidence in their position, and in response to the challenges and rebukes of analysis and existentialism on the one hand, and the friendly attention received from such philosophers as Miss Emmet on the other, they emerge quite suddenly as joint-venturers, and not simply as apologists for their cause. The appearance of the Irish journal *Philosophical Studies* (1951) is in itself a sign of the times, for here is a journal which though Catholic in its editorial board is catholic in other important ways too: writers from all branches of the Church and of none contribute to its pages; the authorship and atmosphere of the journal are international and not insular; and there is no narrow sectarianism in the types of philosophy treated — Ayer, Heidegger, Aquinas; ontology, epistemology, ethics: they are all here. H.F. Davis, who wrote on 'Thomism and the unity of Christian thought' was right: 'Now, more than ever since the Reformation, Catholics and Protestants are showing some sympathy for each other, some attempt at mutual understanding. It cannot be denied that this is greatly helped by the revival among non-Catholics of the study of Thomist philosophy and theology' (*DS*, I, 1948, 107). How, then, did neo-Thomists react to contemporary Anglo-Saxon philosophy and to existentialism?

In an article entitled 'The anatomy of existence' D.J.B. Hawkins welcomes the revival of interest in empiricism on the part of philosophers, but deplores the corresponding distrust of any power in thought capable of transcending empirical data:

> The whole duty of philosophy, after all, is not exhausted by the criticism of common sense and the distinction, within the sphere of what we already hold, of what we genuinely know from what we merely opine. Plato, indeed, in the *Theaetetus*, in the classical discrimination of knowledge from opinion, maintained that real knowledge was altogether outside the sphere of common sense. While not subscribing to this extreme view, we may at least admit that philosophy and a criticism of experience do not wholly coincide, and that there should be room for a metaphysic as well as for an epistemology. (*DubR*, No. 439, 1946, 97)

Hawkins maintains that we cannot contemplate the notion of existence conscientiously without being led into some sort of metaphysics. Our metaphysical analysis of the common notion of existence should lead us to the point at which we transcend the common notion, and contemplate Being itself.

Three years later Hawkins published his *The Essentials of Theism*, a book which has become a classic of its kind — notwithstanding Flew's complaint (*CQR*, CLVI, 1955, 102-4) that he has taken no account of recent developments in logic. Undaunted by post-Hume empiricism, Hawkins presents a deductive natural theology of the traditional kind. He also gave a generally cordial welcome to *Existence and Analogy* (1949) by the Anglican Neo-Thomist E.L. Mascall. Mascall argues that God is to be apprehended in the cosmological relation and not, as some ontologists have held, apart from it. We cannot say how God exists, or how he creates the world; we simply say that unless he exists and is creator, the world would be unintelligible. With all of which Hawkins agrees; but he does question Mascall's labelling of his position as an *existential* approach to theism. For

> The contemporary existentialist, whether theist or atheist, regards existence as a mysterious or even absurd factor which defeats thinking; St. Thomas, on the contrary, found in existence itself the final ground of the intelligibility of the universe. Two so different doctrines hardly merit the same name. (*CQR*, CXLIX, 1949-50, 225)

The Neo-Thomist F.C. Copleston engaged more directly than Hawkins with contemporary philosophy, as is clear from his book *Contemporary Philosophy* which, although not published until 1956, contains articles written in the late 1940s. He points out that the analysis of language has always been a concern of the philosopher, and this is as it should be. He disputes the claim, however, that there is nothing more to philosophy than linguistic analysis. He agrees with the analysts that the philosopher does not discover new facts in the way that an explorer might, but doubts whether this is all the modern analyst wishes to claim. The modern analyst wishes to go further and to maintain that there are no synthetic *a priori* propositions which would enable the philosopher to infer the existence of the unobserved from the data of experience. But Copleston protests that this is a metaphysical view! Not, indeed, in the sense that anything is said about transcendental entities, but certainly in the sense that the belief stated is not the result of any chemical or physical analysis. Copleston maintains that the linguistic criticism of metaphysical and theological propositions has shown beyond all possible doubt the need for the reintroduction into philosophy of the concept of analogy.

With this the Anglican Thomist A.M. Farrer agreed. In an article on 'The extension of St. Thomas's doctrine of knowledge by analogy to modern philosophical problems' he wrote:

> One of the reasons why the Christian thinker may find himself discontented and baffled in the world of modern philosophy is that his appetite is for real being, and not for subjective integrity: and his discontent may find solace with the medieval

philosophers, who did at least prefer the grasp of *what is* to the most spotless intellectual respectability. But it is idle to pretend that we can reassert today the straightforwardness of medieval epistemology. So many centuries of philosophic criticism and scientific development cannot be written off. The modern passion for intellectual clarity really has shown that other realities besides the divine are incurably mysterious: and we have got to wrestle with the mystery, and not deny it. If we want to borrow from the medievals, let us borrow what can help us. They did develop an instrument for wrestling with mystery, where they saw mystery, viz. the analogical method. It is for us to apply it in fresh fields. (*DR*, LXV, 1947, 22-3)

Copleston returns to the subject of analogy in his discussion of the problems attaching to logical positivism. He draws a distinction between subjective and objective meaning, illustrating this by reference to the proposition 'God is intelligent'. Now the theistic metaphysician cannot give the objective meaning of this proposition; that is, he cannot inform us of the nature of the divine intelligence in itself; but he can provide the subjective meaning: he can tell us what the statement means to him. It is this latter meaning which is necessarily analogically expressed, and although there will always be a certain imprecision about such modes of expression, the theistic metaphysician must endeavour to minimise the imprecision (for example, by the way of negation) as much as possible. The question remains whether such analogical utterances are significant. Copleston thinks that they are meaningful, and he cannot agree with the logical positivists that 'meaning' is to be construed univocally. In more than one place he insists that a metaphysical theory must be stated before it can be shown to be meaningless, and he feels that, despite the onslaughts of the critical analysts, metaphysical questions will continue to be raised. They are thrust to the fore not so much by linguistic confusion as by man's existential situation, accompanied as it is by an awareness of dependence or contingency.

This existential situation receives specific attention towards the end of Copleston's book. He finds that 'existentialism mingles triviality with theatricality' not least by its use of emotive language. But at least existentialists do draw attention in a traumatic way to human finiteness, dependence and instability, all of which are factors so obvious as frequently to escape attention. The existentialist seeks to change the perspective in which we see facts of human existence and therefore of the Transcendent. Elsewhere, in an article on 'Existentialism and religion' (*DubR*, 440, 1947), he argues that the analyses of man as a self-transcendent being are far more adequate in Kierkegaard and Marcel than they are in Heidegger and Sartre; for the former bring out the implications of man's spiritual activities, thereby witnessing in a sense to God. Nevertheless, as far as Copleston is concerned, existentialist analysis cannot provide rational justification of belief and religion. It requires to be supplemented by the intellectual approach of natural theology.

Two Non-Thomist Anglicans

Copleston's distrust of existentialism as a final philosophy is shared by Alan Richardson and J.V. Langmead Casserley. It may at first sight seem strange that in view of my aim in this book I should concern myself with Richardson's work entitled *Christian Apologetics* (1947) — did not Clement Webb caution us to beware of apologetic masquerading as philosophy? But one of Richardson's important contentions is that the science of apologetics is to be distinguished from the practice of apologising:

> Apology in its Christian meaning implies the defence of Christian truth. It meets an accusation, explicit or unexpressed, by stating the facts of the case and pointing out the rational conclusions to be drawn from them . . . Apologetics deals with the relationship of the Christian faith to the wider field of man's 'secular' knowledge — philosophy, science, history, sociology, and so on — with a view to showing that faith is not at variance with the truth that these enquiries have uncovered. (19)

Whereas apologies are addressed to unbelievers, apologetics is primarily a study undertaken by Christians for Christians. In a wide sense it is akin to what used to be called natural theology, and in a narrower sense it is concerned with 'the implications of the Christian revelation for the rational understanding of the world and of our existence in it'. Since every constructive philosophy selects a certain key idea and then employs it analogically to interpret the whole universe, the role of the student of Christian apologetics becomes that of delineating the faith-principle which underlies the Christian *Weltanschauung*. In the exercise of this function he may today enjoy considerable freedom, for whereas in the past Christians have felt it incumbent upon them to come to terms with the dominant metaphysical outlook of their day, there is no dominant metaphysical outlook now. Thus the Christian may give full play to the biblical faith-principle without feeling under obligation to accommodate it to an alien thought form.

Richardson reminds us that 'Christianity does not come to men . . . as a fully fledged metaphysic which they are asked to adopt as the basis of their own philosophy of life. It comes to them with the offer of the *possibility* of constructing a philosophy' (38). While it does not supply the data of empirical knowledge, faith does supply the categories of interpretation by which alone such data may be understood. As for those philosophers who do not acknowledge their debt to a faith principle of some sort — to them must be attributed the present 'general paralysis of metaphysical speculation'. As to the character of a Christian philosophy, Richardson argues that it will be unashamedly Augustinian; that is, it will never undermine the conviction that Christian faith alone enables a man to be rational, for 'faith is a light and guide without which reason cannot work' (233). (At this point Richardson quotes Gilson with approval: 'to be Christian *qua* philosophy a philosophy must be Augustinian or nothing'.) The Christian philosopher does not employ his reason in order to seek a faith by which to live; he has faith, and this seeks understanding:

> Between faith and reason there can be no conflict, for faith is ancillary to reason; faith cannot oppose reason; it can only oppose other *faiths*, which are being used as rival conditions or pre-suppositions of reason, such as the faith-principle of Marxism or scientific humanism or anti-Christian rationalism. (235)

This exaltation of faith is not intended by Richardson to deposit us in an unwholesome subjectivity whose foundation is some vague mystical intuition, or inner light, or special faculty: 'Christian faith is not *formally* different from the faith-principles which operate in other systems of thought and philosophies of life. It is a judgment of significance upon the recorded biblical facts' (236). It is grounded in history, and it receives its most powerful expression and its greatest significance within the community of the Church. On the other hand, the employment of reason along Augustinian lines cannot issue in mere rationalism: herein lies the major distinction as between Augustine and Aquinas. For whereas the latter maintained the theoretical possibility that man without faith could still think rationally within certain restricted fields, the former insisted that apart from revelation received by faith reason cannot function. Hence

> The fallacy of Thomism and of all forms of rationalism is that they obscure the classical Christian understanding of human nature as fallen: according to the insights of biblical religion the *whole* of human nature is fallen, and there is no part of it, such as the reason, which is capable without divine grace of fulfilling the purpose for which it is created. (247)

The question of the basis of a Christian philosophy is taken a stage further by Casserley in his book *The Christian in Philosophy* (1949). He suggests that the Christian philosopher's role may be thought of either objectively or subjectively. In the former case the relevant concerns are the nature of language, the meaning of metaphysics, and the analysis of the Christian concept of revelation. But Casserley himself finds the latter mode of approach more congenial, for the questions which his own experience of life has posed are:

> What must be true about the world of man and human language in a world in which the Bible and metaphysics are both valid? What must be true about the Bible and metaphysics separately if it is possible for the same person to devote himself to each of them without tearing his mind and soul in two? (184)

Casserley seeks to answer his questions by showing that the secular philosopher, no less than the Christian, must work in the light of a revealed faith-principle. Furthermore, so long as philosophers realise the uniqueness or singularity of the situation which we may perhaps describe as 'man-in-receipt-of-revelation' they will not be tempted to adjudicate upon the worth of a man's faith, but will rather try 'to give an ordered, coherent account of what he sees from his point of view, which is selected partly by and partly for him on levels of life and experience even more profound than those of philosophical reflection' (188). Such an understanding of the philosopher's role entails the view that metaphysics is not a demonstrable science, but is an analogical art in which the choice of analogies results from a prior decision to embrace a particular revelation. This revelation affects the whole person and *produces* (rather than is derived from) a philosophy: 'The response to the singular is the characteristic spiritual act', and we, who are so familiar with inductive and deductive logic, need to recognise our need of a logic of the singular — an historical logic.

In the earlier part of his book Casserley had argued that since Descartes rationalistic metaphysicians had taken their stand upon clear and distinct ideas. Modern critical philosophy has shown that it is possible to doubt what seems clear and distinct; and so we have three reactions; that of the logical positivists, that of the historical relativists, and that of the neo-scholastics. The first are faulted on the ground of their attitude towards metaphysics — 'which is not unlike that of the Deity towards the tree of knowledge in the Garden of Eden. The positivists bear no other particular resemblance to the Deity, but the rest of us have much in common with our first parents!' (200). The weakness of the metaphysics of historical relativism is that it confines itself merely to enquiring what is the nature of presuppositions that are in fact made, and takes no account of whether or not such presuppositions are true. Finally, the principle defect of the neo-scholastic approach is not so much that it is pre-scientific, but that it is pre-historic:

> Until metaphysical thought has learned how to think about singulars by identifying itself with historical thought it can only be philosophical about God by universalizing and conceptualizing Him. Of course, it is always possible to treat the idea of God in a devout philosophy as a universal concept, but such a position must necessarily clash with the religious attitude in its moments of actual devotion and consciousness of vocation. (221)

Thus Casserley returns to his plea for a logic of the singular — a logic which will perforce employ the doctrines of negation and analogy, classically formulated in Christian thought, and the conceptions of paradox and indirect communication as derived from Kierkegaard. By the employment of such a logic we may construct a philosophy which will be hypothetical and analogical, as are all metaphysical systems, but which will be Christian in so far as the Christian philosopher chooses 'a particular realm or layer of human experience as the quarry from which he derives his analogies — the realm of self-conscious personality in history rising, for him, to its supremely self-revealing climax in the Bible and biblical religion' (249).

Interlude

It will be of some assistance if at this point we remind ourselves of the main philosophical approaches as at 1950. The following list is not presented without reluctance, for as I have insisted throughout, philosophers are hard to categorise, and summaries may give too hard-and-fast an impression. With this caution firmly in mind, however, we may say that at about the year 1950 it is possible to find:
(1) Analytical philosophers who distrust metaphysics.
(2) Analytical philosophers who do not in principle object to metaphysics, but who are otherwise occupied.
(3) Philosophers who are more interested in speculative philosophy, but who recognise the need for careful analysis of concepts.
(4) Philosophers who, besides being generally sympathetic towards metaphysics are also giving attention either to neo-scholasticism, or to existentialism, or to both.
(5) Neo-scholastics who are paying attention to anti-metaphysical onslaughts, and highlighting the question of analogy.
(6) Neo-scholastics who are pondering existentialism in relation to the perennial philosophy.
(7) Non-scholastic philosophical theologians who, taking advantage of the absence of any one widely accepted metaphysical dogma, are exploring the possibility of constructing a genuinely Christian philosophy, without at the same time failing to evaluate both the main contentions of the anti-metaphysical movements and older varieties of metaphysics, both medieval and modern.

What we have so far failed to find is any *widespread* enthusiasm on the part of philosophers of religion for the linguistic analysis of Christian discourse. The 1950s will not be so disappointing in this respect; but before moving into the main-stream work of the new decade, let us note an article which appeared at its opening: David Cox's, 'The significance of Christianity' (*M*, LIX, 1950, 209-18). Cox here goes as far in the direction of logical positivism as a Christian might reasonably do. Some, indeed, thought that he went too far.

Whereas the positivists had urged that non-tautologous propositions were meaningful if and only if they were (in principle at least) verifiable by *sense* experience, Cox widens the criterion to include human experience generally. He recognises that on this basis some Christian doctrines may be found to be non-significant, but he considers that this risk is more than outweighed by the negative advantage that the sting of adverse empiricist criticism is drawn, and by the positive advantage that henceforth statements of doctrine will be directly related to Christian experience. On his principles, for example, 'God exists' will come to mean 'Some men and women have had, and all may have, experiences called "meeting God". '

By no means all Christian philosophers were persuaded by Cox. On the contrary, it was pointed out that the more closely religious language is related to scientific language the more incumbent it becomes upon those who effect this relationship to spell out, or to find a way of predicting, the conditions under which the experience of 'meeting God' may occur; and this is notoriously difficult to do. Moreover, how should we know that God was being met? In any case, as Thomas McPherson pointed out to Cox in an article entitled, 'The existence of God' (*M*, N.S. LIX, 1950, 547), assertions in which such 'meetings' are reported require *sense* experience for their verification; yet Cox has deliberately widened his criterion so that it embraces more than this. Finally, and more theologically, to confine the existential claim to occasions of human encounter precludes the assertion (which, presumably most theists wish to make) that God existed before man existed.

Towards analytical catholicity

We begin now to find that analytical philosophers are becoming less dogmatic than once they were both in respect of the possibility of there being discovered a perfect language in which everything logically sayable may be said, and in respect of the legitimate variety of uses of language. In other words, we find evidence of a more catholic spirit: philosophers begin to analyse concepts and discourse whencesoever they come, and will not neglect on principle the discourse of ethics, aesthetics and religion, which some had prematurely relegated to the realm of the emotive. It is on this basis that, as far as the philosophy of religion is concerned, neo-scholastics and non-scholastic Christian philosophers are able to enter into discussion with philosophers who may or may not be Christians. Whereas in the early part of the century discussion between at least some non-scholastic theologian-philosophers and some secular philosophers was possible because each was a dogmatician of a kind, now in the absence of shared 'isms' it is an agreed, or more or less agreed, way of philosophising that makes debate a viable proposition. Since the bulk of religious philosophising now begins to take account of, if not always to adopt wholesale, the techniques of linguistic philosophy, we shall do well to turn first to discussions of these techniques, bearing in mind that there is but a 'family resemblance' between linguistic philosophers, and that a general similarity of approach to philosophising may, and does, admit of a wide diversity of opinions upon particular philosophical points.

We shall make little headway until we have noted the way in which philosophers of language employ the term 'logic'. They are not concerned with formal, still less with symbolic, logic; but, as Ryle says in his paper 'Ordinary language',

> We are interested in the informal logic of the employment of expressions, the nature of the logical howlers that people do or might commit if they strung their words together in certain ways, or, more positively, in the logical force that expressions have as components of theories and as pivots of concrete arguments. That is why, in our discussions, we argue *with* expressions and *about* those expressions in one and the same breath. We are trying to register what we are exhibiting; to codify the very logical codes which we are then and there observing. (*PR*, LXII, 1953, 186)

This theme is pursued by A.G.N. Flew in his paper, 'Philosophy and language', reprinted in *Essays in Conceptual Analysis* (1956). He draws attention to Ryle's distinction between the various forms the 'appeal to ordinary language' may take. It may consist in an appeal to ordinary use(s); it may consist in a plea for plain English as opposed to jargon; it may express the intention to concentrate upon everyday rather than technical matters; or it may express the protest that the logic of everyday statements cannot adequately be represented by the formulae of formal logic. Flew concludes that

> Oxford philosophers who incline to all four policies together may be thought of as trying to preserve a balance: between this 'formalizer's dream' that non-formalized language really is, or ought to be replaced by, a calculus; and the Humpty-Dumpty nightmare that there is, at least in those parts of it which most concern philosophers, no logic or order at all. (18)

Within the same circle of ideas are those of F. Waismann who, in his contribution to *Contemporary British Philosophy* (1956) entitled, 'How I see philosophy' made his celebrated utterance: 'A philosophic question is not solved: it *dissolves*. And in what does the "dissolving" consist? In making the meaning of the words used in putting the question so clear to ourselves that we are released from the spell it casts on us' (458). The philosopher is more than a fog-dispeller, however: his work may lead to a more profound understanding of language, and may even pass into science. This is not to suggest that the philosopher sets out to *prove* things — his arguments do not have the rigour of deductions. Rather, he seeks to build up a case, and to prompt his reader to give a verdict:

> To put the matter in a nutshell, a philosophic argument does more and does less than a logical one: less in that it never establishes anything conclusively; more in that, if successful, it is not content to establish just one isolated point of truth, but effects a change in our whole mental outlook so that, as a result of that, myriads of such little points are brought into view or turned out of sight, as the case may be. (484)

A still more positive approach is outlined by P.F. Strawson in his contribution to *The Revolution in Philosophy* (ed. A.J. Ayer, 1956) entitled, 'Construction and analysis'. He argues that the philosopher's first task is to exhibit the ways in which our concepts and thought forms actually operate, and then to consider why this should be. After this comes the constructive work of the philosophical imagination — the function of considering how, 'without the nature of the world being fundamentally different, we might nevertheless view it through the medium of a different conceptual apparatus . . . ' (107).

In his 'Some types of philosophical thinking' (in *British Philosophy in the Mid Century*, ed. C.A. Mace, 1957) S. Körner reminds those who would justify their use of analytic criteria of the fact that this can be done only by the employment of philosophical arguments that do not fall within the scope of analytical philosophy: 'In other words, it is not true that all philosophy is analytical philosophy or even that analytical philosophy is independent of other types of philosophical thinking' (122). John Macmurray was another who offered 'Some reflections on the analysis of language'. He welcomes the fact that the *locus* of analysis has been moved from thought to language, because this reinstates the second person, as the recipient of any communication, in the frame of reference for logic. Nevertheless the trouble with analytical philosophy is that 'It tends to combine a utopian faith in the techniques of philosophical analysis with a radical scepticism of their ability to perform the functions for which they were devised' (*PQ*, I, 1950-1, 319). Since language is a human activity which it *used*, the analytical tendency to exclude all teleological considerations is to be deplored. After all, 'There can be no *empirical* objection to treating human beings as if they behaved like human beings' (320), yet in the name of empiricism this is done. Macmurray thinks it imperative that attention be paid to the context out of which discourse arises, and in his view the options are either that we make language as much like mathematical symbolics as possible, thereby creating a new scholasticism; or else we concentrate upon the experiences to which the words used refer, and which they report, and let the words take care of themselves. For his part P.L. Heath in 'The appeal to ordinary language' tilts at those philosophers of ordinary language who seem not to have noticed the fluidity of ordinary speech, or the difficulties attaching to such phrases as a 'sense of linguistic propriety'. Heath finds no grounds for the analyst's assumption that rules for correct discourse are embodied in ordinary language; and to him the biggest obstacle in the analyst's path is the fact that when he tries to chart ordinary language he finds that he has no effect upon common parlance. People still use 'illegitimate' locutions; they are part and parcel of ordinary language; and consequently they help to comprise the standard to which the philosopher of ordinary language appeals? (*PQ*, II, 1952, 1-12).

Writing 'On the state of modern philosophy' J. Hartland-Swann assessed the contribution made by analytical philosophers during the quarter of a century which ended in 1950. What remains, he concluded, is the unexciting though important maxim that language must be carefully examined and problems stated in such ways that they can be profitably discussed. There is no conviction that the time is ripe for philosophical construction, though there is increasing recognition of the fact that all philosophising rests upon presuppositions (*P*, XXVII, 1952, 78). While philosophy must never neglect the lessons taught by the analysts, it must ever seek a more synoptic outlook. Hartland-Swann expresses his hope that within a few years we shall see 'a renaissance which, in its own modest way, will be every whit as significant as that which followed the tiresome dogmatism of the Middle Ages' (79).

Before turning to describe how philosophers of religion followed up analytical clues, mention ought to be made once more of A.C. Ewing and of H.J. Paton, both of whom continue to think that there is more life in metaphysical bones than some of their contemporaries would allow. In *The Fundamental Questions of Philosophy* (1951) Ewing maintains as strongly as ever that the business of the philosopher is to build up a consistent and systematic picture of human experience and of the world, and that his criteria are to be coherence and comprehensiveness. Elsewhere, in an article on 'The necessity of metaphysics', Ewing rejects the verification principle on the grounds of its own unverifiability, but retains and assents to two opinions held by verificationists: first, that there are no affirmative existential *a priori* propositions, and therefore that empirical premises are required for any argument which is to establish positive facts about the real. Secondly, that all content is derived from some experience, and that we can have no idea of anything not given in, or constructed from, experience. He will go no further towards the verificationists than this; and over against them he holds to the possibility of our asserting trans-empirical facts, there being no evidence producable against this given the falsity of the verification principle. There is nothing to prevent our admitting metaphysics 'without claiming absolute certainty for it or anything at all approaching that' (In *Contemporary British Philosophy*, ed. H.D. Lewis, 1956, 149).

In similar vein Paton writes in his *The Defence of Reason* (1951):

> Whether for good reasons or simply because I was brought up when the fashions were different, I cannot bring myself to believe that analysis is the only, or even the main, work of philosophy. I hold that the business of philosophy is to be synoptic, to see things in their togetherness, to fit our different experiences and our different theories, as far as may be, into a consistent whole. Philosophical analysis seems to me to be valuable, not primarily for its own sake, but as a means to this wider end. (13)

A legitimate conclusion to be drawn from our enquiry so far is that philosophers are united in asserting the necessity of analysis; they differ as to whether or not analysis is the sole function of the philosopher. How far was the positive contribution of analytical philosophy appropriated by philosophers of religion? Two important contributions by H.A. Hodges will pave the way to the answering of this question.

Philosophers of religion and analysis

In *Languages, Standpoints and Attitudes* (1953) Hodges points out that at one time it was assumed that God, as supreme reality and goodness, was the proper goal of philosophy, but now philosophy has become more critical in its aims and methods, and more man-centred. We can trace a development of interest from God to man; and then from man the knower to (where linguistic analysis prevails) man the speaker. Hodges does not think that philosophy can properly stop short here, however, for human thinking is conditioned by human purposes. Hence,

> At the centre of philosophy will finally stand not man the thinker, nor man the speaker, but man the purposeful. And then much will depend on whether man the purposeful is conceived as a unit in the prudentially-guided satisfaction-seeking mass of humanity, or as an individual capable of questioning the assumptions of that human mass, and responsible before conscience for what he is and does. (10)

Man is a purposeful, responsible individual, who takes up a certain attitude towards life and the world around him: 'The basic assumption, the resulting aims and methods, and the way of seeing things to which these in turn give rise — all this together is what I mean to designate by the word *standpoint*' (15). A standpoint need not be wholly expressible in cognitive statements, and may include elements of value-judgement or volitional determination. Thus 'Every philosophical or religious system, every intellectual or aesthetic tradition, every civilization or culture, may . . . be seen as the embodiment of a distinctive standpoint' (16). Every standpoint is characterised by its peculiar language, and by elements of vocabulary which are especially its own. When this point is not appreciated metaphysical bewilderment results. Hodges cites the 17th century as providing an example of this. In that century the language of traditional metaphysics was confronting the language of the new physics. Trouble arose because the languages had key words in common, and the false impression was created that there was but one language.

Behind language as used there lies a standpoint. Accordingly, while philosophy today must certainly study words and other symbols, philosophers must appreciate the fact that linguistic confusions are merely symptomatic of confused standpoints. Hodges proceeds to discuss various standpoints, and concludes that whereas we can provide supporting arguments for the choices we make, these arguments are persuasive only, and do not demonstrate logically the rightness of our choices. To say this is not to open the gateway to irrationalism; it is simply to recognise the fact that 'will, in the form of interest, attention, and acceptance, goes before *ratio*, and determines its possibility' (61-2). How then are we to judge between standpoints? Hodges denies that the criterion can be consistency, for rival standpoints can be consistent. The best test is the existential test — that is, the standpoint 'should open up possibilities of life, experience, and activity' (63).

In his review of Hodges's book I.T. Ramsey felt that more attention ought to have been paid to coherence and comprehensiveness in the matter of the commending of a standpoint (*PQ*, IV, 1954, 339); while A.G.N. Flew objected that when Hodges claims that if a rival standpoint dismisses as meaningless a standpoint which stimulates purposeful enquiries in the world this is a decisive point in favour of the criticised standpoint, he is arbitrarily stacking the cards 'against denial that religious experience or revelation really discloses the Management of the Universe' (*M*, N.S., LIII, 1954, 113).

Hodges's contribution to *Contemporary British Philosophy* is entitled 'What is to become of philosophical theology?' He here deals more directly with linguistic questions. He reminds his readers that there are three strands in current philosophy: a concern for formal logic and its relation to both mathematics and to scientific induction; an interest in the functions of language; and a desire to reinterpret what used to be called ontological problems as problems about speech, to be solved by linguistic analysis. He feels that in formulating these concerns contemporary philosophy is 'speaking an important word, which yet is not the final word, about the methods, aims and functions of philosophy' (217). In the light of this new approach the concern of religious philosophy must be to elicit the logical character of theological inferences, to examine religious discourse, and to determine the extent to which problems in this field may be resolved by the employment of the techniques of linguistic analysis.

Hodges deems it important that in considering religious language we distinguish between utterances that are intended as statement, and those that are not; and he draws attention to that 'inherent obscurity' which unavoidably attaches to statements which ascribe personal characteristics to God. For this reason among others

> there is little to be gained by presenting theism as a quasi-scientific hypothesis, to be accepted as true because it

explains certain facts of experience and because it can be verified in action . . . The facts and experiences to which theists or Christian apologists appeal are not comparable with real scientific observations or experiments. (228)

It follows that religious discourse cannot be defended with empirical logic. If we use religious language sincerely we are expressing a preference for one thought paradigm rather than another, and therefore for the accompanying life pattern: 'And when we come to balancing rival life patterns against one another we are surely not far from ethical (or should I say existential?) questions' (232-3). In short, we are back to standpoints once more.

I.T. Ramsey likewise realises that the sincere use of religious discourse gives a certain slant upon a person's total viewpoint, but he wishes to discover whether the theistic policy thus expressed is justifiable. In 'The challenge of contemporary philosophy to Christianity' he asks,

Have theological words any sort of empirical fact whatever to which they can appeal in defence? The challenge the falsification problem makes is to demand on the one hand that we establish some integral connection between theological words and the rest of language, and on the other hand that we give some account of the sort of fact to which theological words can appeal for their empirical relevance. We must discover the logical status of theological words — including, e.g., their relation to, and difference from, the words of scientific assertion. (*MC*, XLII, 1952, 258)

The 'falsification problem' here is a reference to the challenge posed by Flew to the effect that if religious assertions are not empirically falsifiable (that is, if no actual or possible circumstances are permitted to count against their truth) then they cannot be meaningful. We shall return to this issue shortly. Meanwhile we note that Ramsey's response to the challenge is to suggest that there are levels of language, and that each level has its own structure and its own associated brand of 'fact'. A total language map will have index words which give clues to, and are definitive of, the total language scheme, and link and supplement the several language levels. It is in worship, for example, that we justifiably use the index word 'God' — the word which brings unity to our metaphysical system. We shall see in our next chapter how Ramsey developed the views here sketched.

Basil Mitchell's paper on 'Modern philosophy and theology' provides one of the most useful accounts of the change of attitude on the part of many philosophers towards religious questions.[2] He shows how the original positivistic programme has been modified until few philosophers would hold that theological statements are in principle unworthy of their attention: 'The modern philosopher would claim that he is concerned with an entirely neutral analysis, which is preliminary to any examination of the truth or falsehood of theological doctrines' (*Soc.*, V, 1952, 7). Such analysis may be undertaken by people with widely differing temperaments and basic attitudes, 'and this should warn us not to assume prematurely that it cannot consort with Christian Faith' (8).

H.H. Price and H.J. Paton were among those philosophers who insisted that the question of the nature of religious experience was not to be excluded from any analysis of religious claims. Price is clear that

> The two alternatives that *either* religious faith is capable of being justified by arguments from non-religious premises *or else* it is just a matter of feeling, are not exhaustive. There might be such a thing as *religious experience*, and I believe there is. And I mean by the word 'experience' something cognitive, not just an emotion though doubtless emotion accompanies it. I mean a mode of awareness, a unique one, not reducible to any other — and certainly not reducible to reason of any kind . . . If we *must* classify it under one of the familiar heads, I would rather call it 'a sense' myself, *a sense of the divine*; for it does have this in common with the ordinary senses, that it is an original source of *data*, though, in other ways it is not at all like them, e.g. no sense organ is connected with it. (*Soc.*, V, 1952, 43)

In *The Modern Predicament* (1955) Paton pays attention to the question of the justification of religious belief. For him, 'The philosophy of religion . . . is concerned primarily with the norms or standards which religion must follow and by which it must be judged — with the conditions necessary for a religion to be genuine and not spurious' (27). He emphasises the importance of religious experience for such a study, for herein lie the data — principles and acts of belief — whose origin and worth the philosopher seeks to determine. In the course of his exposition Paton returns to the attack upon both theological and logical positivism, roundly declaring that 'Complete scepticism is a poor support, and a dangerous ally, for religion. The marriage between religious experience and philosophical reflexion . . . has been too fruitful of blessings for any wise man to approve a divorce' (58).

Though not advocating the divorce of religious experience from philosophical reflection, R.B. Braithwaite, in his Eddington Memorial Lecture, *An Empiricist's View of the Nature of Religious Belief* (1955), made many more concessions to empiricism than did Paton. Braithwaite agrees that religious assertions are not meaningful in the ways in which statements of empirical fact, scientific hypotheses, or logically necessary statements are. However, they are meaningful if they are construed ethically, that is, as declaring the user's intention to act in appropriate ways. This is not to say that there is no difference between religious and moral assertions. For one thing, 'the behaviour policy intended is not (usually) specified by one religious assertion in isolation'. Again, the moral teaching of religion is often given by way of concrete examples — the parables of Jesus, for example — rather than in abstract terms. Yet again, in the higher religions the moral resolutions are made to bear upon the inner life as well as upon outward conduct. Finally, as between the different religions, the intentions to pursue behaviour policies are associated with different stories or sets of stories. Thus 'A religious assertion will, therefore, have a propositional element which is lacking in a purely moral assertion, in that it will refer to a story as well as to an intention.' The function of these stories is psychologically to undergird the will, and they may so serve whether or not the propositions contained in them are true.

A number of philosophers, including A.C. Ewing and R.M. Hare, felt that Braithwaite had minimised the crucial matter of *belief*. Ewing pointed out in 'Religious assertions in the light of contemporary philosophy' (*P*, XXXII, 1957, 206) that one's power to act is related to the strength of one's faith-commitment; and it is difficult to see how this power could be sustained if the stories relied upon were not true. Hare drew the general moral: 'The moral judgments . . . arise out of the religious belief; they do not constitute it' (in 'Religion and morals', *Faith and Logic*, ed. B. Mitchell, 1957, 180). It was further pointed out to Braithwaite that on his premises there can be no rational grounds for preferring one story or set of stories to another — something which a number of theologians found objectionable. Moreover, if Christian stories, for example, are deemed to be more adequate than others (and Braithwaite confessed Christian allegiance), it is difficult to see what this means if it does not have reference to their content, context and truthfulness. Indeed, Ronald W. Hepburn, whose account of religious language is similar in important respects to Braithwaite's, finds no grounds for preferring Christian stories to others.[3]

How, then, are religious assertions to be understood — and are they assertions? Some of the most influential replies to this question are collected in *New Essays in Philosophical Theology* (1955), edited by A.G.N. Flew and Alasdair C. MacIntyre. This book demonstrates as no other book of its period does the way in which Christian and non-Christian philosophers are enabled, by virtue of their shared analytical approach to philosophical questions, to discuss religious issues. Not the least interesting feature of the book — as a sign of the times — is its title. The editors seem unduly sensitive to the need to distance themselves from things old fashioned:

> We should like to have used the expression 'Philosophy of Religion' for its analogy with 'Philosophy of History', 'Philosophy of Science', and so on . . . But this expression has become, and seems likely for some time to remain, associated with Idealist attempts to present philosophical prolegomena to theistic theology. So we have borrowed from Professor Paul Tillich the expression 'Philosophical theology'; which has a welcome analogy to 'Philosophical Ethics' and 'Philosophical Aesthetics'. . . (x)

This explanation is not entirely satisfactory in view of the emphasis — not least by Tillich — upon the fact that the theologian is a committed person who works within a tradition. Moreover, the *general* absence since the 1930s of attempts to produce idealistic prolegomena to theism (and what of realist attempts to do the same thing?) suggests that the term 'Philosophy of Religion' is not as misleading as they would suggest. At all events it can hardly be denied that Flew himself is a philosopher, that he writes considerable amounts of philosophy of religion, and that he is not committed to the Christian faith.

Returning to our question concerning religious assertions we note first the papers under the title 'Theology and falsification'. The story begins (I speak advisedly!) with Flew's amended version of a parable originally told by John Wisdom in his article 'Gods' (*PAS*, XLV, 1944-5, 185-206). In brief the story goes that two explorers, arriving at a clearing in the jungle, find flowers and weeds growing there.

One explorer declares 'Some gardener must tend this plot.' The other disagrees and, moreover, no empirical tests (electrified fence, dogs) ever reveal the gardener. The first explorer persists in believing that the gardener exists, though he now qualifies his original claim by contending that the gardener is invisible, intangible, insensible to electric shocks; he has no scent, makes no sound, and tends the garden in secret. At which his sceptical friend expostulates: 'But what remains of your original assertion? Just how does what you call an invisible, intangible, eternally elusive gardener differ from an imaginary gardener or even from no gardener at all?' (96).

Flew's argument is, then, that the first explorer ends by saying nothing at all — his 'fine brash hypothesis' is 'killed by inches, the death by a thousand qualifications'. This, he urges, is 'the peculiar danger, the endemic evil, of theological utterance' (97). Once the believer denies that any actual or possible circumstances could falsify his assertions the believer has tacitly admitted that his assertions are (since they are not analytic) meaningless. Flew's concluding question, posed after the introduction of the problem of unmerited suffering, is: 'What would have to occur or to have occurred to constitute for you a disproof of the love of, or of the existence of God?' (99).

R.M. Hare's answer to the question involves the telling of another parable. A lunatic is convinced that all dons wish to murder him, and no matter how many mild, respectable dons are introduced to him, he persists in his belief. He is deluded — but what is he deluded about?

> Let us apply Flew's test to him. There is no behaviour of dons that can be enacted which he will accept as counting against his theory; and therefore his theory, on this test, asserts nothing. But it does not follow that there is no difference between what he thinks about dons and what most of us think about them — otherwise we should not call him a lunatic and ourselves sane, and dons would have no reason to feel uneasy about his presence in Oxford.
>
> Let us call that in which we differ from this lunatic our respective *bliks*. He has an insane *blik* about dons; we have a sane one . . . Flew has shown that a *blik* does not consist in an assertion or system of them; but nevertheless it is very important to have the right *blik*. (100)

According to Hare, Flew mistakenly regards theistic language as *explanatory*, whereas, following Hume, we must say that 'without a *blik* there can be no explanation; for it is by *bliks* that we decide what is and what is not an explanation' (101). Moreover, whereas Flew's explorers do not *mind* about their garden, Hare's lunatic minds about dons, and 'It is because I mind very much about what goes on in the garden in which I find myself, that I am unable to share the explorers' detachment' (103).

In his reply Basil Mitchell points out that the theologian

> *does* recognise the fact of pain as counting against Christian doctrine. But it is true that he will not allow it — or anything — to count decisively against it; for he is committed by his faith to trust in God. His attitude is not that of the detached observer, but of the believer. (103)

Mitchell agrees with Flew that theological utterances are and must be assertions, and in so far as they make sense of the believer's behaviour they are explanations too. Thus an assertion such as 'God loves us' is not conclusively falsifiable, and may be treated in at least three different ways: as a provisional hypothesis to be discarded if experience tells against it; as a significant article of faith; or as a vacuous formula removed from experience and with no influence on life. The committed Christian cannot regard his assertions in the first way, and is in constant danger 'of slipping into the third. But he need not; and, if he does, it is a failure in faith as well as in logic' (105).

Mitchell does not fully satisfy Flew, who thinks that the danger of death by a thousand qualifications still presses those who maintain that religious language is assertorial. As for Hare's *bliks*, Flew declares that if Hare's religion really is a *blik* 'involving no cosmological assertions about the nature and activities of a supposed personal creator, then surely he is not a Christian at all?' Further, unless religious utterances are intended as assertions many religious activities would be fraudulent or silly.

I.M. Crombie discusses some matters arising from the above debate. He argues, against Hare, that theological statements *are* assertions, and, against Mitchell, that they *can* be falsified (and are therefore on Flew's terms meaningful) — *except that* such falsification is possible in principle only and not in practice, for we do not in this life have access to all the relevant facts. This idea of eschatological verification was subsequently to be advocated by John Hick in his book *Faith and Knowledge* (1957) and in his article

'Theology and verification' (*TT*, XVII, 1960, reprinted in *The Existence of God*, ed. J. Hick, 1964).

We have it on the authority of W.D. Hudson that Flew has latterly reviewed his position.[4] The crux of the matter is Flew's recognition that in his original paper he wrongly regarded 'counting against' as equivalent to 'being incompatible with'. That is, on the strength of his supposition (which Mitchell showed to be not universal) that believers cannot state what counts against their beliefs, he wrongly concluded that those beliefs therefore had no incompatibles and could not be meaningful. However, the question how far are religious believers prepared to qualify their assertions remains. To put it another way: *how much* of what seems to count against theism (even if it is not incompatible with it) may a believer properly tolerate before his belief becomes irrational or silly? This question remains as a standing challenge to the Christian, and I see no satisfactory approach to an answer except by the way of unfolding the Christian story, of elucidating the framework of convictions against the background of which the religious assertions are made. For in the last resort the question is not so much one of intellect or understanding, but of standing-ground. It is a question of what respective disputants 'see'.

Our final reference to *New Essays* is to the contribution by Thomas McPherson, 'Religion as the inexpressible'. McPherson is impressed by the way in which believers wish to make apparently contradictory claims — such as that God is 'wholly other' and also that he is 'in us'. His way out of the 'worry' posed by such claims is to say that 'There are some things that just cannot be said. As long as no-one tries to say them there is no trouble. But if anyone does try to say them he must take the consequences. We ought not to try to express the inexpressible. The things that theologians try to say (or some of them) belong to the class of things that just cannot be said' (132-3). To brand religious assertions 'nonsense' in this way is not necessarily to be anti-religious. On the contrary, following Otto's understanding of the numinous (the experience of confrontation by the wholly other), we may say that the essential feature of religion is its non-rational side.

Not all were persuaded by McPherson, and certainly no systematic theologian to my knowledge resigned his post under the impact of this argument! Frederick Ferré put many of the objections to McPherson in a nutshell in his *Language, Logic and God* (1962), and I briefly list them. If McPherson is right: (1) there can be no such thing as religious truths; (2) there can be no public worship, for this requires the use of language; (3) there can be no proclamation of good news; (4) there can be no 'private religion' for this too requires language. Ferré concludes: 'Abandoning language would be tantamount to dismissing religion as an important human activity and substituting, not the mystic's high ecstasy forged in discipline, contemplation, and study, but the formless "rosy glow" of "positive thinking" — without even the thought to think positively!' (37).

Neo-scholastic contributions

We turn now to some Roman Catholic philosophers who have taken account of analytical trends in philosophy, but who would never claim that linguistic analysis is the only task of the philosopher. In *An Essay in Christian Philosophy* (1954) Dom Illtyd Trethowan faces the charge lodged against Christians by certain modern philosophers that Christians, because of their presuppositions, are too biased to be able to perform philosophical functions effectively. In contrast with those who rebut this charge by pointing out that the philosopher also has his presuppositions and his 'faith', Dom Illtyd admits that the Christian philosopher is conditioned by presuppositions, and asserts that these enable him to be a better philosopher: 'the theologian is in a position to answer questions which arise in philosophy from a standpoint higher than that of pure philosophy. He has materials to work on to which the philosopher who is not also a theologian has no access' (12).

This is not to say that theology unwarrantably interferes with philosophy; indeed the former saves the latter from error. Philosophy can reach true results as far as it goes, but theology goes further; yet the two can never conflict when each is being true to its mission, for in a sense philosophy is based upon theology: 'the relation between philosophy and theology, between reason and faith, is that between nature and grace, and so far we have merely been adverting to the famous principle that grace raises and fulfils nature without damaging it' (14). The gift of faith is conditional upon our choosing it, and having chosen it a new world is opened up to us. From the standpoint of one who inhabits this new world (though he does not reside in the Thomist quarter of it) Dom Illtyd surveys positivism and existentialism, concluding that it is not enough for the Christian philosopher simply to oppose irrationalism; he must manifest his positive concern for that '*wisdom* which ought to be the aim of Christian philosophy . . . Christian philosophy must have something to *show* for itself' (182). Augustinian rather than Thomist, Dom Illtyd argues that our knowledge of God is not gained *via* induction or syllogistic deduction, but is given in experience. Our reason brings us face to face with the God who is presupposed in all knowledge; for our knowledge is of particular existents and they in turn owe their being to the source of being.

It is interesting in passing to note that Dom Illtyd's book was widely reviewed — a further indication of the increasing ecumenicity of philosophy; and a wide diversity of opinions was passed upon it. If to A.C. MacIntyre 'This is an arrogant book in which certain genuine insights are sacrificed to a quite unneccesarily polemical style' (*PQ*, VI, 1956, 378), to Mascall it is a 'brilliant and unconventional book' (*HJ*, LIII, 1954-5, 93). Ninian Smart, adverting to Buddhism and Jainism, denied that religion is necessarily bound up with the view that God exists (*M*, N.S., LXV, 1956, 418); and John Macquarrie concluded that although Dom Illtyd is an intellectualist he is not a dry one, for he allows the idea of 'union with and participation in that which is known' (*T*, LVIII, 1955, 115).

D.J.B. Hawkins, an avowed though not an uncritical Thomist, takes a more traditionally Catholic view in his *Being and Becoming* (1954). He seems less keen than Dom Illtyd to take advantage of the worthy insights of analytical philosophy, and more concerned to lament the demise, and to reassert the merits of, metaphysics:

> The notion of a general metaphysic or ontology, which is the science of being and of those aspects of being in its generality which transcend the opposition of mind and matter, has fallen into oblivion. Yet it does not seem unreasonable to suppose that, starting from the world of experience, we should be able to refine our concepts sufficiently to construct such a science. The reasons for its contemporary neglect are reasons of history and not of principle. (19)

Hawkins cites as reasons for this neglect the fact of the unreality of Suarezian and Wolffian presentations of Thomist metaphysics, with their over-neat conceptual constructions, and the criticisms that have been handed down from Hume and Kant. He pays particular attention to the latter, and believes that once Kant's criticisms have been met the worth of Aristotelian metaphysics will be displayed.

Languages, Standpoints and Attitudes, 1945-55

Emergent existentialism

So far in this chapter we have seen how, to a greater or lesser extent, philosophers of all kinds — Christian and non-Christian, scholastic and non-scholastic — were beginning to employ, or at least to react to, the techniques of linguistic analysis. We have seen that undogmatic analytical philosophy (or, some would say, covertly dogmatic analytical philosophy) has succeeded in erecting a platform whereon many find it possible to converse. It remains to note the increasing attention being paid to that more exotic phenomenon, existentialism. The bulk of the contributions in this field are still of an expository or evaluative kind, and include such works as J. Collins, *The Existentialists* (1952); K.F. Reinhardt, *The Existentialist Revolt* (1952); H.J. Blackham, *Six Existentialist Thinkers* (1952); J.B. Coates, 'Existentialism' (*P*, XXVIII, 1953, 229-38); E.L. Allen, *Existentialism from Within* (1953); and F.H. Heinemann, *Existentialism and the Modern Predicament* (1953).

When existentialism has been applauded in Britain it has usually been because of its general underlining of the idea of commitment, and because it has been construed as a plea for the philosophic consideration of the issues of life as it is, and of man in — or over against — his environment. It has sometimes been contrasted favourably with what is taken as the over-precious British preoccupation with analysis. Two things are clear: those who consider existentialism at all do not seem easily able to remain neutral towards it; and such considerations sometimes appear to have curious side effects. Thus, for example, existentialism draws from Hawkins his kindest words about linguistic analysis, whilst for Paton it almost serves as a rock of refuge. In *The Meaning of Existentialism* (1951) Hawkins writes,

> A common feature of existentialism, indeed, seems to be the abdication of the quest for clearness. M. Marcel is there to tell us that mysteries must not be degraded into problems. We would like to suggest, in opposition, that the business of philosophy is with problems and not with mysteries. If the apostles of clearness have sometimes been trivial, this is not because they have confined themselves to problems, but because they have not approached the most important problems. (3)

And Paton:

At its best existentialism is an attempt to defend, both in thought and action, the liberty and dignity and creativeness of the human individual. It may well be doubted whether it is possible to sustain this attitude without at least a minimum belief that it is part of the *essence* of man to be rational. But those of us who hold this belief do not find too many allies at the present time; and we cannot afford to despise the help of those who remind us that philosophy has other problems to face besides those which arise from the methods of mathematics and of physical science. If the existentialists provide us with no coherent solution of these human problems, perhaps they may help to prepare the way for something better. (*In Defence of Reason*, 1951, 228)

B.M.G. Reardon is even less grudging in his appreciation of the phenomenon. He reminds us that existentialism is not one self-consistent doctrine, it is more like an intellectual atmosphere: 'The true existentialist *lives* his beliefs: to philosophical analysis, classification, and system-building he is instinctively opposed . . . Existentialism is a doctrine of human beings — singular, diverse, and irreplacable — and of their relations with each other' (*ET*, LXVI, 1954-5, 112-13). Reardon claims that when the Christian faith has been true to its biblical heritage it has always taken adequate account of the existentialist emphases upon uniqueness, individuality, personal encounters and relations, and so on. For his part the Thomist F.C. Copleston considers that the metaphysician should imbibe the logical positivist lesson concerning the need for careful analysis and worthy speculation, and the existentialist concern for problems of human life and existence which science and logic can all too easily neglect. But in his *Existentialism and Modern Man* (1953) he does not doubt that a new metaphysics will arise. Neither does Philip Leon who, in 'Existentialism and metaphysics' (*P*, XXVIII, 1953), argues that the primary lesson to be learned from existentialism is that philosophy must start with the living subject and with the lived object or reality, and not with Descartes's abstractions, the *cogitans* and the *cogitatum*.

We shall find that the matters raised in this chapter, together with some fresh ones, are pursued with vigour in the decade from 1955.

Notes

1. Among the many contemporary studies of questions so far raised in this chapter see B.A. Farrell, 'An appraisal of therapeutic positivism', *M* N.S. LV (1946); A.C. Ewing, 'Philosophical analysis', in *Philosophical Studies: Essays in Memory of L. Susan Stebbing* (Allen & Unwin, London, 1948); M. Black, *Language and Philosophy* (Cornell University Press, Ithaca, New York, 1949); and (ed.) *Philosophical Analysis* (Cornell University Press, Ithaca, New York, 1950).

2. See also H.D. Lewis, 'The philosophy of religion 1945-1952', *PQ,* IV (1954); and the useful piece of 'public relations' work performed by Margaret Masterman, 'What *is* philosophy nowadays?', 'The philosophy of language, or the study of framework', and 'Linguistic philosophy and dogmatic theology', in *T*, LIV (1951).

3. See R.W. Hepburn, *Christianity and Paradox* (Watts, London, 1958), chap. XI.

4. See W.D. Hudson, *Wittgenstein and Religious Belief* (Macmillan, London, 1975). On p. 145 Hudson refers to an unpublished paper by Flew entitled, 'Theology and falsification in retrospect' in which the point made in my text is elaborated.

7

Widening Horizons, 1955-65

In an article entitled, 'The debate on the relationship between Christianity and existentialism' (*T*, LXVII, 1964, 15-21), James Richmond urges theologians to examine the accuracy or otherwise of existentialist analyses of human experience. If they fail to do this because of predispositions against existentialist extremes they may themselves produce equally exaggerated descriptions of 20th century man as being thoroughly integrated, guilt-free, and so on. To those who might suggest that existentialism is a purely local, temporary phenomenon which could not have emerged apart from war-time desperation, Richmond replies that even if this were true it would still leave open the question of the validity of existentialist claims. More positively, he points out that existentialist emphases are to be found in varying centuries and traditions. Hence, 'It seems to me to be extremely difficult to dismiss existentialism as a purely *local* (geographically speaking) or *temporary* (historically speaking) point of view' (19). Even if the theologian is not convinced by what he reads, he ought at least to understand how his fellow Christians, such as Bultmann, are undertaking the risky business of exposing themselves to the situation in which modern, dechristianized, unchurched man finds himself.

That some theologians had already listened intently to existentialist voices is clear from John Macquarrie's book, *An Existentialist Theology* (1955); and by the time Richmond's article appeared a number of philosophers of religion had begun to take stock of the phenomenon. We have already noted references to existentialism in the writings of D.M. Emmet, F.C. Copleston, and others; but the decade with which we are presently concerned is the decade *par excellence* during which the close analysis of at least some varieties of existentialism took place in Britain. The factors prompting this analysis were, as might have been expected, exotic, and we would draw particular attention to the influence of Kierkegaard; the challenge of Paul Tillich's methodology; and Willem F. Zuurdeeg's attempted marriage of linguistic analysis with existential concern. We shall investigate these from the point of view of our interest in the nature and methodology of the philosophy of religion.

Kierkegaard, philosophy and faith

In tracing the antecedents of existentialism it is customary to refer to the biblical emphasis upon *krisis*, decision, commitment; it is almost mandatory to advert to Luther's opposition to that variety of medieval scholasticism which would appear to objectify God: no, said Luther, *habere deum est colere deum*. Luther's emphasis upon faith as trustful commitment (*fiducia*) over against faith as propositional assent (*assensus*) is entirely compatible with this. Pascal too is often applauded as one whose defiant assertion that God is not the possession of the philosophers and wiseacres places him in the pre-history of existentialism. My view, however, is that the mental shift which Kant effected can make it more misleading than helpful to look too far back for thinkers who resemble *modern* existentialists. For modern existentialism originates in the acceptance of Kant's divorce of the noumenal from the phenomenal realms on the one hand, and in the opposition to Hegel's attempted resolution of the dichotomy on the other. Thus one of existentialism's most sensitive interpreters, David E. Roberts, concluded in his *Existentialism and Religious Belief* (1959, 4) that its chief value was as a corrective. It seeks to prevent our overlooking that encounter-based knowledge which Kant called 'practical', and at the same time it discourages us from attempting to pass in argument from the existential to the theoretic. Between these two a great gulf is fixed. For this reason Kierkegaard used the term 'dialectic' to encompass both that existential knowledge which can never be rationalised, and that unavoidable linguistic objectifying of God which must occur if there is to be any proclamation, anything other than silence.

Although he was indebted to Schelling (1775-1854), and *via* Schelling to Franz von Baader (1765-1841), Kierkegaard could not rest content with romanticism. To him it was too comfortable; it occupied the aesthetic ground; it did not adequately accommodate such realities as pain and suffering. Further, as is well known, the conventionally orthodox Danish establishment of his day gave him no satisfaction at all. Complacency and hypocrisy were everywhere evident to Kierkegaard, and it appeared that the transition from death to life was devoid of challenge, was all too automatic. As he wrote in his *Concluding Unscientific Postscript* (1968), 'An objective acceptance of Christianity is (*sit venia verbo*) paganism or thoughtlessness' (116). But of all his battles, that against Hegel is most important for our present purpose.

Kierkegaard contends that Hegel cannot make room in his system for the individual. The Hegelian monist is in the 'comical' position of having forgotten

> in a sort of world-historical absent-mindedness, what it means to be a human being. Not indeed, what it means to be a human being in general; for this is the sort of thing that one might even induce a speculative philosopher to agree to; but what it means that you and I and he are human beings, each one for himself. (109)

Again, Hegelian monism overlooks the infinite qualitative difference which separates man from God, and which intellectual agility can never span. The only existence open to an Hegelian is conceptual existence. Hegel, in fact, abstracts from real existence, and hence his contention that the real is the rational is absurd. For Kierkegaard the real subject is the ethically existing subject, and God is the holy one with whom sinful I have to do. John Heywood Thomas has well said in his *Subjectivity and Paradox* (1957) that 'The quarrel [Kierkegaard] has with Hegel is . . . that Hegel would try to make God a purely public word' (71).

Above all, Hegel's philosophy was, to Kierkegaard, aristocratic and gnostic; it was grievously ill-fitted to do justice to the paradox at the heart of Christianity, namely, the paradox that God became man. Hegelianism's resultant failure to do justice to the complexity of that faith which alone was adequate came as no surprise to Kierkegaard. For Hegel's view that the terms of Christianity were symbolic of a higher metaphysic he had nothing but contempt. He declared that, far from smoothing away the paradox, reason's task was to exhibit it in all its stark offensiveness. By faith alone is revelation grasped, and that with passionate inwardness. The God-man alone brings the transcendent to us, and in him we have faith 'in virtue of the absurd'. What is the absurd? 'The absurd is — that the eternal truth has come into being in time, that God has come into being, has been born, has grown up . . . ' (*Postscript*, 188).

The Christian needs to know the limitations of reason, and he must believe *against* reason. What is important is not what one believes, but how one believes; the crucial thing in not to believe that x, y, z, are true, but to *be* in the truth. It is by no means the case that had the individual Christian lived in Jesus's day he would inevitably have recognised him for who he was. In any generation faith alone thus recognises him and, moreover, faith makes him our contemporary *now*. Once we have believed the paradox is absurd no more. Faith is 'the objective uncertainty due to the repulsion of the absurd held by the passion of inwardness, which in this instance is intensified to the utmost degree' (540).

It is important that we recognise that for Kierkegaard there *is* a cognitive element in the existential encounter. It is an *objective* uncertainty with which we have to do. He is no mystic, and his paradox is as historically rooted in the actual Jesus as it could conceivably be. When he speaks of truth as subjectivity he has in mind his view of man as an ethical, decision-taking subject. He does not at all wish to defend subjective relativism, or to incur the charge of psychologism — that is, to be accused, when making assertions about God, for example, of reporting only upon his subjective state, and of not being informative concerning anything that is the case. Far from it: 'authentic subjectivity on the part of man, he held, is only possible when he collides with the objectivity of the divine Subject'.[1] Kierkegaard rebuked his own age on this very point — faith had been made 'into something so inward that it disappears completely in the end'. Roberts strikes the right balance thus:

> Unquestionably, Kierkegaard believed that God is real and that He has revealed Himself in history in Jesus Christ, apart from what any individual may think, will, or believe. But he refused to refer to the reality of God and historical revelation as 'objective' because the latter word connoted for him demonstrable, conceptual knowledge, an abstraction from passionate commitment, personal decision, and the 'I-Thou' encounter. Indeed, although he believed that God was real apart from Sören Kierkegaard; he recognised that there was no way of *his* entering into relationship with God apart from Sören Kierkegaard's faith. And with such a recognition it is difficult to quarrel. (84–5)

As Kierkegaard put it in *Either-Or*, 'Only the truth which edifies is truth for you' (1944, II, 294). All of which, to repeat the point, harmonises well with an abhorrence of Hegelian intellectualist objectivity, and with dismay at a careless Church sitting at ease in Zion.

Since philosophy can neither bring man to God nor remedy sinful man's spiritual malaise, it can neither support nor confound the subject matter of theology. Christianity may be presented as being in the interest of man, or of God, but the latter approach alone is adequate, and Tertullian is an exemplar of it. Theology's business is to deal faithfully with the paradox: 'the idea of philosophy is mediation — Christianity's is the paradox' (*Papirer*, IA, 94). This is not to say that philosophy and theology cannot tolerate each other; they can — and at this point Kierkegaard, who by insisting on the anthropological starting-point had qualified for membership of the Augustinian tradition, now adverts to the Thomist distinction to the effect that something can be true in philosophy which is false in theology. But whereas scholasticism spoke of faith as going 'beyond' reason, Kierkegaard takes delight in elaborating the position that it goes 'against' reason. The absurd cannot be known, it can only be believed. Reason's importance in this context is that it is that against which faith is pitted.

Although Kierkegaard abhorred Hegel's system it would be premature to conclude that he had no place for system of any kind. He operates his dialectic method to show against Hegel that the sharp contrasts of eternity and time, holiness and sin, cannot be filed away; he admits the necessity of reason as the means of assuring the Christian that 'he believes against the understanding' (*Postscript*, 504). It would seem that although philosophy cannot be used as a stepping-stone to faith, for there is an unavoidable discontinuity between philosophy and religious experience, Kierkegaard does wish to allow a place to reason. Why, then, have some regarded him as an out and out irrationalist?

Gordon H. Clark, for example, is convinced that Kierkegaard and those influenced by him are irrationalists. They by-pass the requirements of intelligible speech and thought in the interests of the divine-human encounter. Clark declares that 'A meeting in which no conceptual knowledge or intellectual content was conveyed would not give the subject any reason for *thinking* he had met God.'[2] But, as we saw, Kierkegaard did wish to maintain objectivity; the faith-experience does have cognitive import; the paradox is a matter of ontological fact. If reason prompts us to see this, as Kierkegaard says it can, then reason is not redundant and Kierkegaard is not, on his own terms, an irrationalist.

What is disquieting, however, is the fact that in opposition to the Hegelian religion of immanence (Kierkegaard's religiousness A — the religion of God-man continuity) Kierkegaard launches into an interpretation of God as absolutely other which does violence both to biblical teaching and to Christian experience. For Kierkegaard God is absolutely unknown apart from the faith-encounter; for traditional Christianity God, though never exhaustively known, is truly known — and is known even by sinners. His image, though defaced, is not obliterated. Man is both like and unlike God — a paradox which, perhaps, Kierkegaard rather overlooked. Far from upholding the creator-creature distinction he has insisted upon the disjunction of the parties. This cannot but threaten the gospel of the God-man and vitiate the mission of the Church — that corporate undertaking for which, incidentally, Kierkegaard with his model of the lonely knight of faith has little room.

But I must resist the temptation to stray further into doctrinal matters, and advert once again to the lucid exposition of Kierkegaard's central concepts, *Subjectivity and paradox*, by J. Heywood Thomas. Heywood Thomas brings the methods of analytical philosophy to bear upon Kierkegaard's thought, and makes good the following points: first, that faith is not proof:

> religious faith is unlike (a) the method of the lawyer who seeks to establish something, (b) the method of the scientist who wants to discover something, (c) the method of the mathematician who seeks to construct a system that will be true. (139)

Whereas a mathematical proof is a demonstration, faith is a 'persuasion resulting in conviction'. Moreover, existential statements, such as that God exists, cannot be proved; and again, 'in the case of faith there can be no such certainty about its belief as there must be in the case of demonstration' (139). Faith is unlike a scientific hypothesis because it 'is not an explanation which enables us to predict anything' (140). Nor will the model of legal proof suffice, for we do not in religious faith seek to establish beyond reasonable doubt that such and such is the case. Kierkegaard reminds us that religious faith is *sui generis*.

Secondly, Kierkegaard rebukes the rationalist's error that the religious man's decision to believe requires to be justified, or could be justified by the speculative philosopher. Essential religion is not to be identified with reason or metaphysics, and the philosopher does not set out to produce a picture of reality. Thirdly, the empiricist error is rebutted by Kierkegaard. The post-Schleiermacher emphasis upon religious feeling was repugnant to him. He was opposed to an inward faith which did not make a man *do* anything, and to the way in which 'faith' could be evacuated of content. With reference to the theistic argument from religious experience Heywood Thomas writes

> if we say that what faith consists of is feeling then we shall also be found to say that when we say 'I have faith in God' or 'I have faith that there is a Providence whose grace sustains me', all we are saying is that this is our feeling. Thus we are not saying anything about God at all and saying nothing about the sustaining grace either. We see that this does indeed make faith disappear. On this analysis religious statements are made quite the reverse of what they are. Kierkegaard insisted that faith is a real relation to God in the same way as an assertion about physical objects or people is an assertion about my relation to something other than myself. He felt that people were so 'busy about getting a truer and truer conception of God' that they had forgotten 'the first step, that one should fear God.' Worship is a relation to God. (148-9; cf. *Postscript*, 391)

The upshot is that the religious man's claim to know God is both autobiographical and ontological. It is born of his experience — whether cosmological (the mystery of the world) or ethical (sin and guilt) — but its reference is to the One who is over against him. Kierkegaard's outstanding contribution, according to this sympathetic yet searching interpreter, is that he has made this clear, and that he exhorts us to *live* the faith.

Authorial angst

At the beginning of Chapter 5 existentialism was briefly characterised. In that chapter, and again at the end of Chapter 6, reference was made to some philosophers who noticed continental existentialism. In this chapter I have introduced Kierkegaard, who has been called the father of existentialism. We now encounter a problem as far as this book is concerned. There can be no doubt

Widening Horizons, 1955-65

that Paul Tillich (1886-1965), one of the most influential of 20th-century philosophical theologians, was indebted to existentialist thinkers, themes and categories. Tillich's influence in North America is considerable — indeed, it has been said that to this day the number of doctoral candidates who are writing on Tillich outnumbers those who are writing on Barth — though how reliable a measure of influence this is, or which of the two thinkers derives the greater benefit from the alleged fact is not made clear. Equally, there can be no doubt that as far as British secular philosophers are concerned Tillich's labours have produced very little by way of positive or negative response. He did not become a significant talking-point between philosophically inclined theologians and their secular counterparts in the way, for example, that Wittgenstein and, to a lesser extent in Britain, Whitehead did. It is more than likely that Tillich's underlying idealism, and even more his indebtedness to existentialism sufficed to dampen any enthusiasm British secular philosophers might have had for him. For as John Passmore wrote in the decade with which we are at present concerned:

> The fact we have to live with, then, is that if most British philosophers are convinced that Continental metaphysics is arbitrary, pretentious, and mind-destroying, Continental philosophers are no less confident that British empiricism is philistine, pedestrian, and soul-destroying. Even when existentialism reflects certain aspects of British empiricism — as in its emphasis on contingency — it does so in the manner of the distorting mirrors in a Fun Fair; what seemed eminently rational and ordinary suddenly looks grotesque. (*A Hundred Years of Philosophy*, 460)

Tillich must nevertheless be included in this volume, not least because having complained that religious thinkers have not always responded adequately, in time, or at all to their secular counterparts we may not overlook what is perhaps the paramount example of culpable neglect from the secular side. At the same time, it will be a truncated Tillich that I present. I shall focus upon methodological questions only, for these are most germane to the theme of this book. Sadly, this will inevitably make Tillich seem 'flatter' and less fecund than he actually is. Concerning his challenging exposition of traditional Christian doctrines, and his perceptive political, social and cultural analyses

I shall have nothing to say.

It is first necessary to develop certain points concerning existentialism and in particular to clarify the terms 'existentialism' and 'essentialism' — both of which are important for an understanding of Tillich.

Varieties of existentialism

Existentialism has variously been described as a trend, a mood, an attitude, a fashion — even a mess. What no-one has mistaken it for is a system. It sets its face against both the older rationalism and the older and still current empiricism; for both of these presuppose that by the use of reason the dispassionate observer can probe the secrets of mind and reality. In existentialism there are no dispassionate observers, and for many existentialists there is no fixed universe either. What there is, is the individual in his existence, his alone-ness, his finitude, his freedom to choose, his anguish, his guilt, his dread, his fear of death. Existence is no abstraction to be serenely contemplated. For some existentialists existence is a challenge to be faced, and in facing it we move from 'fallen', 'inauthentic' existence to 'authentic' existence; for others, existence cannot be transcended, but only submitted to: the individual is constantly threatened by societal and other pressures to which he is ever subject. (We can see at once why existentialism has lent itself as much to dramatic and literary expression as to philosophical.) Some existentialists are subjectivists after the manner of Kierkegaard, whilst others, of whom Martin Heidegger (1889-1976) is the most notable example, move from existentialist analysis to essentialist or ontological construction.

Heidegger (who, although influenced by Kierkegaard, did not regard himself as an existentialist) was indebted to Edmond Gustav Albert Husserl (1859-1938), and he in turn had been impressed by his teacher Franz Brentano (1838-1917). Brentano's doctrine of intentionality, according to which mental acts such as perception entail the direction of the mind to an object, was particularly influential. In his turn Husserl focused upon consciousness, to the exclusion — 'bracketing' — of 'external' matters, whilst at the same time denying that he was simply encouraging introspection. He saw himself as making an *a priori* investigation of those essences which are present to our consciousness and common to all minds. The study and analysis of these phenomena — of judgement, for example — has come to be known as phenomenology. Husserl was consciously indebted to Descartes's method of systematic doubt, and his analogous argument is that whereas we are able to 'bracket' or 'think away' anything about which we may think, we cannot 'bracket' consciousness itself. This is the Absolute — and it cannot be 'thought away'.

Drawing upon this heritage, and denying the mind/external world duality, Heidegger turned his attention to what was for him the basic concept: being. The individual has certain characteristics and opportunities which are uniquely his; there is a fundamental 'givenness' about his existence: he is 'thrown' into being at a particular time and in a certain place. Furthermore, the individual is ever confronted by the fact of his transience, of his death. As he is he is not complete. He is 'fallen', marked by 'inauthentic' existence. He is nevertheless impelled towards his essential nature which is a possibility lying ahead of him, awaiting realisation. At this point we can see to what existentialists are referring when they say that existence precedes essence. To refuse the quest is to languish in 'inauthentic existence'; to rise to the challenge is to be on the way to 'authentic existence'. Heidegger's anthropocentric vision leaves no room for a personal God — indeed, he considered that Christianity had erred in conceiving God as *a* being; but he denied that he was an atheist.

The fact is, however, that as we noted in Chapter 5 existentialism can take either an atheistic or a Christian direction. Of Kierkegaard's profoundly Christian commitment there can be no doubt; and Gabriel Marcel (1889-1973) set his face against the existentialist atheism of Jean-Paul Sartre (1905-80). Marcel concentrated his thought upon the human community which, he contended, is characterised by fidelity, and rooted ontologically in God. By contrast, Sartre is pessimistic in the extreme: my existence is threatened and constricted by that of others; the world is fundamentally absurd; and we have no recourse to anything or anyone outside ourselves. There is, in Sartre, no possibility that we may transcend the situations of dread, guilt and anguish which confront us — and at this point Sartre is at the diametrically opposite position to that of Karl Jaspers (1883-1969). Jaspers maintained that we *are* free to transcend our circumstances and thus to have communion with others. He also took a more optimistic view of man's reasoning abilities than other existentialists, maintaining that reason was competent within the realm of the sciences, and only protesting when attempts were made to squeeze truths of existence into a rationalistic strait-jacket.

We can now turn to Tillich, and view him against the background of our sections on Kierkegaard and existentialism.

Paul Tillich

Tillich's experiences as an army chaplain during the First World War convinced him that the old social order was crumbling, and with it the old idea of God. He felt impelled out of his earlier idealistic theorising into contemplating the realities of existence. He studied Schelling, Kierkegaard and Heidegger and, in his autobiographical sketch, *On the Boundary* (1966, 56) he tells us that he adopted existentialism. Again, in his *Systematic Theology* he writes, 'The attitude of the theologian is "existential". He is involved — with the whole of his existence, with his finitude and his anxiety, with his self-contradictions and his despair, with the healing forces in him and in his social situation' (I, 23).

Tillich saw himself as a boundary-man, standing in the dialectical tension between philosophy and theology, theory and practice, Church and world. But it is the first of these polarities which immediately concerns us, and presents us with the most intriguing of interpretative puzzles. For while Tillich's debt to existentialism is clear, it may also be said that he exemplifies the truth that, undeterred by the onslaughts of the positivists and the linguistic analysts, idealism's soul goes marching on. It is not without significance that Tillich confessed a wistful attachment to the 19th century: 'I am one of those in my generation who, in spite of the radicalism with which they have criticised the nineteenth century, often feel a longing for its stability, its liberalism, its unbroken cultural traditions'.[3] Indeed at the risk of being accused of insubordination I would go so far as to suggest that in certain respects Tillich is a thinker of whom one may say that the more things change the more they remain the same.

Is not this a perverse judgement? Has not Tillich surpassed his contemporaries in his utilisation of the insights of existentialism and psychotherapy? Does not his method of correlating the message of the gospel with the challenge of 'the human situation' imply a degree of sensitivity to culture not often found among philosophical theologians? Affirmative answers to these questions might at first sight seem to be required; but after sifting the evidence I find myself on the side of those of Tillich's critics who find that his theology, and even his method of correlation, are in the end subservient to a framework of thought which owes much to Hegel, more to Schelling, and which is inadequately clothed by, and is strictly independent of, existentialist and psychotherapeutic terminology. When Tillich's modern terms lie mouldering in their archaic grave, the soul of his theology will be able to go marching on, re-enfleshed by what will pass in successive generations for suitable modern concepts. Some have gone so far as to regard Tillich as but the last in the long line of Christian neo-Platonists — this was certainly the implication of Sidney Hook, who regards Tillich's God as the 'all-in-all of pantheistic spiritualism'.[4] Or again, H.D. McDonald reminds us of the similarity which Professor Kroner finds between Tillich and Eriugena,[5] whilst he himself discovers in Tillich's thought a mysticism reminiscent of the Pseudo-Dionysius.[6] Others have found in Tillich's ground of Being echoes of Boehme's indeterminate void,[7] and others again have found in the same idea something resembling the world soul of Emerson and Theodore Parker.[8]

Tillich's philosophical inheritance induces him to set out from the 'ontic shock' which the contemplation of Being administers to man — and in this connection Tillich acknowledges a debt to Santayana. Then, and now under the influence of Heidegger, Tillich borrows the term 'angst' from Kierkegaard, though he leaves behind Kierkegaard's denotation. For the latter employed the term in connection with the sinful individual's predicament in face of a holy God, whereas Tillich generalises the term so that it becomes a way of describing man's condition *vis-à-vis* Being. In this way existentialist terminology becomes subservient to idealist ontology and, despite the fact that in his *Systematic Theology* II (1957) Tillich wishes to retain the term 'sin' as expressing 'the personal act of turning away from that to which one belongs' (II, 46), and despite all his efforts not to equate sin with finitude, sin does in his hands become something like an impersonal ontological necessity. Thus he can say, 'It is not the disobedience to a law which makes an act sinful but the fact that it is an expression of man's estrangement from God, from men, from himself' (II, 46-7). He can also say, 'Man is never cut off from the ground of being, not even in the state of condemnation' (II, 78). This last seems a thoroughly monistic assertion.

What, then, of Tillich's understanding of the relationship between philosophy and theology? The more lethargic students of philosophy may not feel immediately sympathetic with Tillich's view that philosophy is something to which one is impelled: 'It is always a driving force in the depths of his being that makes the philosopher a philosopher.'[9] What stimulates him is the question of being. Philosophy may be defined as 'that cognitive endeavour in which the question of being is asked'.[10] The question is thrust before man's attention by his existential situation which is one in which finitude and estrangement press upon him, and the answer to the question is provided by theology (I, 64). Already we are on the verge of establishing a relationship between theology and philosophy; but before we go further we must look again at the variety of ingredients which go into Tillich's understanding of philosophy.

His testimony is clear: 'I am an idealist if idealism means the assertion of the identity of thinking and being as the principle of truth.'[11] In adumbrating the system which such a view implies he draws heavily upon idealist predecessors. In much of his talk of being we hear echoes of Hegel, to whom being, passing through a dialectical process first became Nothing, and then, by opposing Nothing, emerges victorious. Many of Tillich's insights concerning the nature of man bear clear marks of post-Kantian ethical dualism. Thus man enjoys a 'Freedom in polarity with destiny' which is 'the structural element which makes existence possible because it transcends the essential necessity of being without destroying it' (I, 182). Again, in the phenomenological explication of man's freedom the disciple of Husserl comes into view, and we are informed that 'Freedom is experienced as deliberation, decision, and responsibility' (I, 184). In the phenomenology lies the foretaste of that dash of realism which existentialism was more adequately to offer Tillich. But if, because of the all-pervasively idealist cast of his mind, he cannot be classed as a phenomenologist pure and simple, by the same token he cannot be labelled an existentialist in any straightforward sense.

Tillich's essentialist ontology takes him into places where many existentialists would not follow; his utilisation of 'death' in the service of Christianity was not endorsed by Heidegger, from whom the notion was borrowed. But above all, his attachment to system in philosophy, and his view that the philosopher describes the nature of reality, place him far from the spirit of Kierkegaard. (In this connection it is interesting to note that Tillich's adoption from Kierkegaard of the term 'existential' to describe his work was prompted by the fact that in his view the term 'practical' had been *anti*-theoretically abused by the Ritschlians.)[12] As Tillich himself assures us, 'I have never been an existentialist in the sense that

Kierkegaard or Heidegger is an existentialist;' on the contrary, because of the requirements of the system 'my present enquiries are predominantly essentialist'.[13] Hence Kenneth Hamilton's engaging comment, 'Just as Henry Ford of the Model "T" days allowed his customers to choose any colour provided it was black, Tillich will join forces with all existentialists provided they support essentialism.'[14] It is also significant that Kierkegaard found Schelling's philosophy but a half-way house between Hegelianism and existentialism, and that Tillich's acknowledged debt to Schelling is so considerable. From the early Schelling he derived his concern with system, and with the view that thought precedes being; from the later Schelling (*ex* Boehme) came the reverse idea, together with the conviction that God is eternally being and becoming. Having reviewed Tillich's writings in the light of this tangled skein of influences, we may well agree with David Jenkins that Tillich 'has an underlying faith in the rationality of things in general which his strong dash of existentialism does nothing to negate'.[15]

Not surprisingly, Tillich will have nothing to do with any Barthian or quasi-Barthian dissociation of theology from philosophy — not least because he does not wish to fall into the trap of psychologism. He is an essentialist, and while he can detect similarities between his 'ultimate concern' and Schleiermacher's 'feeling of absolute dependence'; and his defence of Schleiermacher against the 'mistaken and unfair' charge of psychologism notwithstanding, he does think that Schleiermacher's emphasis upon the religious consciousness was too great. This does not, he thinks, justify the neo-orthodox theologians in turning their backs upon Schleiermacher. Theology can retreat neither into the Word nor into the emotions; there must be some contact with reason, with philosophy.

Tillich finds that philosophy raises the existential question of being to which theology supplies the answer. It must be said, however, that his way of making out his case is ambivalent if not actually inconsistent. He wishes to deny the inevitability of conflict between philosophy and theology, and one of the ways in which he does this is to claim that 'A conflict presupposes a common basis on which to fight. But there is no common basis between theology and philosophy' (I, 26). J. Heywood Thomas, in his *Paul Tillich: An Appraisal* (1963), rightly queries this statement on the ground that if the theologian claims *knowledge* of God the philosopher cannot be blamed for thinking that a term is being used in which he might be expected to have an interest (44). Again, if what Tillich here declares represents his considered judgement, what of his claim made elsewhere to the effect that both theologian and philosopher treat of 'ultimate concern'?[16] Finally, if the ultimate concern of the theologian is faith — as it is said to be — and if the ultimate concern of the philosopher is being itself, how, apart from a common basis, can they comprise one another — as they are said to do?[17] In a word, if there is no common basis, what price correlation?

From Tillich's point of view as an exponent of the method of correlation, 'Natural theology was meaningful to the extent that it gave an analysis of the human situation and the question of God implied in it' (II, 14). The existential-philosophical question is raised by man's experience of finitude; man is surrounded by non-being, hence his ultimate concern. Now the method of correlation 'tries to correlate the questions implied in the situation with the answers implied in the [Christian] message' (I, 8). The answers are given to man's reason by revelation (and at this point Tillich is closest to the neo-orthodox), though not in such a way as to remove all doubt. Still less are they given in such a way that God himself becomes an object. That can never be. He is not *a* being, he is Being itself. To deny this is to indulge in idolatry.

One of the difficulties attaching to the method of correlation is that what emerges is governed by what is put in. Tillich says, for example, that humans are overtaken by 'ontic shock'. But what if *moral* shock, the consciousness of sin and guilt before a holy God, is a man's concern? His answers will presumably differ from those of his ontically shocked neighbour. Further, no matter what the variety of the shock, the truth of the answers is by no means guaranteed. It does rather seem, as some have complained, that we are urged to accept both Tillich's diagnosis and Tillich's answers on the authority of none other than Tillich himself. It has been well said that 'No amount of protesting that the content of the theological answer is given in revelation can remove the offence of regarding theology as having merely the value of providing us with answers to *our* questions instead of being the light that lightens our feet so that even the question is given.'[18]

For all the weight he attaches to it, the method of correlation is not the starting point for his thought — as he himself admits: the 'method is derived from a prior knowledge of the system which is to be built by the method' (I, 60). The theologian can do nothing about the question posed to him by the philosopher, however much it might strait-jacket him. And the system to which all is subservient is idealistic.

God, for Tillich, is the ground of being. In true post-Kantian fashion he teaches that man is surrounded by impenetrable mystery. It is not that man can have only partial knowledge of God; it is not that the historic incarnation and atonement are mysteries which the human mind can never fully fathom. Rather, we have left history behind, and are haltingly contemplating the mystery of being itself. God must never be objectified; though personal, he is not *a* person (I, 245). We may learn from pantheism, provided that we do not make the mistake of identifying God with the world, for this would be idolatrous. In Tillich's opinion traditional theists had brought about the entirely appropriate reaction of atheism, because they had failed to see that it is the God 'above the God of theism' who must be affirmed. Hence, in his now famous phrase, 'It is as atheistic to affirm the existence of theism's God as it is to deny it' (I, 237).

The upshot is that in Tillich's view religious assertions are symbolic. (Whereas at first he said that the statement 'God is Being-itself' was the only non-symbolic statement we might make concerning God, he later declared that the assertion 'Everything we say about God is symbolic' was non-symbolic too (Cf. I, 238-9 with II, 9). He denied that symbols are signs, for unlike signs symbols participate in the reality to which they point (though how they do this is not made clear). I cannot resist the conclusion that this is but a stipulation on Tillich's part which does nothing to make the reality of God any more accessible. Moreover, if that to which our symbols point is absolutely other, and thus beyond our comprehension, how shall we discover what symbols are adequate, or how far our symbols conduce to a true knowledge of that to which they point? Tillich is not the only one to whom this question may be addressed, as we shall see.

Willem F. Zuurdeeg

Zuurdeeg's book, *An Analytical Philosophy of Religion* was widely reviewed when it appeared in Britain in 1959. Zuurdeeg sets out to analyse religious discourse having regard to the existential context from which it takes its rise.

'I. The analytical method is a most appropriate approach in philosophy of religion
  (a) in its conception of philosophy of religion as analysis of language, and

(b) in its disqualification of metaphysics and ontology.
II. The analytical approach to language, in the case of religious and similar languages, has to be qualified by an account of the language situation, to which belong:
   (a) the person who communicates
   (b) the community within which the language functions
   (c) the (subjectively) objective references of the languages
   (d) the 'worlds' within which these elements are related
   (e) the historical backgrounds of these elements.' (17)

Religious language is convictional language. It differs from the indicative language of science, and from the tautological language of mathematics. It is used by 'man who speaks'. We cannot overlook his situation in our analyses. Indeed, it is in speaking that man establishes himself as an existing person.

Most reviewers found Zuurdeeg's work suggestive — even, owing to its non-insularity, refreshing (though none that I could find applauded, though some were repelled by, his diagrams). But John Hick posed the fundamental question in his review (*SJT*, XIII, 1960, 314). Hick rightly sees that Zuurdeeg's analysis raises the question, 'Is religion anything more than a device by which the human animal enables himself to feel at home in the Universe?' Yet this question cannot arise within philosophy's confines as marked out by Zuurdeeg. Nevertheless, he implicitly prejudges the answer to it by his 'crucial assumption that convictional statements are non-cognitive (or non-indicative), and therefore neither true nor false'.

The pros and cons of linguistic analysis

Returning now to the existentially innocent analysis of the British we find that Ernest Gellner's book *Words and Things* (1959, 1979 rev. edn) dropped like a boulder into the philosophic millpond, and that the resulting ripples are just as interesting as the boulder itself. First, the boulder:

> Many professional philosophers — particularly among those who have embraced Wittgensteinian Linguistic Philosophy — are alienated from natural and social science (and hence from the exciting areas of intellectual advance), and are not deeply or originally involved in substantive moral, political and social issues. If philosophy were substantive, they would

have to concede that they are not fit to be good practitioners of it: if, on the contrary, philosophy is shown to be essentially formal, second-order, unsubstantive, this could hardly be more convenient. Linguistic Philosophy can be seen to provide a realm and an activity for philosophers tailor-made for the requirements of some of the people who find themselves inheriting the task of teaching philosophy in the universities: a *neutral* realm, from which no guidance and no commitment on substantive issues is required; a *verbal* realm, which can be studied from the armchair without at the same time making any implausible claims to transcendental insights or faculties; a *conservative* realm, in which no surprising objects or conclusions can be found; and a *polymorphic* realm, in which no daring generalizations are allowed either and in which there is ample scope for continued, *minute* research. (153)

Now the ripples: W.C. Kneale, who quotes the above passage in his review of Gellner's book, cautions us against receiving the impression that Gellner believes that there is an entirely homogeneous phenomenon called 'Linguistic Philosophy'. At the same time, however, Kneale confesses that 'there are individuals and coteries who hold the views he describes and behave in a way that justifies his irritation' (*HJ*, LVIII, 1959–60, 197). Kneale concludes that

Most readers will find Mr. Gellner's book amusing, but it is a safe bet that some of those who are criticised will be angered and that they will accuse the author not only of misrepresentation but also of malevolence and bad taste . . . Although it may generate *odium philosophicum*, this will not be altogether a bad thing if it leads Linguistic Philosophers to that explicit formulation of doctrines and programmes which is what Mr. Gellner rightly demands. (198)

That Kneale was no mean prophet may be confirmed by a glance at Michael Dummett's 'Oxford philosophy', wherein the anticipated charge of misrepresentation and the flush of anger are clearly seen. As to the former, Dummett points out that the positivists, Wittgenstein and the ordinary language philosophers all had different theories of meaning, so that Gellner 'makes a fearful hash of expounding "the" theory of meaning which they all hold in common' (*B*, XLI, 1960, 78–9). As for anger, Dummett complains that Gellner's book 'does not even have the smell of honest or seriously intentioned work' (80). From his somewhat more neutral position, and in a decidedly more temperate manner, Fr. Copleston (*Hey J*, I, 1960, 155-7) suspects that Gellner was wise not to be too positive in his work; had he been more positive some would have taken refuge in attacking him instead of taking adequate account of his attacks upon them! He also felt that it ill-behoved analytical philosophers to complain that Gellner had attacked a man of straw when some of them had been attacking metaphysical men of straw for years. We need stay no longer with this squabble — except to say that with hindsight it appears that the significance of Gellner's book was that it challenged the more precious types of analytical philosophy, and that it was written by one who could not be brushed aside as either an 'old-fashioned idealist' or a 'theological philosopher'.

In his Inaugural Lecture delivered before the University of Oxford, *Philosophy and Language* (1960), A.J. Ayer turns his attention to that department of analytical philosophy which is concerned with ordinary language. He reminds us that most philosophers would now agree that philosophy is, in some special sense, an inquiry into language; it is talk about talk; it is a second-order subject, concerned not with describing, explaining or changing the world, but with the language we use in speaking about the world. He outlines the development and sketches the diversity of linguistic philosophy, and then concentrates upon the inability of ordinary language philosophy to untangle muddled reasoning. For example,

> It has indeed been claimed that examining the use of words like 'inadvertently', 'deliberately', 'mistakenly', 'intentionally', would help us to deal more effectively with the problem of free-will, perhaps even to dispose of the problem altogether. The idea is that we can learn in this way what are the circumstances in which we credit people with responsibility for their acts and on what grounds we are ready to absolve them; and it is agreed that the extent to which they are responsible is the measure of the extent to which they are free. But while this is, no doubt, a useful way of making clear how we do in fact proceed with the ascription of responsibility, it touches only lightly on the problem of free-will. For those who are troubled by this problem are perfectly well aware that we are in fact trained to distinguish between the cases in which an agent can 'help himself', and those in which he cannot.

Their trouble is that they do not see how this distinction can be justified. If all human actions are causally explicable, is there not a very good sense in which no one can help doing what he does? Now it may well be that this reasoning is muddled; and if so that muddle can be shown up. But then some other method must be chosen; it is no answer to the denier of free-will merely to pin-point ways of using language in which the falsity of his position is already presupposed. (17-18)

Ayer avers that the basic trouble with the ordinary language approach is that those who use it forget that there is no sharp dividing line between the description of facts and their interpretation: 'even at the level of common sense our ordinary language will be found to carry a considerable load of theory' (18). Ayer goes so far as to say that the emphasis in current philosophy upon fact as opposed to theory has been too great: 'Too often, the claim to dispense with theory is a way of masking assumptions which, whatever their merit, had better be brought into the open. But, apart from this, the distrust which is rightly felt for speculative metaphysics is not a sufficient ground for limiting the scale of philosophical analysis' (32). Ayer pleads for the application of analytical techniques to the architectonic features of our conceptual system, and in this connection welcomes P.F. Strawson's *Individuals* (1959) and Stuart Hampshire's *Thought and Action* (1959). Such work is 'the best way of preserving analytical philosophy from the scholasticism which has been threatening to overtake it' (35).

In his paper, 'A school for philosophers', R.M. Hare seeks to soften the distinction between linguistic philosophy and other kinds of philosophy. He describes the manner in which philosophy is taught at Oxford, claiming that the bias towards everyday language results from the fact that 'our dealings with our pupils have shown us that it is in the passage from everyday language to technical language that all the most vexatious problems of philosophy have their origin' (*R*, II, 1959-60, 113). Lest any of his hearers (the original version of this paper was given in Germany) should infer from this that metaphysics as such is beyond the pale at Oxford, Hare explains that 'we *do* metaphysics at Oxford; but we *call* it something else — usually "logic" in an eccentrically wide use of the word' (115). He concludes that the subject matter of linguistic philosophy is not clearly divided from that of other kinds of philosophy; that linguistic philosophy is simply philosophy done with a proper awareness of the pitfalls of language; and that what Oxford philosophers share are not tenets so much as standards.

In his article, 'Mr. Hare's paper: A rejoinder' (*R*, III, 1960-1), E.W.F. Tomlin showed that while he was in general sympathy with Hare's position he was not entirely convinced by his case. He thinks it misleading to suggest that metaphysics in the traditional sense is done at Oxford; he warns of the dangers of provincialism — papers written by and for those who know each other; and he advises that the philosopher leave his ivory tower from time to time lest reflection upon the nature and meaning of existence be left to the charlatan and the crank: 'It is a melancholy reflection that the dominance of linguistic philosophy for so many years had not lessened but rather increased the spread of that "propaganda of irrationalism" which R.G. Collingwood, much to the scandal of his fellow-thinkers, held to be promoted by nothing so much as the methods of linguistic philosophy itself' (8).

From his greater geographical and temperamental distance T.M. Knox is even less content to regard linguistic philosophy as a panacea. He insists, in a paper entitled 'Two conceptions of philosophy' (*P*, XXXVI, 1961), that the philosopher cannot keep his own self as historical individual out of his philosophising. This is not to say that philosophy is autobiography, but merely to recognise that we cannot enter into the spirit of a man's work without understanding something of its personal setting. Knox would regard it as legitimate for a philosopher to be interested in justice — not merely the word 'justice' — but justice conceived as an objective fact; and it is this kind of interest which provokes his complaint against the linguistic philosopher who denies, or ignores, such facts — 'and this . . . not at the end of his philosophising but at or even before its start' (298). Nor is Knox's anguish assuaged by those who suggest that linguistic philosophy is not necessarily the foe even of theology. In this connection he refers to H.A. Hodges (in *Contemporary British Philosophy*, ed. H.D. Lewis, 1956, 217), who argues that God is no more the direct concern of the philosopher than matter and energy are, and that in either case the philosopher's task is to examine the language employed. Knox regards this as a drastic limitation of the philosopher's role, for it implies that

> The whole realm of fact is to be handed over to science; but there is another realm, the spiritual world which is for similar reasons to be handed over to theology . . . Philosophy has

no warrant to interfere with either, but only with the varying ways of talking about both. This means that dogmatic theology is to pursue its way uncriticised by philosophy; philosophy may concern itself with clarifying what is said by theologians but never with criticising its dogmas. This implies that philosophy is to accept the scientific dogma so far as the natural world is concerned, and the theological dogma so far as the supernatural world is concerned. In either case metaphysics is dead. (305-6)

H.D. Lewis, in his preface to the collection *Clarity is Not Enough* (1963), shows that he is less suspicious of linguistic philosophy than Knox, and that he is equally hopeful of a return to metaphysics:

There has been much talk of late of a return to metaphysics. This I, for one, very much welcome. But we have also to be exceptionally careful to ensure that it is the right sort of return. No one wants to revive the absurdities, the vagueness and allusiveness and the irresponsible play with metaphors which brought much metaphysics in the past into ill repute and provoked very sharp reactions in our time. (10)

W.H. Walsh went further in the same year by publishing a whole book on the once scorned pursuit, *Metaphysics* (1963). He underlines the contentions formulated earlier by such philosophers as Miss Emmet, that the metaphysician is a committed man — he is committed to a set of categorical principles, the denial of which he would regard as absurd. But this absurdity is not a formal absurdity, for the principles are not *logically* compelling. Walsh has no illusions about the difficulty of the metaphysician's task; it is to try to give a connected account of the world as a whole, and this in such a way that both the metaphysician *and* experts in the several fields of enquiry are satisfied that the facts of experience have been adequately accounted for. Like Lewis, Walsh would learn from the analysts, criticising them only for their exclusiveness, and he concluded that the contrast between metaphysics and analysis is overdrawn: 'One can perhaps occupy oneself with problems of analysis without beating a metaphysical drum, or at least without beating one very loudly: but there is no clear dividing line between the two activities, for metaphysicians necessarily engage in analysis whilst analytical philosophers tend to make covert metaphysical assumptions' (194).

Analytical philosophy of religion

We come now to the successors of those philosophers of religion mentioned earlier who found that a general sympathy with, or at least interest in, analytical philosophy provided a platform upon which many philosophers from diverse 'confessional' backgrounds might meet.

For an example of Anglican philosophy of religion in this style we may turn to the symposium *Faith and Logic* (1957), edited by Basil Mitchell. In the introduction Mitchell describes briefly how the analytical approach has superseded the earlier and more dogmatic positivism of the 1930s, and explains that philosophers who approach theological questions from the standpoint of analytical philosophy will tend to adopt the following stances:

(1) They will not, as did the Idealists, put forward (at least explicitly) a world-view or philosophy of life, which might conflict with Christianity; because they regard the development of such world-views as no part of the philosopher's business.

(2) They will not (at least they should not) rule out theological statements from the start on the ground that they are meaningless, as the Logical Positivists did.

(3) They will ask the same sort of questions about theological statements as they do about statements of other kinds, viz. 'How are they verified?' 'What sort of arguments or observations tend to confirm or refute them?' In short, 'What is their logic?' (5)

The policy adumbrated under (3) is pursued with reference to the possibility of theological statements (I.M. Crombie), and to such concepts as the soul (J.R. Lucas) and the grace of God (B. Mitchell).

By far the most sustained application of the techniques of linguistic analysis to religious discourse is that provided by Ian Ramsey in a series of books: *Religious Language* (1957); *Freedom and Immortality* (1960); and *Christian Discourse* (1965). Ramsey is persuaded that the methods of logical empiricism can provide a useful way of dealing with certain religious problems, and that the analysis of religious language can do theology nothing but good. His case is that the purpose of religious language is to evoke a situation which involves the discernment of something which is spatio-temporal *and more*. The final outcome will be a 'cosmic disclosure' which prompts total commitment to the whole universe. In working out his theory Ramsey introduces us to models and qualifiers. A model is that which grounds a theological story in empirical fact, while a qualifier both develops the model in a certain direction until 'the penny drops' or 'the ice breaks' — a disclosure takes place — and then claims an appropriate, logically odd, placing for the word 'God'.

Ramsey examines the attributes of negative theology — 'immutable', 'impassible'; the characterisation of God by 'Unity', 'Simplicity' and 'Perfection'; and such other characterizations as '*First* CAUSE', and '*Infinitely* WISE' — with a view to showing how words work that profess to speak of God and his attributes. Thus, for example, in 'Infinitely wise' the word 'wise' names a model situation. We can root it empirically by thinking of a third-form boy who is 'scarcely wise', the sixth-form prefect who is 'rather wise' — and so on; and we see that however wise a person is it is always possible that there is a wiser person or a greater wisdom. Enter the qualifier, 'infinitely', which develops the model in a particular direction until the 'penny drops' and we 'see' the point of the reference to One who is the fount of all wisdom. At this point the qualifier is claiming for 'God' a distinctive logical placing — it presides over the whole of whatever languages express wisdom.

Ramsey applied his technique in a number of directions — to biblical and doctrinal language in *Religious Language*, to ethical and eschatological language in *Freedom and Immortality*, and again to biblical language and also to atonement theology and the *Honest to God* debate in *Christian Discourse*. His work is highly stimulating, and there can be no doubt that he treats of language which believers would regard as genuinely *theirs*. Nevertheless he failed to satisfy philosophical and theological colleagues at certain points.

Some have detected a pull towards undue subjectivism in Ramsey's writings, which results from his desire to provide firm empirical anchorage for religious discourse. That he himself was aware of the pitfall is clear from this passage in *Religious Language*:

> There is no question of a characteristically religious situation being merely 'emotional', if that word is thought to claim that the characteristic features we have been mentioning are entirely (in some sense or other) 'subjective'. Let us emphasize, without any possibility of misunderstanding that all these situations, all these characteristically different situations when they occur, have an *objective* reference and are, as all situations, *subject-object* in structure. When situations 'come alive', or the 'ice breaks', there is objective 'depth' in these

situations along with and alongside any subjective changes. (27-8)

It is clear from this both that Ramsey does not wish to be a mere subjectivist, and that we have only his assurance that things are as he says they are. He does not, therefore, answer the possible charge of psychologism; and when he came to concentrate upon 'I' as a model which was so appropriately odd that it could be taken as an analogue for 'God' he was, in the opinion of some critics, bordering upon a Cartesian autonomy of thought which would make it even more difficult to conceive of God (minus inverted commas) — that is, of God as an ontological reality over against the individual.[19] As D.D. Evans has so strongly argued in *The Logic of Self-Involvement* (1963), 'Questions of theological truth are not replaceable by questions concerning the internal logical "grammar" of biblical [or, I would add, of religious] language' (24). W.D. Hudson raised an associated difficulty when he wondered how far 'cosmic' disclosures' can be shown to constitute grounds for a claim to objective knowledge: 'We cannot predict their occurrence and so the test of predictive reliability — so fundamental to any claim to scientific knowledge — is excluded. Can the concepts of "objectivity", "reality", "knowledge" make sense in the absence of predictive reliability?' (*T*, LXVIII, 1965, 535).

A number of reviewers of Ramsey's work wondered whether he had adequately analysed the nature of the discernment which, he says, characterises the religious situation. J. Macquarrie, for example, suggested that the metaphor of dropping pennies needs much qualification before it can be applied to what older theologians spoke of as the 'inward testimony of the Holy Spirit' (*ET*, LXIX, 1957-8, 140); and R.N. Smart was concerned by the dubious immunity purchased for religious discourse by Ramsey. On Ramsey's account, he said, religious statements are unfalsifiable because the fact that the penny has yet to drop for a person is no guarantee that it will not drop. Smart allowed that this kind of unfalsifiability may be native to religion, but still wondered what would count for or against one set of doctrines rather than another (*PQ*, X, 1960, 93-4). — a question also raised by H.D. Lewis (*P*, XXXIV, 1959, 266-7).

The radically empiricist approach of T.R. Miles in his *Religion and the Scientific Outlook* (1959) brings us no nearer an answer to this question. Miles argues that empirical statements alone are factually significant. Hence, the language of 'literal theism' — for example,

'God walked in the garden' taken literally, is excluded. Also excluded is the language of 'qualified literal theism' — for example, 'it was God — but not a visible God . . . ' Miles maintains that the only solution open to the Christian is to qualify his otherwise unavoidable silence by the use of parables. Ronald W. Hepburn is among others who seek to show the parabolic significance, though not the literal meaningfulness, of religious assertions. In his contribution to *Metaphysical Beliefs* (ed. A. MacIntyre, 1957) entitled 'Poetry and religious belief' he suggests that from a consideration of poetic imagery we may see why metaphysical and religious concepts retain their momentousness and solemnity even after their literal significance has been exploded. This is by no means to justify the use of religious language, still less to reinstate a defensible apologetic; but it is to show that 'the theologian need not despair of the sense of his expressions on the sole score of their violation of ordinary language. For such deviations are the staple of poetic inventiveness' (1970 edn, 155). In his *Christianity and Paradox* (1958) Hepburn refines the approach to religious statements adopted by Braithwaite who, we recall, regarded such statements as morality-supporting stories. Hepburn agrees so far, but adds that the parables (his word) must be *adequate* to command the believer's supreme loyalty; they must determine 'his total imaginative vision of nature and man' (195).

In a paper entitled, 'Religious assertions in the light of contemporary philosophy' (*P*, XXXII, 1957, 206 ff.) A.C. Ewing criticises Braithwaite in some detail, but also, by implication, replies to Hepburn. He states the point he challenges thus: 'it has been suggested that what religion does is, like poetry, just express certain more or less emotional states of mind which need have no more objective or intellectual basis than the poet's delight at kinship with nature on a sunny day or the awe he may feel at the sight of storm-capped mountains' (207). Against this, Ewing urges (a) that emotion (except in pathological cases and perhaps even then)

> requires some objective belief, true or false, about the real to support it for long, and if it exists without knowledge or a rationally founded objective belief with which it is in agreement, it is to be condemned as irrational and unfitting . . . if there is no warrant for thinking that the world is really controlled for the best, the feeling of security and peace which a religious man has can only be described as the enjoyment of a fool's paradise.

(b) According to all highly developed religions it is very evil to worship what is not worthy of worship. Yet if there is thought to be no objective justification for belief in God all worship of God becomes idolatory. Nor is it easy to see how a religious attitude could long survive the conviction that reality is not such as to warrant it. (208)

It is interesting in passing to note that from D.J. O'Connor there comes a warning addressed in the first place to the contributors to *Metaphysical Beliefs* — S.E. Toulmin, R.W. Hepburn and A.C. MacIntyre — but applicable to all philosophers who might be tempted along a somewhat sentimental path:

The danger of the new fashionable 'Let's not be beastly to metaphysics' movement is that it encourages the growth of irrationalism in philosophy. Philosophy is nothing if it is not an exercise of reason. It is not a matter for 'sensitivity' or 'imagination' or any of the other nebulous and euphemistic disguises for intellectual muzziness.

O'Connor is wary of these writers'

habit of decorating their essays with quotations from Donne, Eliot, Leopardi, Proust, Mrs. V. Woolf and the rest of the cultural circus of the day. As models of philosophical writing, Aquinas, Spinoza, Russell or Carnap are perhaps a little austere for present tastes. But at least they give no encouragement to confuse philosophy with belles lettres. (*P*, XXXIV, 1959, 56)

But if T.R. Miles leaves us with silence qualified by parables, and if R.W. Hepburn resorts to parables of importance, G.F. Woods and Gordon Kaufman continue to seek ways of rehabilitating religious language as meaningful by elucidating its empirical anchorage. Woods develops his theme in his careful work *Theological Explanation* (1958), and in his paper 'The idea of the transcendent' (in *Soundings*, ed. A.R. Vidler, 1962). He grants that if the transcendent is defined as that which lies outside of human experience, then it can never be experienced. But he disallows this definition, and finds no justification for the assertion that the transcendent is what we can never understand. By means of analogical explanation, based upon our experience of self-transcendence, and of being transcended by beings other than ourselves, he comes to the view that the problems of transcendence are the problems of being. It is not suggested, of course, that the divine being needs something to transcend in order to be; but

> In our experience of the changing, we have also a curious experience of the unchanging. I believe that we are gradually driven towards an awareness of some being, which is variously styled pure, absolute, or transcendent. The conclusion is being itself. It is difficult to say whether one experiences this pure being or whether more usually one experiences being transcended by it. (*art. cit.*, 63)

The last sentence here reiterates what Woods had said two pages earlier, and I feel that he is hovering on the brink of an appeal to revelation, yet fears to take the plunge. Accordingly I sympathise with his pupil Rupert Hoare who, in 'The idea of the transcendent: G.F. Woods as a theological teacher' (*T*, LXX, 1967), questioned whether the move from our experience of other human beings to being itself was legitimate, and who regretted that Woods excluded a Christocentric base for language concerning the 'other' with whom we have to do: 'It is the changelessness of God's love as revealed in Christ that is best described by the analogy of transcendence' (402).

In his article 'On the meaning of "God": transcendence without mythology' (*HTR*, LIX, 1966), Kaufman likewise seeks to provide empirical anchorage for the concept of transcendence, maintaining that 'our speech about this Other arises because certain features of experience force us up against the limit(s) of all possible knowledge and experience' (112). In terminology which, though ethical rather than ontological, is not far removed from that of Woods, he holds that 'Talk about God appears when the ultimate Limit is understood on analogy with the experience of *personal limiting* as known in the intercourse and interaction of personal wills' (122). Kaufman's objective is to show how the cognitive *meaningfulness* of religious language may be defended. As to its *truth*,

> Only on the ground that God had in fact revealed himself could it be claimed that he exists; only if there were and is some sort of movement from beyond the Limit to us, making known to us through the medium of the Limit the reality of that which lies beyond, could we be in a position to speak of such reality at all; only if God actually 'spoke' to man could we know there is a God. (132)

Here once again is the question of the transcendent's self-revelation; and bound up with this is the question of authority. Kaufman takes more account than Woods of the fact that apart from an authoritative revelation we cannot (dare I say it!) get airborne. Moreover, the revelation we need must be one which confronts us in history — how otherwise could it be revelation to man?

Empirically grounded though Ramsey, Woods and Kaufman sought to be, they by no means placed a dogmatic embargo against metaphysical questions. Indeed, Ramsey edited a book, *Prospect for Metaphysics* (1961), in which philosophers from a number of backgrounds found continuing life in the metaphysical bones. Ramsey reminds us that whereas 25 years ago 'metaphysics was no more than a topic for ridicule and abuse', now a broader empiricism leaves room for significant metaphysical discourse, so that the questions to be answered are, 'Is the time now ripe to take measure of what for some twenty-five years has been a challenge to metaphysics? Are we able to face squarely this critical and empirical challenge and yet to say something positive and constructive in support of metaphysics?' (7). The authors of the several papers hold in common the view that natural theology can no longer be regarded as a 'tight, rigorous, deductive system, taking us to God by a process of unmistakeable inference' (7), but they are equally convinced that irrationalism is not the only viable alternative to this. In so far as the symposiasts reach any shared conclusions they are that some kind of 'intuition' is the foundation-stone of any empirically based metaphysical theology, and that 'the aim of a metaphysical philosophy should be to cultivate a reasonable currency for, and a due appreciation of, "mysteries". In doing this it will somehow relate and bring together, in all their variegation, many diverse ways of reliable reasoning' (11).

Among the most suggestive papers in the symposium is that by Howard Root, 'Metaphysical and religious belief'. He discusses *inter alia* MacIntyre's contribution to *Metaphysical Beliefs*, 'The logical status of religious beliefs' — an essay which is among the most antimetaphysical of all writings from the pens of philosophers of religion in the decade with which we are here concerned. MacIntyre argues that a man becomes a believer by conversion; there can be no arguments for belief, and to suggest otherwise is to destroy the essential nature of religion. (It is only proper to point out that in the 1970 edition of *Metaphysical Beliefs* MacIntyre admits to blemishes in his earlier work. Whereas in the original paper 'Christianity, as I defend it here, becomes a belief which is in practice irrefutable at the cost of becoming a belief that is in practice vacuous', he has since come to see that since traditional Christianity is not vacuous, and 'does claim in unambiguous terms to be true', 'the philosophy of religion of my essay is . . . inconsistent with the faith it tried to elucidate' (xi).) Against the early MacIntyre Root points out that people do lose faith — are we to say that they were never believers really because their faith was not permanent? Root wishes to maintain that there may be good reasons for belief, though he is careful to distinguish between rational grounds and constraint:

> Such reasons are of various types; they do not fit neatly together into any unified system. They may be moral or aesthetic, or even scientific. We elaborate them sometimes for apologetic purposes, sometimes simply to satisfy our own minds that our particular theology deserves continued belief . . . If we continue to say that there are reasons for accepting one set of beliefs rather than another, we are so far committed to something which I should call metaphysics. But it will have to be a metaphysics which can somehow do justice not only to our desire for a Natural Theology but also to our religiously inspired distrust of Natural Theology. Just what it would look like is very much worth finding out. (79)

Root continues the search for such a metaphysic in his essay, 'Beginning all over again' (in *Soundings*, ed. A.R. Vidler, 1963). He paints a picture of an uneasy relationship between philosophy and theology. The lot of the philosophical theologian is unhappiest of all, for both theologians and philosophers are suspicious of him; the former, because metaphysics has a way of seeking to accommodate Christian truth to its own cherished systems, the latter, because apologetics are suspect. Despite the difficulties of his vocation, however, Root urges the philosophical theologian to stick to his guns, not merely so that natural theology may be defended for its own sake, but because 'Christian theology without metaphysics (that is, for our purposes, natural theology) is an illusion' (13); and because in any case, 'Metaphysical construction, crude or polished, is natural to human beings' (14). The task of natural theology is to show the grounds for placing reliance upon the Christian world view, and Root is hard put to understand why theologians should scorn such a discipline: 'If natural theology is out of court and there is no appeal to metaphysical reasoning, what rational basis can there be for opposing, say, the most illiterate varieties of fundamentalism?'

(14). When biblical theologians, by appealing to revelation, place themselves beyond the reach of rational argument, 'they invite all the terrors which they, of all men, have most reason to fear. In abandoning natural theology they have lost the only weapon which could ward off their adversaries' (15). Not indeed that all is well with natural theology. Root feels that for too long the medieval approach to the subject has been confused with the subject itself, and he suggests that the remedy lies in natural theology's taking seriously the principle of Incarnation. It must begin with the real world as we know it now — not with the world as St Thomas Aquinas knew it. We must turn to those areas where we find 'faithful, stimulating, profound accounts of what it is to be alive in the twentieth century'. We look, in short, to creative works of art. These will nourish a viable and relevant natural theology.

I am not aware that D.J. O'Connor responded to this proposal in print, but E.L. Mascall certainly did. In his *Up and Down in Adria* (1963) he wrote, 'I should myself find Mr. Root's programme exciting if he had given us any clear indication of what it involved and what principles of discrimination it proposed to apply' (23). Again, 'I suspect that our failure has lain not in insulating ourselves against the questions, or in failing to contemplate and absorb the disturbing visions of modern literature, but in failing to contemplate and absorb the inspiring visions and profound truths of the Christian relevation' (24).

Returning once more to Ramsey's symposium, we are not in the least surprised to find D.J.B. Hawkins on the side of those who would reinstate and strengthen metaphysics. He shows himself well aware of the confusions which render traditional metaphysics unsatisfactory as a final resting-place, and his empirical approach emerges as clearly as that of any of the other symposiasts:

> We must not be bogged down in a thought-world tenanted by universals rather than by things. Otherwise we shall be tempted to suppose that the *being* with which ontology deals is a portmanteau-term covering the real, the merely possible and the merely logical. There is no such unitary concept; there are only the analogies by which we are led to think of the merely possible and the merely logical through their relationship to the real. The primary object of the metaphysician, as it is the primary object of thought in general, is the real in the sense of the existent singular . . . The fundamental task . . . is to recall philosophy to attempting a systematic account

of the problems of being on a clear empirical foundation . . . the anti-metaphysical tendencies in modern philosophy have not been a protest of experience in its purity against the vagaries of the *a priori* but the result of an undue impoverishment of the scope and power of human experience and thinking. (119-20)

This last point echoes what Hawkins had earlier written in his *Crucial Problems of Modern Philosophy* (1957): 'The problem of being and the problem of substance and attribute arise as directly out of our ordinary experience as they are clearly enshrined in the structure of our ordinary language . . . What we need is an empiricism which does justice to the whole of experience, an empirical approach to metaphysics and a consequent renewal of metaphysical thinking upon more completely explored epistemological foundations' (133-4). With this F.C. Copleston agrees, as may be seen from his series of five articles entitled, 'Man and metaphysics' (*HeyJ*, I and II, 1960-1). He argues as follows:

That man can raise *metaphysical* questions or problems is due to his capacity to stand back from or out of the world . . . But that he raises metaphysical *questions* which have the empirically given as their point of departure is due to his involvement in the world, to his nature as embodied or incarnate spirit. (I, 111)

As well as observing how philosophers of religion adjusted themselves to analytical philosophy on the one hand and metaphysics on the other, we have made reference to such specific issues as the meaningfulness or otherwise of religious assertions, the notion of transcendence, and the device of analogy. There are, however, two further matters to which I should like briefly to draw attention: 'mystery' and 'encounter'.

Two writers in particular discussed the concept of mystery during the period under review. In *God and Mystery* (1957) Michael B. Foster grants that he knows no philosophical method other than the analytical. He nevertheless feels that the analysts have wrongly assumed that everything that can properly be said can be said clearly; and they have been so wedded to the view that all philosophical thinking consists in solving problems that they have overlooked the claim which he himself wishes to make good, namely, that 'there is another kind of thinking which depends on the revealing of a mystery' (18). Foster argues that this revelation takes place *via* the medium of language, and that faith is the appropriate response to it. It is not that by faith we discover truths supplementary to, and similar in kind to, those of science. Rather, faith 'is directed upon mystery, as revelation springs from mystery, and as prayer seems properly to be directed upon mysterious objects' (94). Confronted by Foster's work I.T. Ramsey was left wondering what *understanding* can be had of a mystery? How, and using what logical rules, can we talk about mystery? (*HJ*, LV, 1956-7, 415).

H.D. Lewis writes on 'Belief and mystery' in his book, *Our Experience of God* (1959). He says that the traditional arguments for the existence of God fail because they 'break into a series of steps what is in fact one insight', and because they seek 'to start from purely finite factors and reason to conclusions about the infinite' (41). His case is that 'at the very heart of religion lies this quite unique notion of something of which we cannot conceive at all without seeing at the same time that it must be' (44). Though elusive, this insight 'has the same compelling character as the apprehensions we have in logic or mathematics' (47). The upshot is that 'There is then a sense in which God is not known by evidence, and in which the reply to those who ask us "What would need to be different for your belief not to be true?" must be "nothing". But there is a sense also in which we have abundant evidence of what God is like and what He does' (59).

Lewis makes it clear that he is not concerned to build an *argument* for God's existence on religious experience; that he does not think that religious experience is a matter of such literal union with God as would entail the supersession of the limitations of our finite nature; and that we cannot reach a religious view by reflecting on 'the human situation'. Above all, he does not think that our having or not having a religious approach to the world is determined by the way in which we view matters which are in themselves neutral. Rather, the religious man sees something *different*. In fact he becomes aware of transcendent being, of God: 'all existence as we know it stands in a relation of dependence to some absolute or unconditioned being of which we can know nothing directly beyond this intuition of its unconditioned nature as the source of all other reality' (107).

This last point is developed by Lewis in his contribution to *Prospect for Metaphysics*, 'God and mystery': 'The point that most needs to be stressed is the quite radical character of the difference between the idea of God and any other idea we may entertain' (207). Thus,

God 'is "other" not merely in the sense in which we are so to each other, but in the sense that we cannot know at all what it is to be God. The mystery is *total*' (218). Despite this, the Christian makes some very bold affirmations about God. This he is able to do because 'we know and do not know at the same time, or know without knowing what we know. The religious apologist must just not be daunted by this paradox, but rather realize how essential it is to maintain it and to indicate how it should be taken' (234).

In his lucid and comprehensive Teach Yourself book on *Philosophy of Religion* (1965) Lewis confronts the question which Ramsey directed to Foster. Lewis phrases the question thus: 'if God is as incomprehensible to us as religious thought and religious experience and prophecy alike make Him out to be, if He is essentially hidden and invisible, how do we come to make such intimate claims about Him as we do in much of our religious life and worship?' (155). The crux of his answer is that in revelation God makes himself known, and here 'The reference is to a mystery which we cannot fathom but the counters or notation, as it were, are not elusive or strange; they are drawn from the content of common experience. God thus makes Himself known within the world or within the lives of men' (227).

Thus in a number of works, and by means of the analysis of finite experience, Lewis seeks to make good the claim to our awareness of a unique mystery. But how, asked N.H.G. Robinson in his review of *Our Experience of God*, from such a base can we *justify* the claim to uniqueness? If there is no religious norm at the beginning, how can there be one at the end? (*PQ*, XII, 1962, 94-5). Even so, Lewis has attempted, with greater success than many, to speak of the realities with which many religious persons would declare themselves to be acquainted; and as A.C. Ewing said in his paper, 'Awareness of God', 'even if the philosopher cannot prove [the religious point of view] justified, it is a very important task of philosophy to analyze what it involves, since very many people even today feel themselves ultimately bound to accept it and it cannot be shown to be wrong' (*P*, XL, 1965, 17).

At one point Lewis avers, 'We cannot just cry "encounter" any more than we can just cry "mystery" ' — and in the former word here we have the second issue to which I wish to refer. It is the issue left over from our earlier consideration of H.H. Farmer's book, *The World and God*. Theologians and ministers of religion had been greatly influenced by Farmer's work, and to his voice were added those of Emil Brunner and John Baillie. But the concept of encounter surfaces for us here because secular philosophers, notably C.B. Martin and R.W. Hepburn, begin to subject it to close scrutiny.

In 'A religious way of knowing' (*New Essays in Philosophical Theology*) Martin refers both to Farmer and to Baillie, and criticises encounter theology for its claim to constitute an unique and incommunicable way of knowing. For 'Just in so far as the experience of God is unique and incommunicable in this way, then just so far is it not to the point in supporting the existential claim "God exists" ' (82). Martin is concerned by the empirical untestability of the religious man's experience of God, and concludes that the person who claims such an experience is making a psychological claim only; he is saying that he feels in a certain way, he is not asserting a fact concerning the source of his experience. If he persists in his claim he cannot be proved wrong, but his unassailability has been purchased at the price of his making no claim about the word 'beyond the claim about his own state of mind' (86).

Martin's paper drew a number of responses. Some pointed out that his fundamental *metaphysical* assumption that an existent reality is and must be available to empirical testing is open to question. Others suggested that if — as Lewis, for example, holds — the religious experience is unique then it may be self-verifying in ways that other experiences cannot be. This would not, of course, amount to a demonstration of the fact of self-verifying experiences, but it would encourage the delineation of the background against which language about such experiences is, on empiricist assumptions, being oddly used. Thirdly, it has been argued that much of Martin's case is beside the point once we realise that encounter theologians are not attempting to construct an argument from religious experience to the existence of God. This last point was brought out by John Hick in an article entitled, 'A philosopher criticises theology'. The philosopher in question is R.W. Hepburn, and the reference is to his book, *Christianity and Paradox*. Hepburn's arguments are along similar lines to those of Martin, though he concentrates upon the possibility of our being under the illusion that we are experiencing even other persons as they really are; and if this possibility is real in respect of other human beings, how much more with God? How can encounter theologians legitimately build upon an experience which is self-authenticating?

Hick's reply is that Hepburn has 'considerably simplified and overstated the position which he opposes'. Farmer does not set out to argue for the existence of God — indeed, he contends that the theistic proofs are 'as religiously improper as they are philosophically inadequate'. Rather, he is 'seeking to present Christian theism as a coherent possibility, which gains the believer's allegiance through the compelling quality of his own religious experience, and which finds confirmation both in the pragmatic outworking of his faith and in rational reflection upon human experience as a whole. This is not a way of thinking which eschews logic and relies solely upon a unique, incommunicable, self-certifying experience of encounter with God' (*LQ,* April 1962, 105). As with Martin so with Hepburn: underlying his critique is his *declaration* that 'Theological language is . . . continuous with ordinary language' (84). As John McIntyre pointed out, this is to beg a crucial question (*SJT*, XII, 1959, 198), and by begging this question Hepburn makes his task of demolition too easy.

An odd man out

Having caught up, sometimes belatedly, with the times, theologians and philosophers are sometimes apt to indulge in bland 'of course-ism'. '*Of course* we must employ analytical techniques'; '*of course* metaphysical questions cannot be suppressed'; '*of course* we cannot *prove* the existence of God'; and these assertions are made in a tone which suggests that only fools would think otherwise. In such a climate it is refreshing when a 'fool' hoves into view. I have in mind F.H. Cleobury, who was described by A.R. Vidler as 'an impenitent Christian rationalist' (*T*, LXVI, 1963, 397). Cleobury stands in the line of Rashdall and Tennant, and states his position in *Christian Rationalism and Philosophical Analysis* (1959) in language which is nothing if not direct: 'If there are no valid reasons for believing in God, there are equally no valid reasons for interpreting any human writings or experiences as His revelation' (19). Cleobury suggests that since we do not restrict the meaning of 'proof' to logical proof in our consideration of the real world, there is no reason why we should restrict it in religious matters: 'the constructive proof of God's existence is as strong as many other beliefs which no one in practice dreams of doubting' (20–21). As he looks back across this century Cleobury feels that Christian apologists have been too gentle. They have suggested that the scientific picture of reality needs to be *supplemented* by spiritual values: 'This is a tactical error. We should never concede the self-existence of the spatio-temporal framework and its alleged contents. If we do, the most we can hope for is that "spiritual values" will be tolerated as more or less irrelevant' (27).

It would seem that some theologians cause Cleobury as much agony as do some philosophers::

> Those theologians who disparage the use of reason as a basis for Theism, and who appeal solely to mystical states or (as in the case of those theologians of "crisis" who disparage both reason and mysticism) to the experience of being "confronted" by God, have failed to see that in the act of saying *anything at all* about these experiences we are attempting a rational, i.e. a consistent and coherent construction, and that therefore there is no reason to interpret either of such types of experience as an experience of God unless there are *reasons* for believing in God. (63)

The data upon which reason works are supplied by experience and history, and the element of judgement cannot be eradicated from the awareness of any personality, whether that of God or of anyone else. In his *Liberal Christian Orthodoxy* (1963) Cleobury resumes these themes. He is shocked by the glib way in which theologians admit that they cannot prove God's existence. He grants once again that so long as we operate in terms of the scientific model no proof is possible — but nor can any of the scientist's assertions about natural law be proved either on these terms. But if we speak of proof as it is daily spoken of in law courts, homes and market places, to indicate that something accounts for what we experience, 'then it is sheer bias, or muddle-headedness, to deny in principle that God's experience can be proved' (27). Cleobury thus proceeds to re-assert a variety of absolute idealism which, he contends, is quite compatible with Christianity.

If in his conclusions Cleobury seems almost alone, there are signs that his appeal for the re-instatement of the rational in theology is striking a chord in other hearts. In 'Beyond all reason' (in *Four Anchors from the Stern* (1963)) James Richmond opined that 'theological advance will depend upon a courageous but careful rejection of what has bedevilled theological work for almost fifty years, a crippling and rarely examined suspicion of all that purports to be "religious" and "rational". There are signs that this advance has already begun' (46).

Analysis and more

The analysis of the proposition 'Philosophy is linguistic analysis' is not altogether straightforward. If it means, 'All philosophy *ought* to consist in linguistic analysis narrowly conceived, and in nothing else,' then we could by now produce the names of many who would dispute the injunction. If, however, the proposition is intended to assert the fact that 'All philosophy is *in fact* linguistic analysis narrowly conceived' then it is patently false. For reassurance on this point we need look no further than Scotland. There we shall find a number of philosophers whose claim upon our attention resides not least in their resolute refusal to succumb to any analytical party line. I shall refer briefly to John Macmurray, C.A. Campbell and W.G. Maclagan.

Throughout his philosophical career John Macmurray has pursued an independent line. In his Gifford Lectures, *The Self as Agent* (1957) and *Persons in Relation* (1961) he sums up much of his earlier work, and pleads for a new kind of revolution in philosophy. For too long philosophers have thought of persons primarily in organic or substantial terms. Let persons now be thought of as purposive agents. This will mean that whereas traditional philosophy has begun with the self as subject — as in Descartes's 'I think, therefore I am' — the new starting point will be the self as agent. Not indeed that persons are isolated selves: they are persons in relation to others. In working out his case Macmurray takes account of the challenges of both linguistic philosophy and existentialism, and in the result earns the unqualified praise of at least one reviewer, A.R.C. Duncan: 'When philosophy re-awakens from its present undogmatic slumbers, Macmurray's work will be recognized to have been pioneer work of the first importance' (*P*, XXXVI, 1961, 234).

None could say that C.A. Campbell has ever feared to nail his dogmatic colours to the mast. In his Gifford Lectures, *On Selfhood and Godhood* (1957) he seeks to work out a constructive idealism, meeting the onslaughts of empiricism and of philosophical analysis *en route*. His purpose is rationally to defend such a notion of the self as will render theology's talk of the soul intelligible — the soul being understood as a spiritual and active entity. He then turns to the question of Godhood and produces his reasons for believing that those symbols which are employed in theistic discourse about God are adequate and valid. Reality is supra-rational, but the mind may be taken as an objectively valid symbol of it, because

> For the religious consciousness . . . there is an affinity between its object, the *mysterium tremendum et fascinans*, and certain 'rational' qualities, which justifies the symbolic representation of its object in terms of power and value in their highest conceivable manifestations. For the intellectual consciousness . . . there is an affinity between that perfect unity in difference which must characterise reality (if reality is to satisfy the criterion of non-contradiction) and the most comprehensive and coherent, but still in principle imperfect, unities actually attainable under the conditions of finite experience. (403)

Not all were persuaded by Campbell; and as a witness to the gulf between the bulk of Oxbridge philosophy and what some in those citadels were wont to disparage as 'philosophy from north of the Tweed' Root wrote, 'in the face of the weight of contemporary opposition to the belief that philosophical speculation gives us new "knowledge" of "the nature of ultimate reality", one feels that to sustain his optimism one would have to make use of a doctrine of Invincible Ignorance and perhaps one of Original Sin as well' (*T*, LXII, 1959, 38). More seriously, and with reference to the analytical philosophy of religion current when Campbell's book appeared, we must ask how the appropriateness or otherwise of religious symbols is to be judged. Campbell suggests that our *feelings* somehow tell us that 'Justice, Mercy and Love' are appropriate symbols to use in relation to God, whilst 'Injustice, Hatred and Cruelty' are not. At this point he lays himself open to the charge of having confused the emotional import of symbols with the rational justification of them.

Nevertheless Campbell does offer a detailed and wide-ranging argument for his view that

> objective philosophical thinking, in which straight metaphysical argument is supplemented by reflections upon the implications of man's moral consciousness, leads independently to belief in an infinite and eternal being who is the sole ultimate reality, the creator of the finite temporal world, and the source of the moral law which has absolute authority over man's conduct in that world; a being who, moreover, though he transcends in nature all human powers of conception, is yet legitimately symbolised as a spirit endowed with the highest conceivable goodness, wisdom and power. (421)

He does not consider, however, that constructive philosophy can either sustain or refute 'the general principle of specific Divine manifestations in human lives'. For its part, critical philosophy 'can do no more than assess, rather roughly, the probabilities one way or the other in the case of individual claims' (421). If this should seem a disappointing conclusion to some, 'it is infinitely better to set sail and sink than never to set sail at all' (422).

Our third Scot is W.G. Maclagan, whose book, *The Theological Frontier of Ethics* was published in 1961. Whereas such earlier philosophers as De Burgh and Taylor had sought to show how our moral experience prompts us to construct a theory which culminates in a theism, Maclagan argues that morality is not dependent upon religion in any sense of 'religion' which distinguishes it from morality. To maintain the contrary is to devalue both religion and morality, and to run the risk of driving men away from morality because of their difficulties with religion, or of encouraging a corrupt fanaticism.

Maclagan posits a real and an objective (though not a spatiotemporal) order of values. This we may designate 'God', though in so doing we are adverting to an impersonal moment in God. However, God is also to be conceived as personal; but Maclagan does not see how an idea of God can be framed which integrates his personal and impersonal characteristics. All of which prompts Hepburn to wonder whether the 'obscure and problematic' impersonal pole is strictly necessary to Maclagan's objectivist theory (*HJ*, LX, 1961-2, 85). Similarly, when Maclagan asserts that 'we must be content to assert, without comprehending, the unity of personal and impersonal natures in God' (179), D.M. Tulloch gently protests, 'But some may wonder what is the value of such an uncomprehending assertion' (*P*, XXXVIII, 1963, 88). For his part Macmurray challenged Maclagan's implicit presupposition that the whole field of morality can be encompassed by the experience of duty, and that a complete ethic can be erected on the base of the concept of duty. Furthermore, 'For Christianity the proper ground of morality is love, not duty. The attempt to identify the two produces not a paradox but a contradiction' (*ET*, LXXII, 1960-61, 365). Such challenges notwithstanding, it was refreshing to have such a careful defence of the objectivity of ethics in the wake of the flurry of positivistically engendered ethical subjectivism and emotivism.

Stock-taking

I come finally to a number of assessments of the philosophico-religious situation which were offered during the years 1955-65. In his article, 'Changing attitudes to religion in contemporary English philosophy', Macquarrie describes the procession of empirical philosophy from logical positivism to more recent linguistic analysis, pointing out that most of the old iconoclasm is now past, and suggesting that while there is a considerable diversity of approach to theological questions on the part of analytical philosophers, their insistence upon clarity provides a salutary lesson for the theologian. Indeed Macquarrie feels able to say that 'We may confidently expect that the present and future discussions will bring useful results for philosophy and theology alike' (*ET*, LXVIII, 1956-7, 301).

To at least one of the analysts discussed by Macquarrie this seemed an over-optimistic attitude. Hepburn both replied directly to Macquarrie (*ET*, LXIX, 1957-8, 54) and, in his *Christianity and Paradox*, cited four reasons why the theologian might well be *uneasy* in face of contemporary analytical philosophy. First, linguistic philosophy has 'restated and immensely sharpened the attack on traditional arguments for the existence of God' (4). Secondly, philosophy has pointed to the failure of natural theology and, moreover, has cut off that theological escape route which consists in parrying with the rebuke: '*Of course* we cannot *prove* the existence of God.' For the philosopher does not now ask how religious claims are to be established, but 'whether they have been given a coherent *meaning*, a consistent use' (6). Thirdly, there is the partial success of therapeutic philosophy. A number of mysteries have been dissolved — ought not the theologian to be a little anxious lest too many of his 'complaints' are cured? Lastly, the philosopher's revival of interest in metaphysics holds a challenge for the theologian, for the former by no means seeks to discover the unseen, but merely to comprehend the familiar.

In a subsequent article on 'The philosophical school of logical analysis' (*ET*, LXXV, 1963-4) Macquarrie admits that he was perhaps somewhat over-confident, but nevertheless mentions four specific points upon which analytical philosophy has 'taken up positions that are more favourable to an affirmative account of religion than would have been at all possible in the earlier stages of the movement' (45). These are first, the general recognition that there is a multiplicity of languages, so that every language, not least religious language, is given the chance to clarify its logic. Secondly, there is the welcome movement away from physicalistic reductionism with which is associated, thirdly, an atmosphere more tolerant of personal, and hence of theological, language. Lastly, there is the welcome emphasis upon the use of words and sentences, and the desire to place them in the situation out of which they arise.

Macquarrie regrets that 'so many of our theologians seem to be either indifferent or impatient towards the school' (47). He feels that there are three areas in particular in which the theologian might well consider whether any light can be thrown on his path by linguistic philosophy. They are the field of self-criticism — for example, the constant asking of himself, 'What do I mean by this that I am saying?'; the field of biblical theology — for example the consideration of the logic of biblical language as distinct from the well trodden path of its semantics; and the construction of a new natural theology which will take full account of situational analysis, and will thereby impinge upon existentialist considerations.

Roman Catholic philosophers are no less concerned that their colleagues shall take stock in ways which *they* deem particularly appropriate. Thus, for example, John Coulson lodges complaints against three kinds of activity that go by the name of philosophy in many presbyteries and seminaries. The article is entitled, 'Catholics and the revolution in philosophy' (*DR*, LXXVI, 1958), and the first complaint is that of indulgence in the art form known as the medieval disputation, which 'relies upon the syllogism which is used as though the terms of the syllogism were *unquestionable* logical constants, and our thinking were actually done by means of syllogisms' (37). In fact 'there is nothing specially ineffable in a logic which is restricted to one simple form' (38). The second unwholesome attitude is that which, when confronted by a problem, consults St Thomas and quotes anything even remotely relevant with an air of finality. The third fault,

> which is perhaps the most alarming as well as the most prevalent is the failure to distinguish between philosophical criticism and dogma, so that what will be asserted is that the Church 'teaches' the metaphysics of St. Thomas Aquinas as definitively interpreted by Fr. Septimus O'Toole, Professor of Philosophy at the Seminary of the Sixteen Sighs, 1850-90 (38).[20]

In his article, 'Theology and philosophy' (*Tab.*, No. 6541,

1965, 1086-7) Timothy Potts resumes this last point:

> Mere repetition is not conducive to intellectual honesty . . . for too long our ecclesiastical education has sacrificed this virtue to what it calls 'intellectual obedience'. But in the long run the Church is not benefited by bad arguments, and we ought not to fall back on them even when we lack better, but rather admit openly that we have not got all the answers, or that we can only give a sketch of how an adequate solution might go . . . One of the reasons why medieval writers can still help us is that they were good logicians and in a wider field than modern logic has yet covered: happily their contributions to logic are now at last becoming known again, and with their help in extending the methods of twentieth-century logic to the analysis of philosophical and moral concepts there could well be a new scholasticism round the corner.

For our final, more general advice, we turn to Julius Kraft, John McIntyre and Donald Mackinnon. Kraft, writing on 'Religion, experience and metaphysics' (*R*, I. 1957-8) is in no doubt that we require a new understanding of 'religion within the boundaries of mere reason'. He reviews 20th century religious irrationalism in both its dogmatic (e.g. Barthian) and existentialist (e.g. Sartrian) forms and concludes that

> it is a house built on sand. Although it keeps mouthing the great word *Truth* it displays a sovereign contempt for reason and for the biblical exhortation that a man's communication be yea, yea or nay, nay. Instead it has raised paradox, i.e. the yea-nay, to the level of a sacred shrine, thus belying its outward show of inner certainty. (45)

Religion begins from experience but points beyond it. The task of the philosopher of religion is to explain this transcendence with clarity and lucidity.

McIntyre takes as Church-orientated a view of the philosopher of religion's task as I have discovered. With the aid of the philosophy of religion the Church makes herself understood as she proclaims her message; with its aid she understands her own message and methodology — particularly her criterion of truth and her methods of proof — not overlooking the question of the relationship between the Church's doctrinal formulations and her final authority, Holy

Scripture. The final suggestion in this article on 'The frontiers of meaning' is that with the aid of the philosophy of religion the Church makes her message relevant — that is, she undertakes the apologetic task, and examines the validity of her claim to truth. (*SJT*, X, 1957, 138-9).

If McIntyre gives the impression of standing within the Church and looking outwards, MacKinnon is more obviously a frontiersman, and he writes on *The Borderlands of Theology* (1960). He urges the philosopher of religion not to be too prompt in supplying answers, but rather to listen carefully to the world questions — particularly those which arise from contemporary views of the cosmos, contemporary analyses of the human situation as portrayed in literature, and contemporary criticism of Christian ethics. Far from being an apologist the philosopher of religion is a man of the borderlands; and this may explain why 'he may perhaps feel a peculiar kinship with those who, from similarly situated territory, make protesting raids upon the theologians' cherished homeland' (27).[21]

Notes

1. T.F. Torrance, *Theological Science* (Oxford University Press, London, 1969), p. 5.
2. G.H. Clark, 'Revealed religion' in C.F.H. Henry (ed.), *Fundamentals of the Faith* (Baker Book House, Grand Rapids, 1959), p. 22.
3. P. Tillich in *The Theology of Paul Tillich*, eds C.W. Kegley and R.W. Bretall (Macmillan, New York, 1964), p. 3.
4. Sidney Hook, 'The atheism of Paul Tillich' in S.H. Hook (ed.), *Religious Experience and Truth* (Oliver & Boyd, Edinburgh, 1962), p. 60.
5. H.D. McDonald, 'The symbolic theology of Paul Tillich', *The Scottish Journal of Theology*, XVII (1964), p. 424.
6. H.D. McDonald, *Theories of Revelation* (Allen & Unwin, London, 1963), p. 97.
7. E.g. D.M. Emmet, 'The ground of being', *The Journal of Theological Studies*, N.S. XV (1964), pp. 280-1.
8. For example, J.H. Gill, 'Paul Tillich's religious epistemology', *Religious Studies* III (1967-8), p. 492. Tillich confesses a 'close affinity' with Charles Hartshorne's process philosophy, 'perhaps because of common intellectual antecedents, for example, Bergson, Schelling and Böhme'. See Kegley and Bretall, *op. cit.*, p. 340.
9. P. Tillich, *Biblical Religion and the Search for Ultimate Reality* (Nisbet, London, 1955), p. 19.
10. *Ibid.*, p. 5.
11. P. Tillich, *The Interpretation of History* (Scribners, New York, 1936), p. 60.

12. P. Tillich, *The Protestant Era* (Nisbet, London, 1951), p. 98.
13. Quoted by K. Hamilton, *The System and the Gospel* (SCM, London, 1963), pp. 38-9.
14. *Ibid.*, p. 53.
15. David Jenkins, *Guide to the Debate about God* (SCM, London, 1966), p. 89.
16. P. Tillich, *Biblical Religion*, p. 58.
17. *Ibid.*, p. 59.
18. J. Heywood Thomas, *Paul Tillich* (Lutterworth Press, London, 1965), p. 9.
19. See I.T. Ramsey, 'On the possibility and purpose of a metaphysical theology' in I.T. Ramsey (ed.), *Prospect for Metaphysics* (Allen & Unwin, London, 1961), p. 174.
20. Among Roman Catholic philosophers who escape Coulson's charges and take a lively interest in contemporary philosophy are Cornelius Ernst, 'Words, facts and God', *B*, XLIV (1963); A. Kenny, 'Aquinas and Wittgenstein', *DR*, LXXVII (1958-9); C.J.F. Williams, 'The marriage of Aquinas and Wittgenstein', *DR*, LXXVIII (1959-60); J.V. McGlynn, 'Philosophy and analysis', *DR*, LXXVIII (1959-60); D. Cleary, 'An essay on G.E. Moore', *DR*, LXXXI (1963).
21. It would be churlish not to mention those who in the decade 1955-65 sought to popularise the philosophy of religion. Among introductory books we may note Geddes MacGregor, *Introduction to Religious Philosophy* (1959); J. Hick, *Philosophy of Religion* (1963); H.D. Lewis, *Philosophy of Religion* (1965); and T. McPherson, *The Philosophy of Religion* (1965). Of these MacGregor and Lewis cover the widest range of themes, though MacGregor, if the most entertaining of all, is also the least philosophically tough-minded of all. Hick and McPherson treat rather fewer issues in a relatively simple manner, yet without distortion. Other more popular works of the period include E.L. Mascall, *Words and Images* (1957); Alasdair MacIntyre, *Difficulties in Christian Belief* (1959); and John Wilson, *Philosophy and Religion* (1961).

8
Almost Open House, 1965-80

At the end of the Introduction I more than hinted that this chapter is a particularly difficult one to write. I have so far sought to trace philosophico-theological relations over 85 years as these appear to one who views matters as from Britain. The attempt has been made to view matters impartially and to record justifiable opinions. In respect of the years 1965-80, however, I am conscious of being engaged in the forlorn task of attempting to freeze the unfreezable, to isolate the unisolable. There has been a profusion of writing in the philosophy of religion. Publishers have been alive to, and have encouraged this, and have devoted entire series to the subject. Thus we have Macmillan's *Philosophy of Religion Series* edited by John Hick; Macmillan's *New Studies in the Philosophy of Religion* edited by W.D. Hudson; Routledge and Kegan Paul's series of *Studies in Ethics and the Philosophy of Religion* edited by D.Z. Phillips; and Sheldon Press's *Studies in Philosophy and Religion* edited by P.R. Baelz. Such has been the liveliness of debate that new journals have appeared to carry articles and comments, reviews and rejoinders. We have *The Heythrop Journal* (1960), which provides ample evidence of philosophical catholicity on a predominantly Roman Catholic base; *Sophia* (1962), in which special attention is paid to analytical matters; *Religious Studies* (1965), which carries often substantial articles from a variety of standpoints; and the *International Journal for Philosophy of Religion* (1970), the pages of which are open to articles of both a contemporary and an historical flavour. Among introductions to the subject that of Terence Penelhum, *Religion and Rationality* (1971) is comprehensive without being superficial. Nor is it simply that philosophers of religion have been writing more and more about the same issues as hitherto. To offer two examples only: both Ninian Smart and John Hick have written widely on the philosophico-theological implications of inter-Faith dialogue; and the latter has entered into Christological debate, as witness *The Myth of God Incarnate* (1977).

As if the proliferation of interest were not enough, there is the further fact that since the work of many of those who might be mentioned in this chapter is still in progress, any judgements pretending to finality would be both premature and unfair. In any case, we are too close to the years under review to see things in their proper perspective. In the course of preparing this book I have read not only numerous books and articles, but many hundreds of reviews. From reviews it is possible to assess something of the way in which a philosopher's work is received by his contemporaries. I have referred in my text to some of these reviews, but to most I have not referred — often because the works under review have not stood the test of time *no matter how eulogistic their original reception*. Who, for example, now dwells much upon Eucken's works? Who, I dare to wonder (at the risk of being branded by some a myopic heretic!) will, in 20 years' time, still be embroiled in Teilhard de Chardin, to whom so much attention was paid in the years covered by this chapter. Conversely, how many of my contemporaries whom I shall not mention are in the position classically exemplified by Kierkegaard — unable to be heard in their time because they are so far ahead of it?

How to respond to this state of affairs? I could allow the lack of historical perspective to intimidate me into writing a brief, fairly uninformative epilogue along the lines: 'The philosophy of religion is very much alive in many of its parts, even if it is not (in my judgement) well in all of them.' This would be a cowardly policy to adopt. Alternatively, I could attempt a catalogue of everything that has happened in the last 15 years — taking special care to mention my friends. This would result in an inordinately long list of items to which no criteria of selection had been applied. It would be turgid, and would simply duplicate the work of existing indices and bibliographies. I shall therefore produce a chapter in which I shall notice a few areas of activity in which *interesting* — or, at least, not altogether uninteresting — work has been done. It will be for posterity to trace the story of philosophico-theological *relations*, 1965-80, and to determine whether what I have selected is more *important* than what I have omitted.

I shall first resume the story of religious language; I shall then note some contributions to the discussion of a perennially interesting question: that of God's existence. Some reflections upon process theology will be followed by reference to some philosophers who are recalling us to thinkers from the past. I shall conclude, as I began, by taking stock of the metaphysics-theism situation, and shall advert to some styles of Christian philosophising to which scarcely any attention has as yet been paid in Britain.

Religious language

Of those philosophers who have devoted themselves to the analysis of religious language many, though by no means all, have worked the seam opened by the later Wittgenstein, with his emphasis upon the use, rather than upon the meaning, of language. It is important to insist that the work of these philosophers, while it exhibits a certain family resemblance, is by no means narrowly partisan. This is precisely what we should expect, given the differences of interpretation to which Wittgenstein is open, and the varying degrees of loyalty which he has elicited. With these qualifications firmly in mind it is permissible to classify Peter Winch, Norman Malcolm and Stewart Sutherland as among those who sail under, or at least within sight of, the Wittgensteinian flag. W.D. Hudson is another who admits to being influenced by Wittgenstein; indeed, he has spelled out the extent of his indebtedness in his article, 'What makes religious beliefs religious?' (*RS*, XII, 1977). But the fact that Hudson has taken one of the most prolific neo-Wittgensteinians, D.Z. Phillips, to task over certain issues underlines the absence of a firm party line.

One of the leading themes in the writings of these philosophers is that religious language is appropriately used by the believer, since he holds to the necessary existence of God. The religious 'language game' is constituted by the word 'God', and religious utterance can and must proceed without raising the question of God's existence at all. Whereas within other areas of discourse — the scientific, for example, it makes sense to seek the justification of the claims made, in religious discourse such a quest is quite misplaced. The believer does not use language which has cognitive import: when speaking of God he is not referring to a being who actually exists, he is rather engaging in a 'form of life' within which religious language is appropriately used. There is thus an autonomy about the various areas of discourse with which Phillips, in agreement with Winch, is entirely happy:

> One can say *within* any such context, whether it be science or religion, 'This is the rule which *must* be observed, this is the meaning which a word *must* have if it is to belong to this conceptual family.' But when philosophers say, 'This is the meaning which a word *must have*' without specifying any context, they are guilty of arbitrary linguistic legislation. The 'must' is not a logical *'must'*, but simply the 'must' of their own preferences, or the 'must' of one context which they have elevated, consciously or unconsciously, to be a standard for all others.

This passage, from *The Concept of Prayer* (1965, 10) is reinforced elsewhere in Phillips's *corpus*. Thus he insists in *Faith and Philosophical Enquiry* (1970) that theology is 'the grammar of religious discourse' by means of which we determine what it is possible properly to say about God. This, he feels, would be a circular and contradictory pursuit only 'if one [mistakenly] thinks of either logic or language as being prior to the other' (6). As Winch said in his article, 'Understanding a primitive society', 'it is *within* the religious use of language that the conception of God's reality has its place' (*APQ*, I, 1964, 309). To seek meaningful use of 'God-talk' outside the form of life within which alone it properly belongs is to commit what Phillips designates 'the naturalistic fallacy in religion'.

The first thing to be said about this general approach to religious language — and here I take Phillips as its most prolific representative — is that a real attempt is made to do justice to the unique nature of religious commitment. It is noteworthy that the exemplars who loom largest is Phillips's thought are Kierkegaard and some of his Christian existentialist successors. Phillips is persuaded (now following Wittgenstein) that all too frequently philosophers content themselves with examining the 'surface grammar' of discourse, whereas if we attend to the 'depth grammar' of religious language we will see that it arises within a form of life to which the user is experientially committed — indeed, the using of the language *is* the form of life. Thus he tells us in *The Concept of Prayer* that 'I want to try to say what people *are* doing when they pray.' The question is, does he succeed in this? Many critics have protested that probably most people who believe in God and pray understand (rightly or wrongly) that there *is* one to whom their prayers are addressed; whereas Phillips seems to speak as if they are using language which is free of ontological implications, and which has simply the psychological result of making them feel better. He writes, for example, 'When deep religious believers pray *for* something, they are not so much asking God to bring this about, but in a way telling Him the strength of their desires. They realize that things may not go as they wish, but they are asking to be able to go on living whatever happens. In prayers of confession and in prayers of petition, the believer is trying to find a meaning and a hope that will deliver him from the elements in his life which threaten to destroy it' (121). Many have felt that the assertion in the first sentence here is false; that that in the second is true; and that that in the third provides only an attenuated account of what most believers understand to be going on when they confess their sins and pray for forgiveness.

On the general point Phillips declares that 'to understand prayer is to understand what it means to talk to God (38). In his article 'Talk about God's existence' Tziporah Kasachkoff has responded thus: 'This glib avoidance of the distinction between *believing* that one is talking to God and talking to God, by maintaining that "to understand prayer *is* to understand what it means to talk to God" will not do. For the fact is that we understand what prayer is if we understand merely what the believer *takes* to be talking to God' (*PS*, XIX, 1970, 185).

It is not difficult to see why Phillips has been charged with reductionism. He is not, indeed, a reductionist in the sense in which Kant has been so branded; he does not subordinate religion to morality; neither does he think that religion can be reduced to anything else — it is *sui generis*. It is his severance of religious language from its ontological roots which reduces the content of what he will permit believers to mean. Some critics have questioned how far the assertions of the Christian neo-Wittgensteininans differ from non-theistic assertions — and how we could know whether they did or did not so differ apart from the procedures of justification which Phillips and others rule out of court. Moreover the recourse to the idea that religious language is replete with 'pictures' by which (some) men guide their lives — a notion sanctioned by Wittgenstein's *Lectures and Conversations on Aesthetics, Psychology and Religious Belief* (1966), is a further dissuasive to those who would, for example, think in terms of a future occurrence when speaking of the Last Judgement. The Wittgensteinian Last Judgement 'picture' can but challenge us *now*. Phillips goes so far as to say in *Faith and Philosophical Enquiry* that 'Believing in the picture means, for example, putting one's trust in it, sacrificing for it, letting it regulate one's life, and so on' (90). This oft reiterated view has seemed more than a little idolatrous to some.

Yet there is a certain ambivalence in Phillips's thought which at times enables him to veer towards the traditional assumption of the existence of God. Thus in *Death and Immortality* (1970) he writes, 'In learning by contemplation, attention, renunciation, what forgiving, thanking, loving, etc. mean in these contexts, the believer is participating in the reality of God; *this is what we mean by God's reality*. This reality is independent of any given believer, but its independence is not the independence of a separate biography. It is independent of the believer in that the believer measures his life against it' (55). But Phillips's more characteristic attitude is encapsulated in *The Concept of Prayer* where he writes, 'To see the world as God's creation is to see meaning in life' (97). Once again the doctrine is a way of articulating the experience of the believer. He would still wish to say that within religious discourse we find what is meant by the reality of God; but this is only to reinforce the feeling that religious language is the language of an 'in group' who share a form of life. We can understand why Flew declared that 'Sometimes the Wittgensteinian "form of life" is a form of lifemanship!'

The upshot is that Phillips appears to translate many assertions made by believers in ways which the latter would not deem legitimate, and to buy immunity from rational justification by recourse to the notion of autonomous language games and forms of life. Thus, as John Hick argued in *God and the Universe of Faiths* (1973), if Phillips's theory were accepted,

> The principal loss would be the irreversible retreat of religious discourse within the borders of its own autonomous language-game, where it must renounce all claim to bear witness to the nature of the universe, and must cease to interact with other departments of human knowledge. Religious language would become a protected discourse, no longer under obligation to show its compatibility with established conclusions in other spheres, because it makes no claims which could either agree or conflict with scientific knowledge or philosophical reflection. (9)[1]

This from a philosopher who is the first to agree with the neo-Wittgensteinians that 'faith stands ultimately upon the ground of religious experience and is not a product of philosophical reasoning'.[2]

Almost Open House, 1965-80

To exemplify the differences between philosophers who share neo-Wittgensteinian emphases I cite W.D. Hudson. Unlike Phillips, Hudson does believe that the question of God's existence is meaningful. However, he does not feel that it admits of an answer. Rather, in *A Philosophical Approach to Religion* (1974) he declares that 'We have to make our own ultimate ontological decision; we have to make up our own minds what criteria we will use for the application of the word "real" ' (104). But is this so? Do believers think of themselves as adverting to an open ontological option when they speak of the existence of God? *Are* they doing that? The debate continues.

One further point is worthy of note: Hudson makes more frequent reference to the idea of language games than does Phillips, and this not least in his useful book, *Wittgenstein and Religious Belief* (1975). The outstanding questions which this book suggests, however, are these: 'Where do the boundaries between the several language games lie?' If there are no boundaries it is not easy to sustain the charge that neo-Wittgensteinians are reductionists. For his part Wittgenstein seems to have held that that there *are* boundaries, but in accordance with what criteria are they to be drawn? Does the reluctance on the part of neo-Wittgensteinians to talk about criteria result from their realisation that criteria could be established only if the alleged autonomy of language games were called in question, and an independent standard of judgement invoked?

Unlike the neo-Wittgensteins, such philosophers as I.M. Crombie and John Hick are concerned to *maintain* the link between religious and other kinds of discourse. This, in part, was the motivation behind their use of the idea of eschatological verification, to which reference was made in the last chapter. The claim was that religious assertions *are* assertions, and that they are, like any other empirical assertions, in principle falsifiable — though with the proviso that in the case of religious assertions we cannot conclusively verify or falsify them, for we do not yet see all of the picture. In the period with which we are presently concerned, Hick has proposed a further doctrine which is consistent with his earlier conclusion. In his symposium contribution, 'Religious faith as experiencing-as' (*Talk of God*, ed. G.N. Vesey, 1969) he argues that '*all* experiencing, involving as it does the activity of recognizing, is to be construed as experiencing-as' (27). The religious believer experiences circumstances and events *as* encounters with God, just as in perception we see a shape *as* a rabbit. Accordingly, 'it is as rational for the religious man to treat his experience of God as veridical as it is for him and others to treat their experience of the physical world as veridical' (35).

Hick's case has been widely scrutinised, not least by L. Bryant Keeling and Mario F. Morelli in 'Beyond Wittgensteinan fideism: an examination of John Hick's analysis of religious faith' (*IJPR*, VIII, 1977), and James J. Heaney, 'Faith and the logic of seeing-as' (*IJPR*, X, 1979). The former conclude that Hick fails to show more than that a person responds to an event with describable behaviour and dispositions: he does not show that the event is an act of God. This, they believe is the standing challenge to those who would move beyond Wittgensteinian fideism. Once again, the debate continues.

One of the most sensitive analysts of religious discourse, Ian Ramsey, died untimely in 1972. It is a tribute to his influence both that his works are still discussed, and that many deem his approach to be of sufficient importance to merit continued probing. Thus, for example, in our period H.P. Owen writes on 'The philosophical theology of I.T. Ramsey' (*T*, LXXIV, 1971); Ramsey replies (*ibid.* 1971); Brian Hebblethwaite offers 'Some further reflections' under Owen's title (*T*, LXXVI, 1973); and Jerry H. Gill offers both articles and a book entitled, *Ian Ramsey: To Speak Responsibly of God* (1976).

A concise statement of Ramsey's philosophical *credo* is to be found in his article, 'Contemporary philosophy and the Christian faith':

> Empirical philosophy today brings with it no grandiose systems — but it is concerned to ask how the theological and religious language talks about what kind of situation and how. Philosophy comes to the language of the Bible or any other religious book, to the language of doctrine, of hymns and of prayers, to see how language does its job, and what guides can be given to its reliable use. Christian assertions are *not* strangled in the grip of some tight, deductive metaphysics, nor made to conform to a supposed ideal of descriptive picture assertions. (*RS*, I, 1965, 61)

To the end of his days Ramsey was providing further illustrations of the way in which religious language is used to evoke 'disclosure situations'. Truth to tell, some critics have felt that all he did was to provide illustrations — he did not offer the detailed analysis of 'disclosure situation' for which they had been pressing. A partial reply is that Ramsey is implicitly (and at times explicitly) repudiating an unduly narrow definition of 'empirical' and 'objective'. He contends that his disclosures are disclosures of that which is objective; and the fact that they are more complex than our recognition of other empirical phenomena in no way vitiate their empirical status. As he says in his posthumous collection of papers, *Christian Empiricism* (1974), 'theological assertions must have a logical context which extends to, and is continuous with, those assertions of ordinary language for which sense experience is directly relevant' (12). Such is his declaration; some continue to wonder whether he *showed* that this is so.

Passing to related questions prompted by Ramsey's work the question arises, does he not emphasise the question of meaning at the expense of the question of truth? The late N.H.G. Robinson, in an article entitled 'The logical placing of the name "God" ', was among many who pressed this point: 'religious language has always been ontologically, not just logically, oriented, that is to say, oriented towards a distinctive reality, not simply towards a word which behaves peculiarly; and to minimise or to eliminate this objective reference would break the nerve of religion' (*SJT*, XXIV, 133). Again, and now with reference to Ramsey's *Models and Mystery* (1964), Robinson argues that

> When in using the name of God we say 'We acknowledge thee to be the Lord,' of course we are *doing* something, of course we are taking a stand; but am I not right in thinking that in doing so we are also coming into line? And coming into line, not with the establishment, but with something like ultimate reality? . . . When Luther said 'Here I stand, I can do no other' it is possible indeed to try to understand the compulsion as that of self-consistency, but that would be to misunderstand him. It seems plain that it was loyalty to his apprehension of objective truth that was the governing force . . . Consequently what I am suggesting is that the ontological attitude which lies at the heart of religion contains as a moment of itself an implicit but indispensable affirmation which is yet distinguishable from the affirmation of an articulated world-view. (139, 142)

H.P. Owen is among others who have been puzzled by Ramsey's disavowal of ontology. In 'The philosophical theology of I.T. Ramsey' he writes,

Now I agree with him wholeheartedly on three points. First, theistic terms do not describe God in the sense of making him intellectually comprehensible; secondly, we must not confuse linguistic analysis (a formal mode of speech) with dogmatic assertion (a material mode); and thirdly, all existential affirmations concerning God are invalid unless they are anchored in a disclosure. However, the basic fact remains that believers intend their statements to signify God as he actually is, even though they cannot give them 'cash calue' in terms of immediate vision. Thus they mean to assert that God really is changeless and loving although they do not claim to know the ways in which he possesses these attributes. Yet Dr. Ramsey's disavowal of 'description' and his preference for a formal mode of speech leave one wondering whether he has *finally* justified the objective reference which all Christians claim for their theistic terms. In fact I doubt whether a *final* justification is possible except through the doctrine of analogy. (*T*, LXXIV, 1971, 72-3)

To this criticism Ramsey himself replied:

I do not intend to disavow description altogether, and on my view most theological assertions — unless they are altogether formal — will have some descriptive force in so far as they include or develop models. Whatever model leads to a disclosure, or is contained in a disclosure, licenses *ipso facto* appropriate currency for God who discloses himself there, appropriate *as far as it goes*. But it can never be used in an unqualified way about God if we want to safeguard God as God and not make him one of ourselves. (*T*, LXXIV, 1971, 126)

Then there are the numerous problems which attend the concept of 'disclosure' itself. Some have felt that Ramsey was insufficiently clear as to the nature of disclosures. In his review of *Christian Empiricism*, for example, Paul Helm asks, 'What is a disclosure? Judging by Ramsey's examples it can be a vision, or an intuition, or an inference, or a sudden thought, or a pang of conscience, or a moral judgement. Isn't it likely to be methodologically disastrous to handle such diverse notions although they were the same, or even members of the same family? (*RS*, X, 1974, 505). Further, do all disclosures disclose the same reality? How may we judge this matter? To which disclosures *ought* we to commit ourselves? The last question here may refer both to the nature of the disclosures in themselves (may not some be inspired by pathological conditions of the psyche, for example), and to the question, 'Can we say that disclosures which occur within "alien" world views are disclosures of the divine in any sense in which Christians would cash the term?' The question of the *truth* or falsity of what is disclosed is raised once again.

It may be, as Norman Pittenger has said, that what Ramsey said 'has more to do with a proper analysis of the religious state-of-mind than with the kind of world in which that state-of-mind makes sense' (*MC*, XX, 1976-7, 55). Even so, Ramsey has provided a permanent reminder of the implications of the mystery which is God for the language in which, however oddly, believers express their most cherished convictions. But to present such a reminder is not to substantiate the reality of God. It may therefore be that in time Ramsey's greatest contribution will be seen to have been the negative one of reminding philosophers of religion of the *limits* of empiricism.

This is by no means to deny that there is a sense in which every philosopher of religion *needs* an A.G.N. Flew; and certainly during our period Flew has promoted the secularist-empiricist cause with gusto, notably in his *God and Philosophy* (1966). As far as religious language is concerned he presses the falsification charge with which we are already familiar but, as H.P. Owen pointed out, he does not prove that 'empirical verifiability or falsifiability is a conditon of either the meaningfulness or the validity of the truth-claims inherent in religious experience' (*RS*, II, 1966-7, 284). In this book, however, Flew is concerned with much more than religious discourse. He probes (*pace* the Wittgensteinians) the heart of the problem: are there rational grounds for believing in the God to whom religious language allegedly refers? To this perennial question I now turn.

The existence of God

To say that the question of the existence of God was much debated between 1965-80 is an understatement indeed. The journals — notably *RS*, *Sophia* and *IJPR* — carried numerous articles on this theme, especially in the early 1960s and the mid-1970s; collections such as *The Ontological Argument* (1965) edited by Alvin Plantinga,

Almost Open House, 1965–80

The Many-Faced [i.e. the ontological] *Argument* (1967) edited by John Hick and Arthur McGill, and Hick's more wide-ranging collection, *The Existence of God* (1964) have appeared; and we have seen a profusion of monographs on the traditional arguments, whether treated independently or in various permutations. There has in addition been much discussion of the viability of natural theology, and of the coherence of theism. In an attempt to find an intelligible way through the mass of material I shall discuss first the ontological, then the cosmological and teleological arguments; and I shall conclude with some brief notes on the moral argument and the argument from religious experience.

As is well known, Anselm set out in his *Proslogion* to answer the Psalmist's fool (*Pss.* xiv: 1, liii: 1) who says in his heart that there is no God. At once we meet a disputed point: how far was Anselm really being argumentative? Walter Kaufmann suggests that the worth of Anselm's words as an argument is diminished by reason of their origin in a meditation. On the other hand, E.L. Mascall and J. Heywood Thomas agree that Anselm's intention was logically to refute the fool.[3] There can be no doubt that the vast majority of those who have spilled ink over the argument in recent years have taken it as an argument (and even, as we shall see, as more than one argument), and that is how I regard it here.

Anselm seeks, by a *reductio ad absurdum* argument, to show the self-contradictory position we should be in were we to deny the existence of God. God is that than which a greater (or more perfect) cannot be conceived. If we deny his existence we are implying that we can conceive of a being greater than the being than which no greater can be conceived; and this is absurd; we cannot conceive of such a being — therefore God exists. In reply to Gaunilo's objection Anselm declared that only in the case of God may we pass unimpeachably from the idea to the assertion of existence. But it was Kant who, although he criticised the Cartesian restatement of the ontological argument rather than Anselm's own version of it, raised the issue which undermines all versions of the *a priori* ontological argument. Anselm, like Descartes, assumes that existence is a predicate, and in this he is mistaken. If existence were a predicate, an attribute which persons or things might properly be said to possess, we could legitimately say, 'This table is hard, round, brown, and it exists.' This sentence is grammatically impeccable, and in it 'exists' is a grammatical predicate. But 'exists' here does not fill out the description of the table in the way that the other words, 'hard', 'round' and 'brown' do. Logically it is not a predicate, for its function is to assert that the description of the table accords with reality.

Professor Norman Malcolm has distinguished two forms of the ontological argument in his paper, 'Anselm's ontological arguments' (*PR*, 1960; reprinted in J. Hick (ed.) *The Existence of God*, to which page references here refer). Malcolm grants that Anselm did not see himself as propounding two arguments; however, Malcolm contends that in the *Proslogion* chapter 2 Anselm advances the doctrine that existence is a perfection. This is equivalent to saying that existence is a predicate, and Malcolm agrees that Kant has demonstrated that this is not the case. But in the *Proslogion* chapter 3 we have a valid ontological proof, says Malcolm. It turns upon the two-fold claim: (1) that a being than which no greater can be conceived must be one whose existence is logically impossible; and (2) that God is that being than which a greater cannot be conceived.

Having rejected the notion that existence is a predicate, Malcolm is at pains to point out that what is being argued here is that

> *the logical impossibility of non-existence is a perfection*. In other words, *necessary existence* is a perfection. [Anselm's] first ontological proof uses the principle that a thing is greater if it exists than if it does not exist. His second proof employs the different principle that a thing is greater if it necessarily exists than if it does not necessarily exist. (53)

Hence the idea of contingency cannot be applied to God: 'His existence must either be logically necessary or logically impossible' (56). It could be the latter only if the concept of God were self-contradictory or logically absurd. Assuming that this is not so, God necessarily exists:

> The a priori proposition 'God necessarily exists' entails the proposition 'God exists', if and only if the latter also is understood as an a priori proposition: in which case the two propositions are equivalent. In this sense Anselm's proof is a proof of God's existence. (57)

Malcolm confesses that he is no more able to demonstrate that the concept of God is not self-contradictory than to demonstrate that either the concept of a material thing, or the concept of seeing a material thing, is self-contradictory; but he does not think it legitimate to demand such a demonstration.

Two comments may be made upon this ingenious case. First, as Thomas McPherson pointed out in his *The Philosophy of Religion* (1965), it is unlikely that when Anselm used the phrase 'Thou canst not be conceived not to be' he implied the philosophically sophisticated notion of logical necessity purveyed by Malcolm. It is more likely that he had in mind what Hick has described as 'kind of factual necessity which, in the case of God, is virtually equivalent to *aseity* or self-existence'.[4] In this realisation lies the kernel of the case opposed by Hick and others to J.N. Findlay's argument that since no proposition of the form 'x exists' can be analytically true, we can determine *a priori* by inspecting the idea that there can be no such thing as the existent posited.[5] By construing 'necessity' as 'logical necessity', goes the counter argument, Findlay's arrows fly wide of the target. Nevertheless, and reverting now to Malcolm, we need not suppose that Anselm was so arrogant as to suppose that he had uttered the last logical word. Accordingly, we must not rule out, on grounds of misplaced piety, Malcolm's re-presentation of the ontological argument merely because it extends Anselm's thought in a way undreamed of by him. Nor, on the other hand, must we hasten to canonise Professor Malcolm on the ground that he has presented Christianity with that knock-down argument which has for so long eluded the faithful. This temptation leads us to the second consideration.

Malcolm admits that while his version of what he calls Anselm's second argument may remove certain philosophical obstacles to faith in God, the fact of accepting the validity of the argument (supposing that we do) is not equivalent to believing in God in the Christian sense of the words. This squares with Anselm's implied view that the difficult thing is not to persuade the sceptic that there must be a being than which a greater cannot be conceived, but to induce him to assign the appropriate content to the term 'God' and to adopt the appropriate attitudes towards God. The validity of an argument may be the vehicle of a disclosure of the reality of God, but the fact of its logical impeccability provides no guarantee that it will be so. Conversely, it is more than likely that some have been stimulated in a God-ward direction by bogus arguments, faulty exegesis and the like.

A further difficulty in the ontological argument, to which I have already alluded, has been fastened upon by Jonathan Barnes in his book, *The Ontological Argument* (1972). He does not think that it has been conclusively shown that 'necessary existence' is a self-contradictory concept, and therefore that the argument fails on that account. Rather, the argument fails because 'it cannot withstand a close scrutiny of the logical role played by the term "God" in its premises and its conclusion' (81). It is circular, and irremediably so.

In a number of articles, but notably in *The Nature of Necessity* (1974), Alvin Plantinga has propounded an ontological argument in terms of modal logic (in which recourse is had to strict implication). If 'God exists' is a necessary proposition then it must be true in all possible worlds. To exist means to be instantiated in a possible world. What exists in the world we inhabit is, in addition, actual. If there were a possible world in which the being than which a greater cannot be conceived did not exist, and if that being did not (therefore) exist in the actual world, then it would not be the being than which no greater can be conceived. Not all have been convinced by this argument. Some have pointed out that it is not self-contradictory to assert that there is *no* possible world wherein a being such as the one in question is instantiated. Further, in his article, 'Plantinga's God and other monstrosities' (*RS*, XV, 1979), Patrick Grim has argued that Plantinga's argument would prove too much were it cogent — all kinds of monstrosities than which no greater can be conceived might be deemed to exist in possible worlds. The debate continues.

Turning now to the cosmological and teleological arguments I refer first to Aquinas's Five Ways (*Summa Theologica*, I, question ii, article 3). It is to be noted that Aquinas does not say that rational argument is the only, or even the best, method of discovering God; nor yet that it is specifically the Christian God who is thereby discovered. He merely claims that the honest use of natural reason by those suitably endowed will, as a matter of fact, lead men to assert the existence of God.

The first three Ways are varieties of the cosmological argument, and it is proper to point out that Aquinas was well aware of the difficulty inherent in this argument. He confesses that Aristotle's argument from an unmoved Prime Mover (first Way) or First Cause (second Way) would be much more satisfactory if it asserted a once-for-all beginning of the world in time. In other words, he is fully aware of the peril of the infinite regress in *a posteriori* arguments of this kind. Hick has adverted to the attempt of certain contemporary Thomists to avoid this peril by claiming that the regress is not to be understood temporally, but as an eternally inconclusive regress of explanations. Otherwise, it is argued, the universe is simply an unintelligible brute fact. But, retorts Hick, that is just what many think it is. That is certainly what Russell thought it was. In his BBC debate with F.C. Copleston in 1948 he said, 'I should say that the universe is just there, and that's all.' In which connection Copleston elsewhere said, 'If one does not wish to embark on the path which leads to the affirmation of transcendent being . . . one has to deny the reality of the problem, assert that things "just are" and that the existential question is a pseudo-question. And if one refuses even to sit down at the chess board and make a move, one cannot, of course, be checkmated.'[6] More recently Flew, in *God and Philosophy* and elsewhere, has wielded his 'Stratonician presumption' with some relish — the presumption that since the world is what there is, it makes no sense to enquire after its cause. It is a brute fact, a datum.

Even those more inclined to sit at Copleston's chess board have still questioned whether we may properly extend the reference of the inductively explanatory notion of 'cause' as applied to sequences of events within the world to the universe as a whole.

The third Way, the argument from contingency, asserts that since there was a time when nothing existed, it may be said of everything that now exists, or has existed, or will come to exist, either that it might not have existed/come to exist, or that it might have existed/come to exist in a different form. But since contingent beings manifestly exist they must owe their existence to that which is not contingent, namely, to God. This argument turns upon the distinction between contingent and necessary being, and those who yield to the temptation to embrace this distinction fall foul of the ever-watchful Flew, who rightly accuses them of attempting to smuggle in a contraband ontological argument to bolster their case.

The fourth Way, says Aquinas, 'is taken from the gradation to be found in things . . . there must also be something which is to all being the cause of their being, goodness, and every other perfection; and this we call God'. It has often been pointed out that this is the most 'Platonic' of Aquinas's Ways. He here introduces the idea of a scale of values, and in some ways he anticipates later moral arguments for God's existence. But to this argument the sceptic may easily retort, 'I grant that certain things appear to me to be better, or more worthwhile, than others; but this is purely a subjective judgment concerning the way in which, as it happens, things seem to me to be. I do not need to posit an original donor of perfections.' Once again a contraband ontological argument comes to the rescue of those who pursue this path.

Finally, the fifth Way — the argument to, or from, design — is open to this fundamental difficulty: granted that there will inevitably be a certain harmony between the parts of any possible universe (even Hume, the arch-opponent of the argument, granted this), with what justification do we posit one, or any, Designer(s)? May not things just have fallen out as they have? Enter the ontological argument. Furthermore, sceptics from Hume and Mill onwards have not been slow to point out that this argument can prove too much. Not all aspects of the grand design are beneficent; indeed, some features of the 'pattern' constitute one of the most prominent of anti-theistic weapons, namely, the problem of evil. Even when such a writer as A.E. Taylor attempts to secure something from the argument — 'Nature is not exactly like a large establishment for the mass-production of Ingersoll watches, but when all is said, is it not more like this than it is like an unending harlequinade with no point in particular'[7] — it is clear that the judgement implicit in his final phrase is not one that can be supported by the argument itself; it is in the nature of an act of faith.

Perhaps the most significant and incisive book on Aquinas's arguments to appear during recent years is Anthony Kenny's *The Five Ways* (1969). Kenny provides a careful analysis of Aquinas, noting in particular the difficulties which arise from the context of medieval cosmology within which the arguments were developed. He does not, however, encompass contemporary varieties of Thomism. Nor indeed does Hick, in his helpful discussion of the *Arguments for the Existence of God* (1970). A reviewer of the latter work (*HeyJ*, XIII, 1972, 111-12) noted the omission, and pointed out that such contemporary Thomists as Rahner, Coreth and Lonergan reinterpret the Thomistic proofs according to a post-Kantian transcendental method. They do not argue by logical deduction from finite experience, nor do they offer a purely formal analysis of concepts. Rather, they analyse the conditions of possibility of our actual experience, and 'This is claimed to lead to the metaphysical insight of God's existence, not as a probable hypothesis, but as a necessary (*a priori*) truth implicit in the reality (synthetic) of that experience' (112).

That Hick is not alone in his neglect of contemporary Thomists is clear from an examination of the reception accorded in Britain to the work of Lonergan. Lonergan's massive work, *Insight*, first appeared in 1957. Philip McShane did useful introductory work in his article, 'The contemporary Thomism of Fr. Bernard Lonergan' (*PS*, XI, 1961), but it is still true that as far as British *philosophers* are concerned Lonergan's work is largely unheeded outside Catholic circles (and in those circles it is not uncritically received) and this despite the efforts of Hugo Meynell who, in a number of articles, and in his book, *An Introduction to the Philosophy of Bernard Lonergan* (1976), has sought to show Lonergan's importance and relevance. (It is only just to point out that Lonergan's subsequent works on theological method have been somewhat more ecumenically appraised by theologians.)

Neither Locke, Berkeley or Hume would have quarrelled with Lonergan's starting-point: 'Thoroughly understand what it is to understand, and not only will you understand the broad lines of all there is to be understood, but also you will possess a fixed base, an invariant pattern, opening upon all further developments of understanding' (xxviii). But, as Meynell points out, Lonergan's denial of the empiricist claim that the intelligible order is a product of the activity of the human mind at once places him in the line of Aristotle and Aquinas, for whom 'both the phenomena which we experience and the intelligible pattern within which they are found to cohere are aspects of the real objective world which confronts the human inquirer, and which would exist even if there were no intelligent beings to inquire into it' (2). Lonergan's analysis of human understanding, and of the phenomenal world leads him to the idea of an 'unrestricted act of understanding' which understands not itself alone, but all actual and possible existents. Here we reach the foundation-plank of Lonergan's theism. No more than the classical arguments does Lonergan's argument lead to the *Christian* God. But in a Thomist-cum-neo-Kantian way he purports to reach *a being*, though not in a logically coercive way.

Apart from the fact that the traditional theistic arguments are to the philosopher of religion as the cuttle fish is to the budgerigar, the most positive thing to be said about them is that they indicate certain aspects of human experience — contingency, order, purpose and the like — which have to be accommodated within any articulation of a world view which pretends to adequacy. They raise the question of the relation between reason and revelation, and (sinful) nature and grace; and they caution us to be very circumspect in our choice of systematic starting-points. Some versions of Thomism, for example, seem to leave us with undifferentiated being, just as some of the older idealisms left us with an undifferentiated absolute. I have a hunch which I cannot pursue here that neither of these are of special help to one who would construct a *Christian* philosophy.

It remains only to add that the relatively more modern arguments for God's existence — the moral, and that from religious experience — have been examined in some detail during our period — the former notably by H.P. Owen in *The Moral Argument for Christian Theism* (1968). The crux of Owen's case is that unless the objectivity of morals can be maintained on purely rational grounds we cannot begin to construct a moral argument for the existence of God: 'Unless goodness can be given an objective sense in the premises (where it refers to finite being) it cannot have this sense in the conclusion (where it refers to the infinite being of God' (30). Owen properly claims that his arguments are neither sufficient nor necessary to inspire belief in God, but believes that dialectic can precede faith.

The argument from religious experience has been discussed (in a somewhat attentuated way) by T.R. Miles in his *Religious Experience* (1972); and C.B. Martin kept up the pressure upon this argument ever since his celebrated article 'A religious way of knowing' appeared in *New Essays in Philosophical Theology*. My own view is that while religious experience is an important factor to be taken into account in the construction of a coherent statement of the theistic position, the *argument* from religious experience cannot surmount the difficulty encapsulated by R.W. Hepburn thus: 'There seems no way, *at the experiential level*, of settling the really urgent questions, most of all the following: Do we have in theistic experience *mere* projection? Or do we have a projection matched by an objectively existing God?'[8]

As I hinted when discussing the cosmological argument, the problem of evil remains the gravest objection to theism. Why do the righteous suffer? Why is there so much suffering — apparently random and inequitable suffering? In face of evil, how can we continue to believe in a good, powerful, loving God? The outstanding survey of the territory in this field is John Hick's *Evil and the God of Love* (1966; rev. edn 1977), though the spate of articles which followed the publication of this book showed that not all were at one with Hick in opting for an allegedly personalist Irenaean type of theodicy, according to which man is on the way, as against an allegedly non-personalist Augustinian type of theodicy, according to which man is a fallen sinner. In a less historical context Plantinga has argued against J.L. Mackie and others that those who object to theism because of the problem of evil have not shown, and cannot show, that their claim that 'no case of severe, protracted, involuntary human pain is ever outweighed by any good state of affairs' is true.[9]

In *Providence and Evil* (1977) Peter Geach argues that the world is planned by the good God; that evil arises because he has given free will; and that sin is a necessary condition of the virtue of redemption. No doubt 'We may think this price too high to pay, but are we in our sloth and cowardice the best judges?' (66). Even as I write Geach's words I hear James Orr's words thundering down the years, 'Sin is that which ought not to be *at all*.'[10] On the broad question, H.P. Owen has reasserted the kind of answer that is open to the Christian — an answer nowhere more forcefully given than by P.T. Forsyth in *The Justification of God* (1917/1948). Owen writes,

> Evil . . . constitutes *prima facie* evidence *against* the existence of an omnipotent and loving God. On the theoretical plane our perplexity remains. But on the practical plane it is overcome by faith in the redemptive power of Christ. If we lack this faith it is, I admit, always possible that the disorder of the world will prevent us from discerning the divine order to which morality, on other grounds, so amply testifies.[11]

This note is lacking in Geach's work, and that it is not the only lack is clear from Jonathan Harrison's lively article, 'Malt does more than Peter can, or On behalf of the damned' (*RS*, XIV, 1978).

Undeterred by the difficulties posed by the arguments for the existence of God, many continue to believe that some form of natural theology is essential. These include the Thomists, of course, but also non-Thomist Catholics such as Trethowan, and Reformed Christians such as H.P. Owen and Hick. Notwithstanding the difficulties in the arguments all of these maintain that it makes sense to seek the rational justification of religious belief; that theism is a coherent system; and that the concepts applied to God are worthy of investigation.

In 1967 F.H. Cleobury's *A Return to Natural Theology* was published. This is an interesting defence of a view which we met near the beginning of this book, namely, that the only real existents are minds, and that all minds are included without confusion in the ultimate, all-embracing Mind. In fact this is a reiteration of idealism which, though interesting, is not typical of the approach to natural theology during recent years. Rather, what we have seen is an increasingly ecumenical attempt to move from the demonstrative-essentialist Thomism of, for example, John Horgan in his articles 'The proof of the existence of God' (*PS*, I and II, 1951, 1952) to the more existentialist-ontological approach of those who, like

N.D. O'Donoghue, maintain that 'we can never arrive at an absolute regressively, along the critical road; we can only find an absolute progressively, along the road of reality as it presents itself to us in experience — the road that leads to the affirmation of existence, that is lighted for us by the light of existence itself' (*PS*, XVII, 1968, 120).

A similar view was expressed by Hick in his *Faith and Knowledge* (2nd edn, 1967), where faith is rightly held to be 'an apprehension of the divine presence within the believer's human experience' (115); and by Trethowan in his *Absolute Value: A Study in Christian Theism* (1970). The latter works out his position in relation to our experience of obligation. Not indeed that he proceeds in a syllogistic or quasi-syllogistic manner: he begins from an apprehension of God as causally present in his creatures. We thus have a direct (albeit mediated) apprehension of God. A similar position is adopted by Owen in his *The Christian Knowledge of God* (1969). Owen argues that the logical gap between inadequate theistic arguments and the knowledge of God is bridged by intuition. This intuition is, when supported by the arguments, veridical: 'Neither reason (*ratio*) nor intuition (*intellectus*) is, on its own, a sufficient ground for faith. Each needs the other. Without intuition belief is empty; but without reason it is blind' (176). It is only proper to point out that not all (including Trethowan) have been convinced by Owen's appeal to intuition at this point.

The implication of the positions just noted — however much their respective proponents may differ from each other — is that the natural theologian is adverting to something which the sceptic has not *seen*. The sceptic neglects, and cannot do other than neglect, important evidence; while the natural theologian is not simply seeking to pile one broken-backed argument upon another. Thus, against Flew, J. Macdonald Smith argues in 'Philosophy and God', that

> the essential difference between the Christian and the atheist is not over the existence of God at all; it is a difference as to the nature of the world . . . natural theology intuits the Creator as the ground of a contingent universe, simultaneously intuiting the universe as contingent. This intuition is later shown to be valid by a rational argument. Now, while in the logical and ontological order God is primary, nevertheless in the natural order it is the intuition of the universe as contingent which is primary. (*CQR*, CLXVIII, 1967, 83)

From a somewhat different perspective comes Basil Mitchell's *The Justification of Religious Belief* (1973). He does not himself set out to provide a rational justification of belief, but rather asks what would be involved in providing such a thing. Strictly, he says, it is impossible for us to *know* that there is a God — or to *know* that there is not a God. Christian theism is thus a world view which is to be judged by the extent to which it makes sense of all the available evidence. Mitchell does not deny that *prima facie* certain factors count against religious belief, but he does not think that these are insuperable obstacles. Mitchell's arguments (though not necessarily his conclusions) have been queried by Michael Durrant in his article, 'Cumulative arguments in theology' (*Sophia*, XV, No. 3, 1976), on the ground that Mitchell does not attend sufficiently to the different types of context in which rational arguments can occur.

Whereas Phillips, for example, does not think it meaningful to look for order in human affairs, Richard Swinburne holds that belief in God demands such an order. He argues his case in *The Coherence of Theism* (1977). He maintains that the existence of God is given — it is not explicable by reference to anything else; and that the belief that God is omnipresent, omniscient, perfectly good, immutable, eternal and free is a coherent belief. Two difficulties in particular have been found by Swinburne's reviewers. The first is that he seems to scale down the connotation of the traditional attributes of God to the point at which God can be only a function of the world. Secondly, it has been pointed out that even granted the coherence of the discourse about God, the question of the reality of God remains, and so also does the question of the verification of statements made about God. Swinburne has made a partial response to the latter point in *The Existence of God* (1979). He adopts a cumulative approach to the traditional arguments, and finds that the evidence of religious experience conduces to the probability of the theistic explanation of the world. Swinburne's views are, at the time of writing, still under discussion, and no doubt he has not uttered his last word on the matter.

Among others who have discussed the attributes of God are H.P. Owen in *Concepts of Deity* (1971) and A. Kenny in *The God of the Philosophers* (1979). The concepts of transcendence and immanence have been discussed by many — the latter not least by Helen Oppenheimer in *Immanence and Incarnation* (1973). I have myself sought to construe 'transcendence' morally, and in relation to distinctively Christian claims in 'Transcendence, immanence and the supernatural' (*JTSA*, No. 26. March 1979).

Process thought

In the wake of the later Whitehead, and variously inspired by such Americans as Charles Hartshorne, John Cobb and Schubert Ogden, some philosophically-minded theologians have devoted themselves to process thought during the past 15 years. In this they have been aided and abetted by Norman Pittenger who, in turn, has been critically pursued by Colin Gunton. For all their differences from each other, the process thinkers unite in regarding classical theism as deficient because static. In the Greek tradition God exists *a se*; the concept of temporality cannot be applied to him. This, so it is alleged by process thinkers, encouraged the unwholesomely transcendent view of God which, passing from the Aristotelian unmoved Mover through the scholastic *ens realissimum*, reached its climax in deism where God was understood as static, external, uninvolved. Needless to say, none of these ideas appealed to those who sympathised with the general trend of 19th-century evolutionary thought and wished to forsake the static view of God for the dynamic, the fixed for the developing.

In approaching process thought it is necessary to keep a sense of proportion. We may justifiably feel that deism and its precursors was but a minority interest, and one, perhaps, which had more to do with religious practice. Thus, for example, the Old Testament tells of a creative God who works through historical events, who addresses his people, who has a purpose for them, and so on. The New Testament is replete with teleological and eschatological motifs and, above all, it has the God-man at its heart. How could the Almighty have become *more* involved and closer, a Christian might ask? In post-biblical times, to take random examples only, we find Duns Scotus correcting an undue Thomistic emphasis on being with his teaching concerning the primacy of the ethical; we find the best of the mystics, Puritans, pietists, Quakers, Moravians and others experimentally persuaded of the reality of God in their midst; and we find the conviction of the presence of God inspiring phenomena as various as the ecclesiologies of Dissent and the testimonies of Christian existentialists. In all these cases the transcendence of God is regarded much more as a matter of his character as holy, than as a matter of the *quasi*-geographical distance between him and men. The process theologians have not, therefore, succeeded where *all* others have failed in bringing God near.

They have, however, made two radically new proposals. First, they have revived the Greek idea, shunned in the orthodox tradition, of a developing God. We recall Plato's words in the *Timaeus* to the effect that 'the Creator, in creating the world, creates himself; he is working out his own being. Considered as not creating, he has neither existence nor concrete meaning.' But, secondly, whereas Plato thought of the self-creating deity as being far removed from the world of matter, with the process thinkers immanence reigns, and part of their inspiration is the doctrine of emergent evolution. Thus Whitehead could say in his *Process and Reality*, 'It is as true to say that God creates the World, as that the World creates God' (1978 edn, 348). Now while it is true, as we saw earlier, that Whitehead wished to preserve transcendence by introducing his concept of di-polarity, according to which God's primordial nature is eternal and beyond human knowledge, whilst his consequent nature is that by which he acts dynamically in the world, lovingly 'luring' it on its evolutionary way towards the goal he has appointed for it, it is the immanentist aspect which exerts the greater pull. Hence Whitehead's follower, H.N. Wieman, in *The Source of Human Good* (1946) can assert that 'The only creative God we recognise is the creative event itself' (7). Here transcendence seems to have become so inconsequential that it is quite impotent to serve any longer as the bulwark between the process thinker's desiderated pan*en*theism and that full-blown pantheism of which he is rightly suspicious.

Undeterred, such scholars as Schubert Ogden and Norman Pittenger persist with process thought, and they both find it necessary to focus on the Incarnation, or on what the latter calls 'the event of Jesus Christ' — this event being regarded not so much as the 'supreme anomaly' as the 'classical instance'. In Charles Hartshorne's view Christ is the supreme symbol of God's activity and meaning in his world. We may agree that 'Jesus is not an isolated "entrance" or "intervention" of God into a world which otherwise is without his presence and action', but this is by no means to agree that 'the "incarnation" of God in Jesus Christ is focally but not exclusively true of him'. Ogden, in his *Christ Without Myth* (1961) and subsequent writings, seems to have no inhibitions at this point. To him God literally participates in man, yet at the same time (following Heidegger) God's being is infinite whilst man's is not. This seems an extreme statement from one who wishes to oppose the idea of temporal infinity. As James Richmond has said, if the philosophical sceptic 'finds "temporal infinity" to be a stark contradiction in terms, he may find "infinite temporality" to be equally, not less, contradictory'.[12] The difficulty of reconciling the absoluteness of God with his alleged temporality, with process, is the most serious obstacle of all. In this connection R. Gregor Smith's criticism of Ogden is reminiscent of Temple's criticism of Whitehead, which was noted earlier:

> Ogden is forced into a very serious inconsistency when he asks us to accept the reality of God as meaning both the abstract principle of all relatedness and the self-creative activity of God. Certainly, this variation of the process philosophies of Whitehead and Hartshorne can help us to grasp the significance of human historical becoming; but it cannot also expect to save the absoluteness of God except as a face-saving gesture, or an idle speculation.[13]

The nub of the criticism is that the abstract conflicts with the personal; the idea of organism with that of history.

Standing somewhat apart in confessional allegiance, professional training and mood from the process thinkers we find Teilhard de Chardin (1881-1955). His works, *The Phenomenon of Man* (1959), *Le Milieu Divin* (1960), *Letters from a Traveller* (1962), *The Future of Man* (1964) — and more than a dozen more published between 1965 and 1970 — have enjoyed a wide sale. The Garnstone Press published 'The Teilhard Study Library', and *The Teilhard Review* (1966) is devoted to the exposition and development of the master's thought.

Many have felt that Teilhard sets out to create a mood rather than construct a logically water-tight system — and no doubt this is what a visionary scientist should do. Beginning *qua* scientist he seeks to promulgate a variety of panentheism based on observation and description. He finds an evolutionary process punctuated by 'thresholds' such as the emergence of life and of man. From this starting-point he looks forward to creation's reaching its 'Omega point' which is Christ, and of which Christ's self-transcending love is for us the earnest. John Macquarrie has cogently argued that if we remain with Teilhard's naturalistic starting-point we cannot legitimately reach his speculative conclusions; whereas if we embrace his supernaturalist conclusions we must support them on other than naturalistic foundations.[14] This conclusion is reinforced by Teilhard's employment of the sacramental principle, notably in *The Future of Man*, and by his vision of a world in which 'Christ cannot sanctify the Spirit without . . . uplifting and saving the totality of Matter' (94). This 'Christification' of all things is anticipated in the Mass.

In declaring against God as 'unmoved Mover', 'ruling Caesar' and 'ruthless Moralist' Whitehead was making a proper protest against deism. Again, process thought facilitates the proclamation of the Christian message in a way that would be impossible if God was exclusively and absolutely transcendent. It proclaims a God who enters into the human lot with victorious potential. As Hartshorne writes in *Man's Vision of God* (1941), 'God has nowhere to hide himself from any sorrow or joy whatever, but must share in all the wealth and all the burden of the world' (198). Above all, it demands an adequate doctrine of immanence; God may not be excluded from any part of his universe, all of which is 'alive with his life' (*John* i : 4).

It is not easy to suppress the feeling that these benefits are purchased at too high a price; certainly they can be expressed equally well by a theology which does not batten itself to process thought. Indeed it seems to me that the peril of reductionism is at least as great here as it was in connection with the idealisms of the earlier part of the century, and with their Tillichian successor. The crucial theological question is, 'Is the creator-creature distinction adequately preserved in process thought?' If it is not then we do justice neither to man's dire need nor to God's gracious provision. David Jenkins has put the point well in his book, *The Glory of Man* (1967):

> Whatever [God's] relationship to continuing processes and developing patterns, he himself is not to be equated with those processes and patterns, and he is not dependent for his being God, or his being as God, in any way on the movements, developments, changes in materiality and history. This insight into the transcendent independence of God in his goodness is, I am convinced, a valid one. The God who is nothing but involvement is not the God of biblical encounter nor the God of theistic worship nor the God who is required by, and the fulfilment of, the mystery of personalness and love . . . God

does not exist in order to guarantee man fulfilment. Such a notion is idolatrous anthropomorphism . . . The true God exists because he is the true God and it is a *consequence* of his transcendentally independent existence both that man exists and that man has the hope of fulfilment as man. (108)

The upshot is that there can be divine immanence (properly dear to process thought) only if God's independence is posited, and there cannot be immanence if it is not. Only because he is over all can he be here or there. Among further questions which may be addressed to process thinkers, and which are in fact under discussion, are these: Can process thought maintain the absoluteness of God, and if God is less than absolute *ought* we to worship him?; Does not process thought place God at the mercy of the contingent, and require him to change course as and when unexpected eventualities arise? The place of the contingent is, I am sure, among the most intractable questions to have been raised by process thought, and it cannot yet be said that the difficulties in answering it have been removed.

The historical interest

We have seen that with the passage of time older 'sectarianisms' in philosophy have become less entrenched if they have not vanished altogether, and a greater degree of openness prevails in respect of what counts as proper employment for philosophers. In my student days I heard a learned tome dismissed as 'not *philosophy*, but *history*!' (Philosophers, it will be recalled, were supposed — in certain quarters at least — only to analyse discourse.) But now we find that a number of philosophers of religion are recalling us to past thinkers. (Moreover philosophers of religion are not alone in doing this. The art of philosophical biography is making a welcome return in the secular quarter too, as witness D.O. Thomas, *The Honest Mind: The Thought and Work of Richard Price* (1977) and Don Locke, *A Fantasy of Reason: The Life and Thought of William Godwin* (1980).) Thus James Richmond takes a fairly broad sweep through post-Kantian philosophy of religion in his *Faith and Philosophy* (1966); M.J. Charlesworth ranges over *Philosophy of Religion: The Historic Approaches* (1972); David Pailin writes on *The Way to Faith, An Examination of Newman's Grammar of Assent as a Response to the Search for Certainty in Faith* (1969); and B.M.G. Reardon has written illuminatingly on Hegel's *Philosophy of Religion* (1977). For my part I have examined some philosophical thinkers who stand broadly within the Reformed tradition, and have published *Robert Mackintosh: Theologian of Integrity* (1977) and a number of articles: 'Arminians, deists and reason' (*FF*, XXIII, 1979), 'John Howe's eclectic theism' (*JURCHS*, II, 1980), 'Priestley's polemic against Reid' (*PPNL*, III, 1979), 'Henry Rogers and the eclipse of faith' (*JURCHS*, II, 1980), and 'The centenary of Flint's *Theism*' (*PS*, XXVI, 1979).

Christianity, philosophy and Christian philosophy

This final section bears out as clearly as any in the book the point made in the Introduction: philosophy (like many other subjects of study) is fashion-prone. Metaphysical questions, which are in any case remarkably durable, are being raised in a quite uninhibited way. Not indeed that there is a widely prevalent philosophical 'ism' in terms of which, or by reference to which, Christian claims may be cashed — as there was in the early part of our century. Nor do we now hear the grandiose synthetic claims of yesteryear. The climate is different; metaphysicians are, for the most part, down to earth; but the positivistic and narrowly linguistic-analytical embargoes have been lifted, and philosophers are free to roam widely and to speak freely — provided they are willing to take the consequences.

During the period 1965–80, in the wake of more tentative enquiries into the prospects for metaphysics, there was increasingly widespread and unselfconscious recourse to metaphysical foundations, and the theme of the relations between theology and metaphysics was rehearsed with renewed vigour. Already in this chapter I have mentioned some of the work of writers as various as Swinburne, Owen and Trethowan. A.C. Ewing's posthumous *Value and Reality: The Philosophical Case for Theism* (1973) is the final collection of papers from one who did not capitulate before the anti-metaphysical onslaught; and in *Christian Theology and Metaphysics* (1968) Peter R. Baelz has provided for the wayfaring man a lucid survey of the metaphysical matters arising from the discussion of the preceding years. The concept of belief has been examined in interestingly different ways in the Gifford Lectures of H.H. Price — *Belief* (1969) — and Brand Blanshard — *Reason and Belief* (1974).

The question of the relations beteen theology and metaphysics has been specifically addressed by James Richmond and Donald MacKinnon among others. In his *Theology and Metaphysics* (1970) Richmond argues that metaphysics is ineradicable and necessary to theology; and that a theism may be propounded which derives its strength and its justification from its success in meeting its objective, which is 'to *connect up*, by the establishment of rhythms, patterns, and relations, the various disintegrated, ontologically diverse areas of the overall map into a coherent whole, whose *total* significance or meaning is expressible only in utterances of a definitely theistic kind' (121). Attention to human experience, history and nature persuades us of the contingency of the world (and this Richmond takes to be the abiding import of the Thomistic 'proofs' of the existence of God). The idea of a personal, transcendent God is the only one to which recourse may be had by those who seek coherence: the theistic explanation is the most satisfactory explanation of all. Richmond's book was kindly received in many quarters (though some reviewers, as often happens, used its appearance as an occasion for reminding us of *their* views, rather than as an occasion for discussing Richmond's). Keith Ward's concise, adversely critical remarks in what was a generally favourable review may be taken as representative of the qualms shared by some. Ward is puzzled by the notion of 'metaphysical explanation', and writes, 'If the world is "obscure, puzzling and unclear", so is the notion of God; so how does one obscure thing explain another? I suspect that the notion of an "ultimate explanation" is senseless; if not, the author needs to show it' (*T*, LXXIV, 1971, 275).

Of all contemporary British philosophers Donald MacKinnon most strikingly exemplifies a determination to *agonise* over the perplexities of human experience — not least the problem of evil. In his Gifford Lectures, *The Problem of Metaphysics* (1974), as in his earlier collection, *The Borderlands of Theology* (1968) — to the title article of which I have already referred — he resolutely takes things as they are. Not for him an 'airborne' metaphysics. But, equally, not for him the mere recognition that things are, and are as they are. He seeks the significance of the phenomena of the world, and of the facts of human experience. As he attends to the latter he is impressed by the way in which what he calls the transcendent impinges upon us. Accordingly, 'If there is anything worthy to be called metaphysical insight, then whatever the form in which it is expressed, it is a finding of what is the case; it is discovery, rather than creation' (28). With Kant he 'sees the metaphysical as something lying beyond the frontiers of intelligible descriptive discourse, yet as something that *presses* on us with a directness and immediacy which requires no argument to convince us of its reality' (55).

In MacKinnon's view we are nowhere more conscious of the pressure of the transcendent than in the ethical sphere. There is here an 'ontological intrusion' of such a kind as to undergird MacKinnon's realism: we are overtaken by that which is *there*; we are not (*pace* the constructivists) creators of the metaphysical insight which we experience. MacKinnon illuminates his theme by numerous references to artists, writers and others, in the conviction that a philosophical theory which excludes the insights into things as they are which such seers offer is impoverished indeed. The writers and artists can help us to grasp the significance of human experience, and when we meet such experience at its most harrowing, 'it is as if we are constrained in pondering the extremities of human life to acknowledge the transcendent as the only alternative to the kind of trivialisation which would empty of significance the sorts of experience with which we have been concerned' (145).

MacKinnon adverts to so much, but is ever humbly tentative. This comes out clearly in his conclusion: 'So at the end of our enquiry we come to see that we have not resolved the problem of metaphysics, only at the level of a continued self-consciousness come to see aspects of it more clearly, come indeed dimly to perceive the sort of aliveness to connections which will refuse facile consolation but find in that refusal that the issues are raised in the engagement' (170). It seems fitting to describe MacKinnon's cadences as almost liturgical for if no other contemporary British philosopher more resolutely faces the anguish of the human condition, no other expresses such an all-pervading consciousness of the *mysterium tremendum et fascinans*.

Passing from general theologico-metaphysical matters we must finally ask, 'Is there a Christian philosophy?' Both Thomas Brophy (*PS*, I, 1951) and R.F. Aldwinckle (*RS*, II, 1966–7) have written articles under this heading; but as yet no British philosophers have presented a fully rounded Christian philosophical system for our inspection. A number of philosophers and theologians have noted some of the constraints upon anyone who would venture to articulate a Christian view of the world. There is, for example, the crucial question of starting-points posed by Austin Farrer in his posthumous volume, *Interpretation and Belief* (1976):

Are we to lay down the precept, 'First judge the evidence of

your facts, then see whether they have any religious bearing?'
or should we take account of the (presumed or possible)
religious bearings of the facts, in estimating the value of the
evidence for them? (160)

But even as Farrer recognises that 'There is no such thing as a
neutral or purely scientific study of Christian origins' (162) N.H.G.
Robinson cautions us in his article 'The logical placing of the name
"God"' that 'the articulation of a world-view is a severely intellectual exercise, and it is important to remember that it can begin only
on the basis of an abstraction from the commitment and concern
which indefeasibly belong to the original situation' (*SJT*, XXIV,
1971, 144).

But if British philosophers have been reluctant to develop Christian philosophical systems, philosophers elsewhere have not been
so inhibited. I shall therefore conclude this section by noting the
contributions of some who, although their theories are by no means
mutually compatible in all respects, and although they are in some
cases at daggers drawn, would claim to be Christian philosophers
in a special sense. Not only have they not been emulated in this
country; they have, apart from the smallest handful of reviews, not
been noticed. In heading this chapter '*Almost* open house' I had
in mind the fact that whereas diverse philosophical views are more
readily accorded a hearing today than in the past, those to whom
I have now to refer are thus far beyond the pale of philosophical
discussion in Britain. Since I should prefer them to be refuted (if
that is what they deserve) than ignored, I mention them now.

The Christian philosophers to be considered are predominantly
Calvinistic in orientation and conservative in their approach to the
Bible (two considerations which are enough to damn them at the
outset in certain quarters). I use the circumlocution 'Calvinistic in
orientation' because it is a moot point how far some of them are
true to *Calvin*, and how far Calvin himself sanctions a Christian
philosophy. This question has been pursued by Charles Partee in
his article, 'Calvin, Calvinism and Classical Philosophy' (*RR*,
XXXIII, 1980); and in greater detail in his book, *Calvin and Classical
Philosophy* (1977). What a number of the Calvinistic philosophers
share is a conviction that if the religious *a priori* is not acknowledged,
we land in an immanentist philosophy which accords far too great
a place to man's sin-inspired, supposed autonomy. Implicit here
is a further reason for the neglect of these thinkers by British
philosophers (assuming that the latter have heard of the Calvinists):

it is, to say the least, not easy to enter into philosophical debate with those who set out from presuppositions which will not even admit the possibility that their opponents can reach true conclusions. But a contrary case might even then be advanced.

Instead, the Calvinistic philosophers engage in a considerable amount of in-fighting. This centres in the question: 'How far, in making Christian truth claims, may we appeal to evidence which is genuinely available to all? Is there such evidence? Does the Christian share any epistemological common ground with the unbeliever? Is the image of God in man utterly obliterated, or merely defaced?'

The impetus towards Christian *a priorism* came from Holland. Appalled by the rationalising theological liberalism of his day Guillaume Groen-van Prinsterer (1801-76) developed a doctrine of sphere-sovereignty according to which there exist such distinct spheres of authority as the family, the school, the church. Each sphere is characterised by certain inviolate responsibilities which are peculiar to itself. Abraham Kuyper (1837-1920) developed this theory, firmly locating the several spheres in the sovereign purpose of the creator God. In turn Kuyper's work was developed by D.H. Th. Vollenhoven (1892-1978) and Hermann Dooyeweerd (1894-1977). Whereas Vollenhoven's main interests lay in logic, mathematics and the history of philosophy, Dooyeweerd investigates the epistemological and ontological aspects of what came to be known as the philosophy of the idea of law, or the philosophy of the cosmonomic idea. His major work, *Wijsbegeerte von de Wesidee* (Philosophy of the Idea of Law) appeared in 1931, and was translated under the title, *A New Critique of Theoretical Thought* in 1953. Dooyeweerd's intention was to be biblical in honouring the God who governs creation by laws given to each of his creatures 'after his kind' (*Gen.* 1: 21), and to maintain the Calvinistic emphasis upon God's sovereignty. Some Reformed Christian philosophers have charged him with exalting the concept of law above that of the Word, but he had no wish other than to be true to his (conservative) understanding of biblical authority.

This variety of Christian philosophy has taken root in certain circles in South Africa, where its best-known exponent is Hendrik Stoker. His Afrikaans works are not readily accessible to the English-speaking world, though it may be said that as compared with Dooyeweerd, Stoker's emphasis is upon creation rather than law. Dooyeweerd's work has been expounded accessibly by A.L. Conradie in her book, *The Neo-Calvinistic Concept of Philosophy* (1960). Professor Conradie does not hesitate to criticise the master where she deems it necessary. From Holland there emanates the party journal (happily multi-lingual), *Philosophia Reformata* (1936); and in Toronto there is located the Institute of Christian Studies and its publishing arm, the Wedge Publishing Foundation. The latter is dedicated to publishing works in the Dooyeweerdian tradition — among them the most readily assimilable exposition of Dooyeweerd's thought which has yet appeared: L. Kalsbeek, *Contours of a Christian Philosophy* (1975). This volume maintains a proper critical distance, and includes an extensive bibliography and a most necessary glossary.

Before adverting to some in America who have been influenced by the Kuyper-Dooyeweerd tradition it is necessary to refer to the Reformed apologetics of 19th-century America, which was associated predominantly with Princeton, and the names of Charles and A.A. Hodge and B.B. Warfield. These scholars by no means ruled out the 'evidences' — miracles, biblical testimony, and the like — to which traditional Christian apologetics had appealed. They were not *a priorists*, and for his part Warfield maintained that far from faith's being apart from, or prior to, the evidences, faith is given in and with the evidences by the Holy Spirit. This tradition, which seeks to support Christian truth claims by appeal to evidence which is genuinely available to believer and unbeliever alike, has been perpetuated in our own century by J. Oliver Buswell Jr in his book, *A Christian View of Being and Knowing* (1960).

Resolutely setting his face against any appeal to objective experience, Gordon H. Clark (1902–85) begins from rational principles which are in the mind. He is convinced that empiricism cannot but end in scepticism; that Kierkegaard and the existentialists are irrationalists; and that the principle of contradiction is the final arbiter in philosophical disputes. His fundamental axiom is the existence of the God to whom the Bible bears infallible witness, and he holds to the possibility in principle of adumbrating a Christian system of thought which is deductively rigorous and logically impeccable. The principles operative throughout his many works are encapsulated in his Wheaton Lectures, which are printed in *The Philosophy of Gordon H. Clark* (1968), edited by Ronald H. Nash. This volume includes critical expositions of various aspects of Clark's thought, together with his replies to his critics. It may be mentioned in passing that if mainstream Anglo-Saxon philosophy has scarcely commented upon Clark's work, he has not been inhibited in the opposite direction. In his *Language and Theology* (1979) he criticises *inter alia* Wittgenstein, Ayer and E.L. Mascall.

Whilst appreciative of some aspects of Dooyeweerdian thought Clark is opposed to the way in which the cosmonomists ground both the logical and all the non-logical modalities in Christ. He elevates logic and *identifies* it with Christ: he has translated the first verse of the fourth gospel: 'In the beginning was logic.'

Precisely because of this elevation of logic, with its implication of something epistemologically sharable by all men by virtue of their creation; and because of his insistence that men are to use logic to judge the validity even of what the scriptures tell them, Cornelius Van Til (1895-1987) opposes Clark. Van Til, influenced by the presuppositionalism of Kuyper and the system of Dooyeweerd, yet parts from the latter, whom he charges with being insufficiently biblical: the idea of law takes precedence over the scriptures at crucial points, and Van Til will have none of this. (The Americans H. Evan Runner, David H. Freeman, Robert D. Knudsen and Calvin Seerveld are among more 'orthodox' — though not uncritical — Dooyeweerdians.) Van Til is equally opposed to the evidentialists, for they — standing as they do in the Aquinus-Butler-Arminius line — assume a degree of common ground as between believer and unbeliever. They do not, he thinks, take due account of the noetic effects of sin; they do not reckon sufficiently with the fact that natural man *suppresses* the truth — an act for which he is responsible and without excuse (Rom. 1). Unless one begins from the presupposition of the self-contained Triune God no facts can be accorded their true meaning; and no one will in fact begin from that point unless God removes the scales from his eyes. The fullest account of Van Til's position is in his *A Christian Theory of Knowledge* (1969). A number of Van Til's friends and (intellectual) foes have contributed to the collection, *Jerusalem and Athens* (1971), edited by E.R. Geehan. Van Til's responses to his critics are always vigorous if not universally convincing. Thom Notaro's book, *Van Til's Use of Evidence* (1980) treats the main methodological issue in a fair and lucid way.

A pupil of both Clark and Van Til, Edward J. Carnell (1919-67) devised a Christian philosophical methodology which is more broadly based than that of either of his mentors. The claim that the triune God of the Bible is the source of all being and knowledge is not an innate idea, or an unquestionable presupposition; rather, it is a testable hypothesis. Carnell finds the hypothesis internally coherent and systematically adequate. It squares with observed facts of history, and it alone honours man's axiological longings, meets his psychological needs, and sustains his moral convictions. The most comprehensive statement of Carnell's position is to be found in his *A Philosophy of the Christian Religion* (1952).

From many other philosophers who stand broadly in the Reformed tradition I select as concluding examples Arthur Holmes and Warren C. Young. Holmes has not as yet offered a fully rounded system, but in *Christian Philosophy in the Twentieth Century* (1969) and *Faith Seeks Understanding* (1971) he sets out his methodological principle with clarity and charity. All philosophy is perspectival, he claims. Accordingly, the Christian philosopher need have no qualms about taking his stand and affirming those insights by which he has been gripped. Men need God for the fulfilment of their manifold needs; Holmes has found his own needs thus met; and his philosophy becomes the working out of a view of the world consistent with his experience. The categories used in presenting Christian philosophy are to be drawn from revelation, and will include God, the logos, creation and personality among others. The Christian perspective both fits all the facts and involved the philosopher existentially.

In *A Christian Approach to Philosophy* (1954: 10th edn 1973) Warren C. Young argues for a Christian realism which is grounded upon divine disclosure:

> It is the Christian realistic contention that only if the revelational postulate be granted is it possible to construct a fully integrated philosophy . . . [The coherence of a philosophical system is always relative]: It always depends on a system of assumptions which are adhered to by faith or conviction rather than by rational demonstration. Christian realism is the most coherent world-view, we believe, if the assumption of special revelation be granted; it is not the most coherent philosophy if the fact of special revelation be denied, as in the case of empirically rooted systems such as idealisms or naturalism. (200-01)

Christian philosophy begins with 'the assertion of a positive, supernatural, and authoritative message' (201). (There is more than enough in that last sentence to prompt a British analyst to feel that Christian philosophy is remote from his concerns — indeed, that it is not genuinely philosophy. Well, let him make out a case accordingly.) Young contends that since all philosophical systems begin with postulates of some kind the Christian philosopher is no differently placed in that respect. Moreover, the insistence on the primacy of revelation in the attainment of truth is defended on the ground that from revelation alone do we learn the *limitations* of the human reason. Man is a fallen rebel. Hence Young takes issue with Carnell, for whom reason is that by which man discerns the philosophical options: 'the natural man is in no position to understand what the Biblical option is' (203). The Christian world view begins from a vital *experience*, not from a supposedly neutral weighing of evidence and starting points. The resulting assurance confirms the truth of the written Word and of the given experience.

Even from these brief statements we can see the variety and the disunity of the philosophies under review. Thus Young, believing as he does that Christian philosophy begins from the divine self-disclosure, cannot accept Buswell's empiricism — how could we reach the supernatural by attending to empirical phenomena? Nor can he accept the rationalism of Clark and Carnell, for they allow too much to blighted reason. Van Til has taken Clark to task for appearing to set logic above the infallible Word, and has charged Dooyeweerd with elevating law above scripture. Clark has had it pointed out to him that a deductive rational system can be *untrue*; Van Til has been shown that for all his denial of common ground as between believer and unbeliever, he conducts vigorous apologetics with 'apostates' of all kinds — an activity which would be pointless were there not some common ground. (To which Van Til replies that man can understand arguments intellectually, but, apart from saving grace, he cannot endorse them.) Young has been seen to run into the difficulties which lie in the path of any encounter theology. As Clark said of his work, 'Instead of asking, Who decides? he should have asked, On what ground can a decision legitimately be made?'[15]

I think it can fairly be claimed that these broadly Reformed philosophers are raising genuinely *philosophical* questions — concerning the possibility of a Christian philosophy; starting points; common ground; the place of evidence; the relation of faith to reason; the concept of coherence; and the place of revelation and religious experience. All of these matters bear examination, and the study of these thinkers has prompted these questions in my mind: 'Can there really be a Christian philosophy? What would such a thing be like? Can it be devised in such a way as to avoid Clement Webb's implied accusation: "I can honestly say that nothing is to me more unlovely, when detected, than apologetic masquerading as philosophy"?'[16] The answering of these questions is a task for another day.

Notes

1. For the issues in a nutshell as between Hick and Phillips see J. Hick, 'The justification of religious belief', and D.Z. Phillips, 'Religious belief and philosophical enquiry', *T*, LXXI (1968), pp. 100-07, 115-22.

2. J. Hick (ed.), *Faith and the Philosophers* (Macmillan, London, 1964), p. 241.

3. See W. Kaufmann, *Critique of Religion and Philosophy* (Faber & Faber, London, 1959), pp. 116-17; E.L. Mascall, *Existence and Analogy* (Darton Longman and Todd, London, 1949), p. 21; J. Heywood Thomas, *Subjectivity and Paradox*, (Blackwell, Oxford, 1957), pp. 78-9.

4. Thomas McPherson, *The Philosophy of Religion* (D. Van Nostrand, London, 1965), p. 46. cf; J. Hick, *Philosophy of Religion* (Prentice Hall, Englewood Cliffs, 1964), p. 21.

5. See J.N. FIndlay, 'Can God's existence be disproved?' in *New Essays in Philosophical Theology* (SCM, London, 1955), pp. 47-56, 71-5.

6. The BBC debate between Russell and Copleston is reprinted in J. Hick (ed.) *The Existence of God* (Macmillan, New York, 1964), pp. 167-91. The further reference is to F.C. Copleston, *Aquinas* (Penguin, Harmondsworth, 1955), p. 124.

7. A.E. Taylor, *Does God Exist?* (Collins Fontana, London, 1961), p. 89.

8. R.W. Hepburn, 'Religious Experience, Argument for the Existence of God', *The Encyclopedia of Philosophy* (Macmillan, New York, 1967), VII, p. 168.

9. A. Plantinga, *God and Other Minds* (Cornell University Press, New York, Ithaca, 1967), p. 129.

10. James Orr, *Side-lights on Christian Doctrine* (Marshall, London [1909]), p. 94.

11. H.P. Owen, *The Moral Argument for Christian Theism* (Allen & Unwin, London 1965), p. 88.

12. See J. Richmond, 'God, time and process philosophy', *T*, LXVIII (1965), p. 241.

13. R. Gregor Smith, *The Doctrine of God* (Collins, London, 1970), p. 157.

14. J. Macquarrie, 'The natural theology of Teilhard de Chardin', *The Expository Times*, LXXII (1960-61), pp. 335-8.

15. G.H. Clark, 'Apologetics', in C.F.H. Henry (ed), *Contemporary Evangelical Thought* (Baker Book House, Grand Rapids, 1968), p. 151.

16. C.C.J. Webb, 'Outline of a philosophy of religion', in J.H. Muirhead (ed), *Contemporary British Philosophy* (Allen & Unwin, London, 1925), p. 342.

9
Epilogue

From an inescapably British — though not, I trust, from a damagingly partisan — perspective I have attempted to chart the course of the philosophy of religion from 1875 to 1980. Our attention has been concentrated upon the relations between Christian and secular philosophy of religion to 1965, and upon a selection of themes which have occupied the attention of philosophers of religion from 1965 to 1980.

A number of general lessons have been learned. First, that the labelling of philosophers and of philosophical systems is a hazardous pursuit. Even in the 'hey-day of idealism' there was much that was not idealism, and no two idealists thought exactly alike. Second, that positivist and other attempted embargoes notwithstanding, metaphysical questions — not least those bearing directly upon religion — are remarkably durable. Third, that the (ostensibly) undogmatic atmosphere of linguistic analysis created a climate in which Thomism, existentialism and process thought could emerge into the arena of general philosophical debate — though in Britain Thomism has had more success in this respect than either existentialism or process thought. Fourth, that the relations between Christian and secular philosophy in Britain in our period have fluctuated widely. There were times, notably in the early years, when an available philosophical 'ism' — idealism — encouraged a number of Christian philosophers to attempt to adumbrate their own philosophy in terms of, or at least in close relation to, that 'ism'. But there were also cases of either side ignoring the other: the theologians, for example, paying little heed to Alexander, the secular philosophers to Tillich; and there were time-lags too, as when the Christian philosophers somewhat belatedly explored the terrain of linguistic analysis, and their secular counterparts allowed some

Epilogue

years to elapse before a minority of them turned their attention to the pronouncements of encounter theology.

Our study may end with good news and with bad news — or, at least, our general optimism concerning the philosophy of religion as such cannot obliterate anxiety regarding the constraints under which the discipline (like other branches of the philosophical family) currently labours.

Our optimism derives from the fact that although philosophers of the kind discussed in the last part of the preceding chapter have yet to be widely welcomed at the British philosophical table, it is nevertheless true to say that Schiller's 'fair maid' Philosophy is more hospitable today than she has been at any time during the past century. J.H. Muirhead's attitude, spelled out in more sectarian days, is now commonplace:

> Philosophy, like heaven, is a house of many mansions, and for my part (supposing myself to be there) I should welcome to a place in it even the movements and methods with which, from a practical and even a philosophical point of view, I have the least sympathy.[1]

This eirenic statement is also realistic; for it reminds us that philosophy, presumably unlike heaven, is a house of many sects, parties and even squabbles. Certainly as far as the philosophy of religion is concerned we cannot say that the challenges of the Enlightenment have finally been met, and it is clear that philosophers will continue to take up differing positions in relation to them.

We may hope that close conceptual and presuppositional analysis will characterise the philosophy of religion of the future. Many spheres of Christian discourse — the ecumenical, liberation and counselling theologies, to name but a few — merit such scrutiny; and what is the analysis of 'Christian education', 'Christian epistemology', 'Christian ethics'? Some may continue to feel that analysis of this kind is not only indispensable, but that it is the only proper function of the philosopher of religion. They will follow in the line of C.D. Broad who, as long ago as 1924, said that the time was not ripe for synthesis. Others may consider that so much linguistic ground-clearing has now been done that erosion threatens. There are signs that the adumbration of a Christian world view is being increasingly attempted, here with reference to other world faiths, there in relation to secular humanism, or to the threat to

Epilogue

creation itself, or to the manifold ethical questions which are posed by scientific and medical research.

The analytical-*cum*-synoptic agenda is so large that a misapplication of the biblical text comes to mind: 'The crop is heavy but the labourers are scarce; you must therefore beg the owner to send labourers to harvest his crop' (Matt. ix, 37). Where matters economic are concerned the government of the day is to a large extent 'the owner' *vis-à-vis* higher education. It is not here suggested that philosophy should be favoured above all other academic disciplines; but it is permissible to record disquiet at the news that 'There are now only two people under 30 in full-time [university] posts' in the United Kingdom.[2] No doubt the philosophy of religion may be studied in some theological courses, and in some polytechnics and colleges and institutes of higher education. Its status is usually that of an 'option', however, and its candidates may come to it with little or no general philosophical background.

However it may be with other professions and callings, it is highly desirable that the churches continue to ensure that at least some of their ordinands encounter the philosophy of religion. In commending the subject we need not be so aristocratic as to extol the worth of the discipline for its own sake whilst overlooking its pastoral usefulness. It is, of course, abundantly plain that countless thousands of Christians have managed to fight the good fight of faith without ever having heard of Wittgensteinian language games or even of Wisdom's gardener; and there is no justification for doing the philosophical equivalent of what the cartoon parson did in the doctrinal field when he peered down upon his unsuspecting flock and expostulated, 'I know what you're thinking — Sabellianism!' The fact remains, however, that church members and others will persist in demanding a reason for their hope; they will crave an account of 'the meaning of life'; and if office and factory sceptics do not challenge them on the problem of evil, the grounds of belief, immortality and the like, the circumstances of life probably will.

Of one thing we may be sure: not all philosophical challenges will be so easily disposed of as the one to which the celebrated Dr Joseph Parker (1830–1902) referred one Sunday morning in London's City Temple. Parker informed the congregation that he had received a letter stating that a certain gentleman proposed to attend worship that day with a view to subjecting the sermon to philosophical analysis. After pausing for effect Parker continued, 'I may add that my trepidation is somewhat mitigated by the

Epilogue

fact that the gentleman spells "philosophical" with an "f"![3]

Notes

1. J.H. Muirhead, 'Letter to the Editor on the present need of a philosophy', *Philosophy*, X (1935), p. 134.
2. Steven Lukes, 'Why the brains of Britain are fleeing', *The Observer*, 3 May 1987.
3. Ernest H. Jeffs, *Princes of the Modern Pulpit: Religious Leaders of a Generation*, Sampson Low, Marston, London, n.d.), pp. 20-1.

Bibliography

In addition to the books and articles referred to in the text, the following minimal list of general books will be of interest. Some of them are now, in some respects, dated; but our purpose has been not simply to survey work in the philosophy of religion, but to monitor its reception at different times during the last one hundred years. For this purpose a Caldecott is as relevant as a Macquarrie.

Alfred Caldecott, *The Philosophy of Religion in England and America* (Methuen, London, 1901).

Thomas A. Langford, *In Search of Foundations: English Theology 1900-1920* (Abingdon Press, Nashville, 1969).

Gordon R. Lewis, *Testing Christianity's Truth Claims* (Moody Press, Chicago, 1976).

John Macquarrie, *Twentieth-Century Religious Thought* (SCM Press, London, rev. edn, 1971).

James Patrick, *The Magdalen Metaphysicals: Idealism and Orthodoxy at Oxford, 1901-1945* (Mercer University Press, Macon, GA, 1985).

Rudolf Metz, *A Hundred Years of British Philosophy* (Allen & Unwin, London, 1938).

J.O. Urmson, *Philosophical Analysis* (Clarendon Press, Oxford, 1956).

G.J. Warnock, *English Philosophy Since 1900* (Oxford University Press, London, 1958).

Index of Persons

Aldwinckle, Russell F. 234
Alexander, Samuel 62-8, 74, 83, 91-2, 97, 122, 242
Allen, Edgard Leonard 157
Anselm 216-18
Anstruther, Godfrey 100
Aquinas, Thomas 2, 84-6, 89-90, 92, 100, 110, 112, 133-4, 138, 186, 190, 201, 219-22, 238
Aristotle 34, 68, 84-5, 90, 219, 222
Arminius, Jacobus 238
Augustine of Hippo 138
Austin, John Langshaw 129-30
Aveling, F. 87-8, 91, 132
Avicenna 85
Ayer, Alfred Jules 4, 79, 109, 114-16, 119, 123, 126, 133, 143, 178-9, 237

Baader, Franz von 161
Baelz, Peter Richard 205, 232
Baillie, Donald Macpherson 94
Baillie, James Black 36, 38-9, 41
Baillie, John 94, 104-5, 193-4
Banks, John Shaw 37-8
Barnes, Jonathan 218
Barnes, Winston Herbert Frederick 132
Barth, Karl 67, 84, 167
Baur, Ferdinand Christian 16
Bergson, Henri 58
Berkeley, George 14-15, 33, 222
Blackham, Harold John 157
Blanshard, Brand 232
Boehme, Jakob 171, 173
Bonaventure 89
Bosanquet, Bernard 40, 46, 48, 54-5
Bradley, Francis Herbert 2, 9, 12, 17-18, 20, 22, 25-6, 29, 33-4, 40, 45-6, 48, 50-1, 53-5, 62
Braithwaite, Richard Bevan 112-13, 150-1, 185
Brentano, Franz 51, 168
Brightman, Edgar Sheffield 64
Britton, Karl William 117-18
Broad, Charlie Dunbar 3, 56, 65, 77, 82-3, 94-5, 123, 130, 243
Brophy, Thomas 234
Browning, Robert 6, 55
Brunner, Emil 94, 193
Buber, Martin 94
Bultmann, Rudolf 104, 160
Burgh, William George de 59, 83, 97, 105-8, 111, 199
Buswell, James Oliver 237, 240
Butler, Joseph 8, 10, 238
Buzetti, Vincenzo 86

Caird, Edward 12, 14, 19-23, 27, 49, 55, 74
Caird, John 15, 21, 27
Caldecott, Alfred 10, 22
Calvin, John 235
Campbell, Charles Arthur 94, 197-8
Carlyle, Thomas 13
Carnap, Rudolf 79-80, 186
Carnell, Edward John 238-40
Case, Thomas 49
Casserley, Julian Victor Langmead 136, 138-9
Cavanaugh, John 92
Charlesworth, Maxwell John 231
Clark, Gordon Haddon 164, 237-8, 240
Clarke, William Newton 4
Cleobury, Frank Harold 195-6, 224
Coates, J.B. 157
Cobb, John 227
Coffey, Peter 86-7
Coleridge, Samuel Taylor 6, 13
Collingwood, Robin George 58, 92-4, 120-1, 180

Index

Collins, J. 157
Comte, Auguste 79
Conradie, A.L. 236
Copleston, Frederick Charles John Paul 134-6, 158, 160, 178, 191, 220
Coreth, E. 221
Coulson, John 201
Cox, David 140-1
Croce, Benedetto 89
Crombie, Ian MacHattie 153, 182, 211

Darwin, Charles 6
Davidson, William Leslie 28-9, 45
Davis, Henry Francis 133
Democritus of Abdera 85
Denney, James 23
DeQuincey, Thomas 13
Descartes, René 90, 139, 158, 169, 197, 216
Dionysius the pseudo Areopagite 84, 171
Donne, John 186
Dooyeweerd, Hermann 236-8, 240
Dummett, Michael Anthony Eardley 177
Duncan, Alistair Robert Campbell 197
Duns Scotus, Johannes 227
Durrant, Michael 226

Edwards, David Miall 30-1, 96-7
Einstein, Albert 69
Eliot, Thomas Stearns 186
Emerson, Ralph Waldo 13, 171
Emmet, Dorothy Mary 71, 102-3, 105-6, 111, 123-5, 130-2, 160, 181
Eriugena, John Scotus 171
Eucken, Rudolf 206
Evans, Donald Dwight 184
Ewing, Alfred Cyril 93-4, 97, 118, 145, 150, 185, 193, 232

Farmer, Henry Herbert 94, 104-5, 193-4

Farrer, Austin Marsden 123, 134, 234-5
Fawcett, Edward Douglas 2
Ferré, Frederick 154-5
Ferrier, James Frederick 13-14
Fichte, Johann Gottlieb 13, 20
Findlay, John Niemeyer 218
Flew, Anthony Garrard Newton 133, 142, 147-8, 151-4, 210, 215, 220, 225
Flint, Robert 8-12, 232
Ford, Henry 183
Forsyth, Peter Taylor 67, 224
Foster, Michael Beresford 191-2
Freeman, David H. 238
Frege, Gottlob 51, 77

Galileo, Galilei 70
Galloway, George 56-8
Gaunilo 216
Geach, Peter Thomas 224
Geehan, Ernest R. 238
Gellner, Ernest 176-8
Gentile, Giovanni 89
Gény, P. 91
Gill, Jerry H. 212
Gilson, Etienne 86, 91, 137
Gladstone, William Ewart 6
Gore, Charles 4
Green, Thomas Hill 8-9, 11-17, 47, 49, 50, 62
Grim, Patrick 219
Grote, John 13-14
Gunton, Colin Ewart 227

Haldane, Richard Burdon 7
Hallett, Harold Foster 118
Hamilton, Kenneth 173
Hampshire, Stuart Newton 130
Hare, Richard Mervyn 150, 152-3, 179-80
Harrison, Jonathan 224
Hartland-Swann, John 144
Hartshorne, Charles 227-30
Hawkins, Denis John Bernard 133-4, 156-7, 190-1
Heaney, James J. 212
Heath, P.L. 144
Hebblethwaite, Brian Leslie 212

Index

Hegel, Georg Wilhelm Friedrick 8-9, 12-15, 17, 19-21, 23, 25-7, 35, 38-9, 42-3, 56, 161-2, 164, 171-2, 232
Heidegger, Martin 103, 115, 133, 136, 168-73, 228
Heinemann, Friedrich Heinrich 157
Helm, Paul 214
Hepburn, Ronald William 151, 185-6, 194-5, 199, 200, 223
Heraclitus 69
Hick, John Harwood 153-4, 176, 194,, 204-5, 210-12, 216-19, 221, 223-5
Hicks, George Dawes 66, 107-8
Hoare, Rupert 187
Hodge, Archibald Alexander 237
Hodge, Charles 237
Hodges, Herbert Arthur 145-7, 180
Hodgson, Leonard 50, 110-11
Hodgson, Shadworth Hollway 34-5
Hoernlé, Reinhold Friedrich 4-5, 62, 67, 80-1, 83, 97, 126
Höffding, Harald 35
Holland, Henry Scott 37
Holmes, Arthur Frank 239
Hook, Sidney 171
Hope, Felix 111-12, 132
Horgan, John 224
Howe, John 232
Hudson, William Donald 154, 184, 205, 207, 211
Hügel, Friedrich von 45, 47
Hulme, Thomas Ernest 39
Hume, David 6, 12, 15, 79, 112, 133, 153, 156, 221-2
Husserl, Edmond Gustav Albert 64, 168-9, 172
Huxley, Thomas Henry 6

Illingworth, John Richardson 39-41
Inge, William Ralph 83
Iverach, James 3, 16-17, 21, 24-5, 28-9, 36

Jacks, Lawrence Pearsall 68

James, William 13, 34
Jaspers, Karl 169
Jenkins, David 173, 230
Jenkinson, Alfred James 27
Jessop, Thomas Edmund 84, 99
Jevons, Frank Byron 98, 118
Joachim, Harold Henry 39-41
Joad, Cyril Edwin Mitchinson 120
John of Damascus 85
Jones, Henry 54-5, 62, 83
Joseph, Horace William Brindley 50
Jowett, Benjamin 14, 19

Kalsbeek, L. 237
Kant, Immanuel 6-7, 9, 11-13, 15, 19-20, 34, 42-3, 47, 49, 56, 90, 122, 156, 161, 216-17, 233
Kasachkoff, Tziporah 209
Kaufman, Gordon 186-8
Kaufmann, Walter 103, 216
Keeling, L. Bryant 211
Kenny, Anthony John Patrick 221, 226
Keynes, John Maynard 29
Kierkegaard, Soren Aaby 102-3, 136, 139, 161-6, 168, 171-3, 206, 208, 237
Kneale, William C. 177
Knox, Thomas Malcolm 180-1
Knydsen, Robert Donald 238
Körner, Stephan 143
Kraft, Julius 202
Kroner, Richard 171
Kuyper, Abraham 236-8

Ladd, George Trumbull 55-6
Laird, John 91, 122-3
Lee, Atkinson 2
Leibniz, Gottfried Wilhelm 33
Leo XIII 86
Leon, Philip 158
Leopardi, Giacomo 186
Levin, Thomas Woodhouse 24
Lewis, Hywel David 145, 180-1, 184, 192-4, 204
Lindsay, James 58-60

Index

Locke, Donald Bryan 231
Locke, John 15, 51, 70, 222
Lonergan, Bernard 221-2
Lotze, Hermann 41, 46-7, 50, 59
Lowrie, Walter 103
Lucas, John Randolph 182
Luther, Martin 161, 213

Mabbott, John David 116
McDonald, Hugh Dermot 171
McDougall, William 39
Mace, Cecil Alec 115, 143
McGill, Arthur C. 216
MacGregor, Geddes 204
Mach, Ernst 79
MacIntyre, Alasdair Chalmers 151, 156, 185-6, 188, 204
McIntyre, John 195, 202-3
Mackenzie, John Stuart 32-3, 38-9, 53, 98, 118
Mackie, John Leslie 223
MacKinnon, Donald MacKenzie 4-5, 121, 202-3, 233-4
Mackintosh, Robert 232
Maclagan, William Gauld 197, 199
Macmurray, John 143-4, 197, 199
McPherson, Thomas Herdman 141, 154, 204, 218
Macquarrie, John 36, 104, 156, 160, 184, 200-1, 229
McShane, Philip 221
McTaggart, John McTaggart Ellis 25-6, 36, 38, 43, 45, 47, 49, 52, 62, 66, 83
Magee, William Connor 6
Maimonides 85
Malcolm, Norman Adrian 52, 207, 217-18
Manning, Henry Edward 6
Mansell, Henry Longueville 14
Marcel, Gabriel 103, 136, 157, 169
Maritain, Jacques 86, 91
Martin, Charles Burton 194-5, 223
Mascall, Eric Lionel 85, 123-4, 133-4, 156, 190, 204, 216, 237
Matthews, Walter Robert 67
Maurice, Frederick Denison 6, 112
Meinong, Alexius von 51
Mercier, Désiré Joseph 86
Metz, Rudolf 77
Meynell, Hugo Anthony 222
Miles, Thomas Richard 184-6, 223
Mill, John Stuart 6, 13-14, 221
Mitchell, Basil George 4, 149-50, 153-4, 182, 226
Moore, George Edward 33, 37-8, 40, 50-4, 60, 62, 92, 100, 109, 112-14, 122
Morell, John Daniel 13
Morelli, Mario F. 212
Morgan, Conwy Lloyd 63
Muirhead, John Henry 12, 82, 91, 119, 243

Nash, Ronald H. 237
Nettleship, Richard Lewis 14, 40
Neurath, Otto 79
Notaro, Thom 238

O'Connor, Daniel John 186, 190
O'Donoghue, Noel Dermot 225
Ogden, Schubert 227-9
Oman, John Wood 89, 94
Oppenheimer, Helen 226
Orr, James 66, 224
Otto, Rudolf 47, 108
Owen, Huw Parri 212-13, 215, 223-6, 232

Pailin, David Arthur 231
Parker, Joseph 244
Parker, Theodore 171
Partee, Charles 235
Pascal, Blaise 161
Passmore, John 66, 167
Paton, Herbert James 145, 149, 157
Pecci, Giuseppe 86
Penelhum, Terence M. 205

Index

Perry, Ralph Barton 39
Phillips, Dewi Zephaniah 129, 205, 207-11, 226
Phillips, Richard Percival 100-1
Pittenger, Norman 215, 227-8
Plantinga, Alvin 216, 219, 223
Plato 34, 38, 71, 74, 85, 90, 92, 95-6, 105, 133, 228
Popper, Karl Raimund 115
Potts, Timothy Cyril 202
Price, Henry Habberley 117-18, 126-7, 149, 232
Prichard, Harold Arthur 37, 50
Priestley, Joseph 232
Pringle-Pattison, Andrew Seth 34, 41-9, 67, 95
Prinsterer, Guillaume Groen-van 236
Proust, Marcel 186

Quick, Oliver Chase 57-8

Rahner, Karl 221
Ramsey, Frank Plumpton 94
Ramsey, Ian Thomas 108-11, 147-8, 182-4, 188, 192, 212-15
Rashdall, Hastings 34, 46-9, 57, 195
Reardon, Bernard Morris Gavin 158, 231
Reid, Thomas 10, 43, 122
Reinhardt, Kurt Frank 157
Richardson, Alan 136-7
Richmond, James 160, 196, 229, 231, 233
Ritchie, Arthur David 94
Roberts, David Everett 161, 163
Robinson, Norman Hamilton Galloway 193, 213, 235
Rogers, Henry 232
Rogerson, John 76
Root, Howard Eugene 188-90, 198
Royce, Josiah 22-3, 26
Runner, Howard Evan 238
Ruskin, John 6
Russell, Bertrand Arthur William 37-8, 40, 50-1, 53-4, 57-8, 60, 62, 70, 77, 81, 92, 100, 109, 112-14, 120, 186, 220
Ryle, Gilbert 3-4, 102, 113-14, 118-19, 121, 126, 142

Sandars, Thomas Collett 12
Sanseverino, Gaetano 86
Santayana, George 171
Sartre, Jean-Paul 103, 136, 169
Schelling, Friedrich Wilhelm Joseph von 13-14, 20, 28, 161, 170, 173
Schiller, Ferdinand Canning Scott 18, 33-4, 38-9, 57, 243
Schleiermach, Friedrich Daniel Ernst 108, 173
Schlick, Moritz 79-80, 109
Schlipp, Paul Arthur 50-1
Scott, John Waugh 91
Seerveld, Calvin 238
Sell, Alan Philip Frederick 226, 232
Sertillanges, Antonin Dalmace 100
Seth Andrew (*see* Pringle-Pattison)
Sidgwick, Henry 6-7, 49
Smart, Roderick Ninian 156, 184, 205
Smith, J. Macdonald 225
Smith, Ronald Gregor 229
Smyth, John 26-7, 29, 35
Socrates 2
Sordi, Domenico 86
Sordi, Serafino 86
Sorley, William Ritchie 59-60
Spencer, Herbert 19
Spengler, Oswald 100
Spinoza, Benedictus (*also* Baruch) de 34, 186
Stace, Walter Terence 118
Stebbing, Lizzie Susan 72-3, 75, 115-16, 120
Stedman, Ralph E. 75, 119-20
Stirling, James Hutchinson 12
Stoker, Hendrik 236
Stout, George Frederick 94
Strauss, David Friedrich 13

251

Index

Strawson, Peter Frederick 3, 143, 179
Streeter, Burnett Hillman 94
Struthers, John Paterson 23
Sturt, Henry 34-5, 46-7
Sutherland, Stewart Ross 207
Swinburne, Richard Granville 226, 232
Switalski, B.W., 91

Taylor, Alfred Edward 19, 33-4, 59, 90-2, 94, 108, 123-4, 199, 221
Teilhard de Chardin, Pierre 206, 229-30
Temple, William 46, 74-6, 94, 99, 229
Tennant, Frederick Robert 94-5, 108, 123, 195
Tennyson, Alfred 6
Tertullian, Quintus Septimus Florens 38, 164
Thomas, David Oswald 231
Thomas, John Heywood 162, 165-6, 173, 216
Thompson, J.J. 70
Tillich, Paul Johannes Oskar 104, 151, 161, 167-8, 170-5, 242
Tomlin, Eric Walter Frederick 180
Toulmin, Stephen Edelston 186
Trethowan, Illtyd William Kenneth 4, 155-6, 224-5, 232
Tulloch, D.M. 199

Urban, Wilbur Marshall 99-100

Van Til, Cornelius 238, 240
Vesey, Godfrey Norman Agmondisham 211
Vidler, Alexander Roper 186, 189, 195

Vollenhoven, Dirk Hendrik Theodoor 236

Waismann, Friedrich 79, 143
Wallace, William 19-20, 40, 83
Walsh, William Henry 181
Ward, James 47, 94
Ward, Keith 233
Warfield, Benjamin Breckenridge 237
Waterhouse, Eric Strickland 96
Watson, John 23, 28, 36-8
Webb, Clement Charles Julian 34, 46-9, 54, 57, 60, 66, 81-3, 89-91, 108, 122, 136, 240
Wells, Herbert George 67
Wenley, Robert Mark 4, 23-4, 28, 32, 38
Whewell, William 14
White, Alan Richard 52
Whitehead, Alfred North 62, 66, 68-76, 83, 90, 92, 97, 123, 167, 227-30
Wieman, Henry Nelson 228
Wilson, John 204
Wilson, John Cook 37, 50
Winch, Peter Guy 207-8
Wisdom, Arthur John Terenco Dibber 113, 126, 151, 244
Wittgenstein, Ludwig 51, 62, 77-80, 97, 100, 109, 112-15, 128-9, 167, 177, 207-12, 237
Woods, George Frederick 186-8
Woolf, Virginia 186
Wulf, Maurice de 86

Young, Warren Cameron 239-40

Zuurdeeg, Willem Frederik 161, 175-6
Zybura, John Stanislaus 88-9, 91-2, 101

www.ingramcontent.com/pod-product-compliance
Lightning Source LLC
Chambersburg PA
CBHW051634230426
43669CB00013B/2293